The Rape Victim

Volume 185 Sage Library of Social Research

RECENT VOLUMES IN . . .
SAGE LIBRARY OF SOCIAL RESEARCH

13 Gelles **The Violent Home, Updated Edition**
78 Matthews **The Social World of Old Women**
84 Gelles **Family Violence, 2nd Edition**
96 Rutman **Planning Useful Evaluations**
126 McPhail **Electronic Colonialism, Revised 2nd Edition**
142 Toch/Grant **Reforming Human Services**
150 Frey **Survey Research by Telephone, 2nd Edition**
152 Estes/Newcomer/and Assoc. **Fiscal Austerity and Aging**
153 Leary **Understanding Social Anxiety**
154 Hallman **Neighborhoods**
155 Russell **Sexual Exploitation**
156 Catanese **The Politics of Planning and Development**
157 Harrington/Newcomer/Estes/and Assoc. **Long Term Care of the Elderly**
158 Altheide **Media Power**
159 Douglas **Creative Interviewing**
160 Rubin **Behind the Black Robes**
161 Matthews **Friendships Through the Life Course**
162 Gottdiener **The Decline of Urban Politics**
163 Markides/Mindel **Aging and Ethnicity**
164 Zisk **Money, Media, and the Grass Roots**
165 Arterton **Teledemocracy**
166 Steinmetz **Duty Bound**
167 Teune **Growth**
168 Blakely **Planning Local Economic Development**
169 Mathews **Strategic Intervention in Organizations**
170 Scanzoni/Polonko/Teachman/Thompson **The Sexual Bond**
171 Prus **Pursuing Customers**
172 Prus **Making Sales**
173 Mayer **Redefining Comparative Politics**
174 Vannoy-Hiller/Philliber **Equal Partners**
175 Brewer/Hunter **Multimethod Research**
176 Chafetz **Gender Equity**
177 Peterson **Political Behavior**
178 So **Social Change and Development**
179 Gomes-Schwartz/Horowitz/Cardarelli **Child Sexual Abuse**
180 Evan **Social Structure and Law**
181 Turner/Turner **The Impossible Science**
182 McCollum **The Trauma of Moving**
183 Cohen/Adoni/Bantz **Social Conflict and Television News**
184 Gruter **Law and the Mind**
185 Koss/Harvey **The Rape Victim**
186 Cicirelli **Family Caregiving**
187 Caves **Land Use Planning**
188 Blalock **Understanding Social Inequality**
189 Gubrium **Out of Control**
190 Albrecht **The Disability Business**
191 Alter/Hage **Organizations Working Together**

The Rape Victim

Clinical and Community
Interventions

Second Edition

Mary P. Koss
Mary R. Harvey

Sage Library of Social Research 185

SAGE PUBLICATIONS
The International Professional Publishers
Newbury Park   London   New Delhi

For information address:

SAGE Publications, Inc.
2455 Teller Road
Thousand Oaks, California 91320
E-mail: order@sagepub.com

SAGE Publications Ltd.
6 Bonhill Street
London EC2A 4PU
United Kingdom

SAGE Publications India Pvt. Ltd.
M-32 Market
Greater Kailash I
New Delhi 110 048 India

Printed in the United States of America

Library of Congress Cataloging-in-Publication Data

Koss, Mary P.
    The rape victim: clinical and community interventins / Mary P. Koss, Mary R. Harvey. — 2nd ed.
    p. cm. — (Sage library of social research ; 185)
    Includes bibliographical references and index.
    ISBN 0-8039-3894-2 (c).   ISBN 8-8039-3895-0 (p)
    1. Rape—United States. 2. Rape victims—Services for—United States.   3. Rape victims—Counseling of—United States.
    4. Community mental health services—United States. I. Harvey, Mary R. II. Title. III. Series.
    [DNLM: 1. Community Mental Health Services. 2. Crisis Intervention. 3. Rape.   WM 401 K86r]
    HV6561.K67 1991
    362.88'3—dc20
    DNLM/DLC
    for Library of Congress   90-9241
                                                                        CIP

    98 99 00 01 02 03 10 9 8 7 6 5

Sage Production Editor: Judith L. Hunter

Contents

Preface   viii

Acknowledgments   xiii

1. The Crime of Rape   1
   Legal Definitions of Rape   2
   Types of Rape   5
   Incidence of Rape   8
   *National Crime Survey Techniques That Undermine
      Rape Disclosure*   16
   Prevalence Studies of Rape   22
   The Causes of Rape   29

2. The Trauma of Rape   42
   An Ecological Model of Rape Trauma   43
   Phases of Response to Rape   47
   The Male Victim   55
   Symptomatic Responses to Rape   57
   Cognitive Impact of Rape   68
   Person Characteristics That Affect Rape Response   74
   Event Characteristics That Affect Rape Response   76
   Posttraumatic Stress Disorder in Rape Victims   77
   *A Behavioral/Cognitive Conceptualization of
      Rape Aftereffects*   80
   Clinical Screening for Assault History   82
   Psychometric Assessment of Rape Aftereffects   85

3. Rape as a Community Issue   89
    Defining "Community"   92
    Functions of Communities   94
    The Community as "Ecosystem"   96
    A Resource Perspective   97
    Case Example: Date Rape on College Campuses   100
    The Adaptive Nature of Community Change   102
    Initiating Change in a Community's Response to Rape   103
    Assessing Local Services   104
    Components of a Communitywide Response to Rape   107
    Social Action, Community Education, and Prevention   113
    A Community Needs Assessment Tool   115
    Conclusion   115

4. The Rape Crisis Center   118
    The Rape Crisis Center Movement   120
    Feminist Origins of the Rape Crisis Center Movement   123
    A Feminist Analysis of Rape   124
    Social Change Initiatives   127
    Empowering Services   133
    Feminist Organizations   135
    Rape Crisis Center Research   139
    A Study of Nine Exemplary Rape Crisis Centers   142
    Conclusion   153

5. The Clinical Treatment of Rape Victims   155
    Challenges of Working With Rape Victims   156
    Single-Session Debriefing for the Victim of Rape   159
    Criteria of Recovery   176
    Integrative Treatment of Nonrecent Rape   177

6. Group Treatment for Survivors   205
    Research on Group Treatment   207
    The Rationale for Group Treatment   208
    Group Treatment and Recovery   217
    A Range of Group Treatment Approaches   224
    Designing a Survivors' Group   231
    Group Treatment Within the Victims of Violence Program   234
    Conclusion   244

7. Preventing Sexual Assault   245
    Preventive Mental Health Care   247
    Prevention, Public Health, and Epidemiology   250

Prevention and the Promotion of Competence   255
The Primary Prevention of Sexual Assault   260
Competence-Based Primary Rape Prevention Strategies   270
Conclusion   279

Epilogue   281

References   285

Index   304

About the Authors   312

Preface

Our motivation in writing this book was to produce a text that moved beyond the consulting room and avoided overemphasis on traditional mental health interventions. Our different backgrounds in clinical (MPK) and community (MRH) psychology contributed to this motivation and compelled our search for a unifying perspective. The result is the ecological perspective that serves as the conceptual foundation of the text, which emphasizes the interconnections of people and their social environments in understanding rape response and recovery. Although the book contains concrete advice about conducting interventions with rape victims, including single-session debriefing in the immediate aftermath of rape, individual psychotherapy with the nonrecent rape victim, and group approaches, only the individual psychotherapy techniques require professional training to administer. Each of the chapters contains a review of current clinical and empirical scholarship on rape, but we have aimed for a readable style that does not presume a graduate level education. Vignettes of individual experiences are included in the text because no one is as eloquent as those actually affected by rape, who raise our awareness that rape happens to real people. Case studies of successful community interventions also have been included to provide concrete suggestions for those readers whose responsibilities include program development within community agencies. We hope that the book will be of interest to a range of specialists including those in counseling, criminal justice, psychology, nursing, social work, and victim assistance.

Some may wonder at our choice of the word "victim" as opposed to "survivor" in the book title. Our rationale is to signify the outrage of rape. Rape is a hostile act done to an innocent person who is changed unwillingly as a result. The word "victim" is appropriate for the person who is raped because it means "one who is acted upon and usually adversely affected by a force or agent, one who is subjected to oppression, hardship, or mistreatment, or one who is tricked or duped" (Webster's Ninth New Collegiate Dictionary, 1985). The word victim, however, also can denote "one that is injured, destroyed, or sacrificed." This is an outcome that all our interventions aim to mitigate or reverse. Immediately postassault, the victim of rape is a survivor only in the sense of preservation of biological life. We believe that surviving "standing up" (in the words of one of our colleagues) entails a hard transformation through a victim-to-survivor process. The survivor is the victim who not only has endured, but who has prevailed and who has rebuilt the meaning shattered by rape.

The text is divided into seven chapters. In Chapter 1, the crime of rape is addressed, including its legal definition as well as the various types of assaults it subsumes. Following this material, the current information on the incidence and prevalence of rape is summarized. This material is important to the development of awareness of the true scope of rape and as a counterpoint to federal data sources that have maintained for years the false illusion that rape is the rarest of all violent crimes. The chapter concludes with a four-tiered conceptualization of the causes of rape including society-wide supports for rape, institutional influences, dyadic characteristics, and individual determinants.

Chapter 2 is devoted to the trauma of rape. It begins with an explanation of the ecological model of rape trauma and recovery that serves as the conceptual foundation of the text. Then clinical observations of the phases of response to rape are described, including a short consideration of the experiences of the male rape victim. Next, empirical studies of the impact of rape are reviewed, including those that have focused on psychological symptoms (anxiety, depression, sexual dysfunction, social disruptions); physical health; and cognitive changes, including the shattering of central beliefs. Many rape victims meet the diagnostic criteria for posttraumatic stress disorder, which is briefly explained. A cognitive/behavioral model of individual response to rape is presented to specify the processes by which diffuse and long-lasting aftereffects are initiated and maintained. The chapter concludes with suggestions for identification of a rape history by clinical interviewing and a discussion of psychometric assessment of the severity of rape aftereffects.

Community influences on rape response are addressed in Chapter 3. We begin by defining communities and delineating their functions. How the community operates as an "ecosystem" is illustrated using the example of date rape on college campuses. Next, community change is considered including its adaptive nature and methods for initiating it. The chapter concludes with a discussion of the components of a community-wide response to rape and an assessment tool designed to evaluate a community's services.

The rape crisis center movement is the subject of Chapter 4. The roots of the rape crisis center movement are traced to their feminist origins. Then, a feminist analysis of rape is presented, and it is demonstrated how rape crisis centers foster social change and provide empowering services. The chapter concludes with an extended discussion of the organizational and programmatic characteristics of nine exemplary rape crisis centers across the United States.

The remainder of the book is about interventions for victims of rape. In the ecological model of rape recovery, we identified four possible outcomes, which included those who recover with and without intervention, and those who remain distressed in the absence of or despite intervention. The individual and group interventions are aimed at fostering survivorship among those victims who seek help. The prevention chapter considers public education campaigns that seek to mitigate the suffering of rape victims who do not seek or cannot find clinical interventions.

Chapter 5 considers two types of individual interventions. The first, single-session debriefing, is designed for use by service providers in the immediate aftermath of rape. At the conclusion of this material, we discuss our thoughts about what constitutes recovery from rape. These criteria are then used as the goals that individual and group interventions strive to accomplish. Because of evidence that many rape victims enter a period of denial following assault during which few seek intervention, our suggestions for psychotherapeutic treatment are designed for use with the nonrecent rape. The suggested psychotherapeutic interventions are developed from an integrative perspective and begin with suggestions for assessing spontaneous rape resolution. Techniques then are presented to build a relationship, foster processing of painful memories, promote reformulation of shattered beliefs, restore lost mastery, and treat target symptoms.

It is the opinion of many experts in the field, however, that group treatment may be the treatment of choice for victims of rape. Therefore, we have provided a separate chapter on group approaches. This material begins with consideration of some of the special advantages that group treatment possesses in achieving our criteria of recovery. Then a range of group approaches are described including drop-in discussion groups, crisis-oriented groups, self-help groups, stress-management groups, and time-limited and open-ended psychotherapy groups. This chapter concludes with a focus on the group treatment program at the Victims of Violence Center[1] in Cambridge, Massachusetts, which was recognized for excellence by a Gold Medal Award from the American Psychiatric Association.

Prevention activities are the topic of Chapter 7. In this chapter we describe the medical and public health models for prevention. Then we contrast deficit-oriented programs with competence-promoting programs. The chapter concludes with several case studies of successful, competence-oriented primary rape prevention programs across the United States.

The text concludes with an Epilogue that summarizes our thoughts about the present climate for provision of interventions against rape. We look back at the field's accomplishments, mourn the setbacks in social programs that have occurred in the last decade, and look forward to the work that remains to be done.

NOTE

1. The Victims of Violence Program is directed by this book's coauthor (Harvey) and was cofounded by Mary R. Harvey, Ph.D., and Judith L. Herman, M.D., in 1984. It is discussed in some detail in Chapter 6.

Acknowledgments

It seems important first to acknowledge the people who brought us together and who nurtured and encouraged our separate and collective efforts in the sexual assault field. These people include staff of the National Center for the Prevention and Control of Rape at the National Institute of Mental Health, including Mary Lystadt, Jean Garrison, Marvin Feuerberg, Ellen Ferris, and Ann Manney, as well as *Ms.* magazine editor Ellen Sweet and her colleagues. Staff members of the Antisocial and Violent Behavior Branch (now called the Violence and Traumatic Stress Research Branch) of NIMH also are thanked for their ongoing support. Also deserving of our recognition and gratitude are the rape crisis centers and rape crisis volunteers who comprise the National Coalition Against Sexual Assault and whose efforts on behalf of raped women have transformed public policy, community resources, and mental health services for victims.

We are deeply grateful to the talented therapists who contributed clinical experiences that were used in the creation of composite case studies and to the many feminist scholars, clinicians, and activists whose work we have cited. Mary Koss would like to personally acknowledge for their generosity of ideas Judith Becker, Barry Burkhart, Edna Foa, Ellen Frank, Dean Kilpatrick, Patti Resick, Nancy Felipe Russo, Susan Sorenson, Lois Veronen, Jackie White, and Gail Wyatt. Mary Harvey extends special thanks to mentor, friend, and colleague James G. Kelly who introduced her to ecological thinking about communities and special appreciation and acknowledgment to her colleagues at Cambridge Hospital's Victims of Violence Program, including Judith Herman, Janet Yassen, Lois Glass, Emily Schatzow, Barbara Hamm, Beth Parsons, Jayme Shorin, and Shirley Moore. Also deserving of recognition are colleagues Bessell van der Kolk, Angela Browne, Susan Schechter, Ray Flannery, and clinicians from the Boston area's Trauma Group Study Group. The additions to the second edition of the book are the direct result of our colleagues' work and the challenging and supportive milieu they have helped develop. The administrative assistance and enthusiastic support of Gwen Johnson and Stephanie Barkas Saponaro are deeply appreciated.

We held in our minds while writing this book clear images of our family and friends whose lives have been changed by victimization. It is for them that we most tried to create a book with a positive impact. In addition, several special people created a haven from which we gathered strength, including our partners Oliver Fowlkes and Paul Koss, our children Eric Harvey, Abby and Maggie Fowlkes, John Koss, and Paul Koss, and our parents Ruth Donald Godshall, Betty and Irv Koss, and Carol and Dick Pease.

ONE

The Crime of Rape

Experiencing sexual violence transforms people into victims and changes their lives forever. Once victimized, one can never again feel quite as invulnerable. Rape represents the most serious of all major crimes against the person, short of homicide. The focus of this chapter is on the crime of rape including its legal definitions, frequency, and causes. Some of this material is technical, but it is our firm belief that those working with rape victims must have accurate information on rape frequency. It may help victims to know that their experience was not a rare event. Knowledge of the processes by which incidence and prevalence numbers are generated also facilitates appropriate rebuttal in instances where statistics are (mis)used to maintain the illusion that rape is an infrequent crime. The chapter concludes with an extended discussion of why men rape. It is important that the person who proposes to help victims has a conceptually sound model of rape that can be communicated in bits and pieces to potentiate re-formation of non-self-blaming beliefs about why the rape happened. (This topic is treated in Chapter 4.) Evidence supportive of external, non-self-blaming interpretations of a sexual assault are best generated by the therapist who has a working knowledge of the multiple factors that support and maintain rape. Finally, a reasoned approach to prevention programming (see Chapter 5) is more likely to result from a thorough grounding in empirical evidence on the causes of rape.

LEGAL DEFINITIONS OF RAPE

The traditional common-law offense of rape is defined as "carnal knowledge of a female forcibly and against her will" (Bienen, 1981, p. 174). Carnal knowledge means penile-vaginal penetration only; other sexual offenses are excluded.

FBI Definition

This definition of rape is adopted by the Federal Bureau of Investigation (FBI) for purposes of compiling the *Uniform Crime Reports* (FBI, 1989). The *Uniform Crime Reports* (UCR) compile the numbers of rape complaints that have been filed with local police authorities that the police considered to be legitimate incidents. The UCR definition of rape also is adopted by the National Crime Survey (NCS), which is the federal data-collection effort that aims at describing the extent of unreported crime (Bureau of Justice Statistics [BJS], 1989). The one exception is that the FBI definition is extended to include "homosexual rape" in the NCS (BJS, 1989, p. 127). This statement contains two problematic elements. First, carnal knowledge refers to penile-vaginal intercourse. The compilers of the NCS have not considered that the carnal knowledge definition cannot be extended to male victims; to do so would require a change in the qualifying forms of penetration. Such changes would have implications for female as well as male victims. Second, it is inaccurate to refer to the rape of men as homosexual rape. Men who rape other men are not always homosexuals.

Reform Rape Definitions

In spite of the existence of an FBI definition of the offense, rape is not a federal crime (except in those instances where the crime occurs on federal property or on Indian reservations). Rather, rape statutes are written at the state level. Recent years have seen extensive reform of these laws (Bohmer, 1990; Searles & Berger, 1987). One of the reforms was to substitute other terms for rape including sexual assault, sexual battery, criminal sexual penetration, criminal sexual conduct, gross sexual imposition, and sexual intercourse without consent. The intent of these reforms was to place emphasis on the perpetrator's acts rather than the victim's experiences and to draw attention toward rape's violent as opposed to sexual aspects (Searles & Berger, 1987). We have retained the use of the term "rape" to refer to the most highly sanctioned form of sexual penetration offense.

In reform statutes, *rape* is defined as nonconsensual sexual penetration of an adolescent or adult obtained by physical force, by threat of bodily harm, or when the victim is incapable of giving consent by virtue of mental illness, mental retardation, or intoxication. Included are attempts to commit rape by force or threat of bodily harm (Searles & Berger, 1987). A representative reform state definition of rape is the following:

> Vaginal intercourse between male and female and anal intercourse, fellation, and cunnilingus between persons regardless of sex. Penetration, however slight, is sufficient to complete vaginal or anal intercourse. . . . No person shall engage in sexual contact with another person not including the spouse of the offender, when any of the following apply:
>
> (1) the offender purposely compels the other person to submit by force or threat of force

(2) for the purpose of preventing resistance, the offender substantially impairs the other person's judgment or control by administering any drug or intoxicant to the other person, surreptitiously, or by force, threat of force, or deception

(3) the other person is less than 13 years of age whether or not the offender knows the age of that person. (Ohio Revised Code, Supp. 1980, 2907.01A, 2907.02)

Among the differences between reform statutes and the FBI definition of rape is that penetration has been expanded from penile-vaginal intercourse to include oral and anal sodomy and penetration by fingers or objects other than the penis. A second difference is the expansion of the methods for obtaining compliance that are considered to be rape. Many reform statutes delineate a category of rape that is nonforceful but takes improper advantage of an incapacitated victim. Often mental illness and mental retardation are considered to render a woman incapable of giving consent to sexual activity. In addition, drug and alcohol intoxication may be considered to be incapacitation, but in some states the offender must have administered the chemicals for the express purpose of obtaining sexual access. "Voluntary" intoxication does not meet this stipulation. A third characteristic of many reform statutes is the modification of the spousal exclusion. There are few states where the spousal exclusion has been totally excised from the law (Bohmer, 1990; Searles & Berger, 1987).

A final characteristic of reform statutes is the avoidance of sexual stereotyping in that they do not specify the sex of the victim or offender. The FBI definition, on the other hand, stipulates that the victim of rape must be female. The new sex neutrality in the laws has been confusing to many young people who never fail at public lectures to ask, "What about men raped by women?" When prompted to give an example, the inevitable result is a story about a man who had sex with a woman when he did not want to because she threatened to say things that would embarrass him if he did not. One certainly never wants to condone coercion; however, such incidents are not rape. Rape is a penetration offense; the victim is penetrated by the offender. The example just cited involves penetration of the offender by the victim! Some therapists believe that the word rape is so inextricably associated with women that it should be reserved for female victims (Masters, 1986). It is properly applied to men only when a penetration offense has occurred, and virtually all of these incidents are perpetrated by another male (BJS, 1989).

Distinctions Among Acts That Meet
Legal Definitions of Rape

Although rape is the most highly sanctioned sexual penetration offense, many other forms of sexual victimization may be psychologically experienced as traumatic. Included are unwanted touching, nonconsensual voyeurism, threatening telephone calls, attempted rape, workplace harassment, and sexual coercion (i.e., ostensibly consensual sexual intercourse that occurred subsequent to menacing verbal pressure, threats to end the relationship, or false promises). The distinctions among these incidents are more apparent to legal scholars than they are to clinicians. Although this book focuses on rape, there are many similarities in response to these other sexual offenses.

TYPES OF RAPE

Even the category of legal rape is heterogeneous, and there are several distinctions that have practical and clinical significance. First, rape differs in form. An *individual rape* involves a single offender, a *pair rape* involves two offenders who act together to rape the same victim, and a *multiple rape* involves three or more offenders. The offenders in a multiple rape include those who actually obtain sexual relations with the victim as well as those who threaten or use force to make the victim submit but do not themselves have sexual relations.

Rapes also differ in the interpersonal context in which they occur. *Stranger rape* involves a victim and offender who have no relationship before the assault and do not even recognize each other. *Acquaintance rape* involves parties who know each other, including coworkers, fellow students, relatives, neighbors, or family friends. These relationships are not ones in which the expression of sexual behavior is appropriate. The term *date rape* is reserved for sexual contacts that occur within a relationship superficially appropriate for intimacy when obtained through the use of inappropriate coercion or violence. *Marital rape* involves a victim and an offender who are spouses. Brief clinical examples of rapes that differ in form and interpersonal context are found in Table 1.1.

Rapes may differ in their spontaneity. A *planned rape* means that the offender arranged the site of the assault, deliberately selected a victim, and employed elaborate tactics to coerce her to have sexual relations. In a *partially planned rape*, the offender made vague plans regarding how to proceed after spontaneously meeting a potential victim. The *unplanned rape* is impulsive, with no planning, and may take place under the influence of alcohol. The search for a stable set of causal factors of rape is made much more complex by the impulsive, unplanned, spontaneous nature of some assaultive episodes.

Finally, rapes differ in the extent to which they become public knowledge. A *reported rape* is one where the victim reports the incident to the police. If after taking her statement and investigating the preliminary evidence, the police feel the complaint is valid (founded), the incident becomes part of the official crime statistics and the investigatory process is initiated. A *hidden rape* is an incident that meets a legal definition of rape but is not reported to police. There are two types of hidden rape. It is *acknowledged rape* when the victim realizes her experience was rape but declines to report for various reasons such as fear of damage to her reputation or fear of being held responsible. *Unacknowledged rape* occurs when a victim does not realize that her rape meets legal definitions of the crime. Although she may describe the incident in very negative terms, she does not see herself as a rape victim. Clearly, unacknowledged rapes are unlikely to be reported to police.

Some of these distinctions affect the applicability of rape law to a particular instance. Thus in some states it still makes a difference whether forced intercourse took place between a

Table 1.1 Types of Rape

Stranger rape	Rose, age 25, was accosted at knife point in a shopping mall parking lot and forced by a stranger into his car. He drove her to a rural area, raped her, stabbed her five times, set the car on fire, and left her. Although severely injured, she survived.
Acquaintance rape	Susan, age 23, went to the door of her house to find a man she recognized from one of her college classes. She opened the door to let him in the house, whereupon he threw her on the sofa and raped her.
Date rape	Diana, age 50, is vacationing in the Caribbean. She spends some of her time learning sailing and walking along the beach with a fellow guest. At a hotel dance, she dances with this man, and he asks to walk outside. Once on the beach, this 6'4" man asks to have sex and forces her to cooperate by holding her down. Diana is too afraid to resist.
Multiple rape	Ann, age 21, was at a friend's home with a group of her peers. There were three men, one other woman, and herself present. When the other woman left, the three men raped her.
Marital rape	Unidentified caller, in her thirties, telephones a radio talk show on which marital rape is discussed. She describes her husband's sexual assaults and asks where to go for help.

woman and a stranger or a woman and her husband. The relationship of the victim and offender also affects prosecutors' willingness to pursue cases. It is much less likely that a prosecution will go forward if the victim was acquainted, even distantly, with the offender (LaFree, 1989). It is likewise difficult to obtain prosecution when there was a delay in reporting a rape, as might occur to the victim who initially did not realize her assault was a crime (LaFree, 1989). Furthermore, the characteristics of the rape often alter the reactions of a victim's social network and may thereby influence the untoward emotional consequences that are experienced. Finally, many of these characteristics affect the average person's belief that a rape has

occurred and influence the likelihood of receiving a serious police investigation and winning a conviction from a jury of typical citizens.

It is also important to be cognizant of the heterogeneity of the
legal category of rape when interpreting professional literature.
It is an inescapable conclusion that a comprehensive model of
rape must be based on a body of research in which victim and
offender samples are recruited by a variety of techniques. No
single sampling technique and no single clinical setting could
make available individual victims and multiple victims, reported and hidden victims, stranger and acquaintance victims,
unacknowledged and acknowledged victims. Comparative
studies of rape that explore the various forms of rape have been
relatively neglected (Deming & Eppy, 1981). Yet, clearly it is
simplistic to expect that a theory of rape could be developed on
a sample of stranger rape victims that will hold equal explana-
tory power when extended to husbands who rape their wives.
Unfortunately, it is quite common in the rape literature to find
authors making unwarranted extensions to all rape victims of
findings that were based on only one particular type of victim.

Now that an overview of the definition of the term rape has
been completed, we turn attention to current data on the incidence of rape.

INCIDENCE OF RAPE

The concept of *incidence* is borrowed from the field of epidemiology. This term has a precise meaning in relation to disease but now is routinely applied to mental health and crime
phenomena. Incidence refers to the number of new cases that
appear within a specified time frame (Kleinbaum, Kupper, &
Morgenstern, 1982). When applied to crime data, incidence refers to the number of separate criminal incidents that occurred
during a fixed period of time—often a one-year period. Incidence often is expressed as a *victimization rate*, which is obtained

by dividing the number of incidents that occurred in the time period by the number of persons in the population. The rate is then set to a standard population base, often 1,000 people.

The Uniform Crime Reports

Statistics on crime reported to local authorities have been compiled by the FBI for the past five decades. The UCR summarizes several violent index offenses that include criminal homicide, forcible rape, aggravated assault, and robbery. Included in the rape rate are attempts to rape where no penetration took place. In 1988, a total of 92,486 reported crimes qualified as rape according to the FBI definition (FBI, 1989). This figure translated into a victimization rate of 73 per 100,000 female Americans. By definition, 100% of the victims of rape in the UCR were female. Approximately 82% of the rapes reported in 1988 were completed by force; the remainder were attempts. Rape accounted for 6% of the total violent crime volume. The UCR presently does not provide any further information on the indexed crimes such as the relationship of victim and offender; however, a conversion to incident-based crime reporting is in progress among the states that will significantly increase the range of data that are available in the future.

It is widely accepted that the reported rapes represent only the tip of the iceberg, and the compilers of the UCR have cautioned, "Even with the advent of rape crisis centers and an improved awareness by police in dealing with rape victims, forcible rape is still recognized as one of the most underreported of all index crimes. Victims' fear of their assailants and their embarrassment over the incidents are just two factors which can affect their decisions to contact law enforcement" (FBI, 1982, p. 14). In addition to these impediments to reporting, the victim who is unaware that a sexual assault qualifies as a crime or fears that the police will express disbelief has little likelihood of reporting.

National Crime Survey

Because it is common sense that not all crimes that occur are reported to the police, the President's Commission on Law Enforcement and Administration of Justice issued a contract in 1966 to conduct the first nationwide, household-based crime victimization survey. The successor of this survey is the NCS (BJS, 1989). The NCS data result from a panel design, which means that respondents are recontacted multiple times. Once selected as a NCS household, a given housing unit remains in the sample for three years with interviews occurring every six months. During each contact, respondents are asked to indicate only those criminal victimizations that have occurred since the last interview, which serves to "bound" or delineate the recall period. Responses from the initial interview are not included in the annual crime victimization estimates. These estimates are based only on respondents' recall of events since last speaking with the interviewer. The first and fifth contact with the housing unit is in person; all other interviews are conducted by telephone. The 15th NCS report was based on findings from a survey of a representative sample of approximately 100,000 inhabitants over age 11 living in 59,000 housing units in the United States (BJS, 1989). These participants included 96% of the eligible households. Respondents are asked only about victimizations that they have personally experienced. Exceptions are incapacitated individuals and persons absent from the household during the entire reference period. In these cases an adult member of the household serves as a proxy respondent.

In successive versions of the NCS, the methodology for questioning about rape experiences has been changed. In part, these revisions were stimulated by the fact that early versions of the survey resulted in only 15 rapes being reported among 10,000 households (Hindelang & Davis, 1977). The present procedures for measuring rape have remained unchanged since 1973. The estimated rape victimization rate for 1987 in NCS data is 1.3 per 1,000 women and girls and 0.1 per 1,000 men and boys (BJS, 1989). Over 90% of the identified victims of rape are women

(Jamison & Flanagan, 1989). All the perpetrators were men (BJS, 1989). Rape represented just 3% of the violent crimes reported in the NCS (BJS, 1985). Of the rapes that were projected to have occurred in 1987, fewer than half were completed; the majority were attempts. Half of the perpetrators (53%) were strangers to the victim. More than three fourths of all rapes reported in the NCS involve one victim and one offender (BJS, 1985). One third involve a weapon (BJS, 1985). Perpetrators who were total strangers to the victim were involved in 45% of the rapes of white women and 70% of the rapes reported by black women (BJS, 1989). On the basis of these data, the compilers of the NCS have suggested that women are twice as likely to be raped by a stranger than by someone they know. Other research, however, challenges this assertion as will be discussed shortly.

The NCS victimization rate for women is twice as large as the UCR estimated rate based on reported crimes. However, the compilers of the NCS admit that these numbers are still too low in terms of accuracy (BJS, 1984). Each year typically only 100 cases of rape *and* attempted rape are identified. To obtain the 1,000 cases necessary to develop a descriptive profile of rape, it was necessary to aggregate *all* the incidents of rape and attempted rape that were reported in *every* NCS interview across the decade from 1973 to 1984 (BJS, 1985). On the basis of these data, the compilers of the NCS characterize rape as "the rarest of NCS measured violent offenses" (BJS, 1984, p. 5) and "relatively rare compared with other violent crimes such as robbery or assault" (BJS, 1985, p. 1). We believe that such assertions create a false illusion about rape and blunt social concern about victimization. In the next section, research is presented that supports the conclusion that NCS estimates of rape incidence are unrealistically low.

Independent Research

Rape incidence also has been estimated in a small number of specialized studies carried out under federal contracts including research that has focused on adolescents (Ageton, 1983); college women (Koss, Gidycz, & Wisniewski, 1987); and adult women (Koss, Koss, & Woodruff, 1990; Russell, 1982, 1984). All of these studies documented rates of rape that are far higher than federal estimates. Russell (1982) conducted a pioneering study in 1978 that involved interviews with a random sample of 930 women residents of San Francisco. Detailed interviews were administered in respondents' homes by a trained female interviewer. Whenever possible, race and ethnicity were matched. There were 38 questions about sexual assault, only one of which used the word rape. Rape was defined according to California statutes as, "forced intercourse (i.e., penile-vaginal penetration, or intercourse obtained by threat of force, or intercourse completed when the woman was drugged, unconscious, asleep, or otherwise totally helpless and hence unable to consent)" (Russell, 1984, p. 35). In the 12 months prior to the survey, 25 rapes and rape attempts occurred among respondents that met the UCR definition, which resulted in an estimated incidence rate of 2,688 per 100,000 women. This figure is 7 times higher than the NCS estimate for San Francisco during the same year (Russell, 1984). In contrast to the picture painted by NCS data of that era, when two thirds of rapists were strangers, in Russell's data (1984) only 11% of the rapes and attempted rapes were perpetrated by strangers, whereas 62% were perpetrated by current or former husbands, boyfriends, lovers, and other male relatives (the remainder were perpetrated by nonromantic acquaintances).

Ageton (1983) inserted questions about sexual assault into the National Youth Study. Boys were questioned about their perpetration of assault, and girls were questioned about victimization. The nationwide sample of 1,725 adolescents age 11 to 17 were interviewed yearly for five years. Sexual assault was defined in this study "to include all forced sexual behavior involving contact with the sexual parts of the body. Attempted sexual assaults were counted" (Ageton, 1983, p. 11). Two questions were used to operationalize this definition of sexual assault. They included the following: "How many times in the last year have you been sexually attacked or raped or an attempt made to do so?" and "How many times in the last year have you been pressured or pushed by someone such as a date or friend to do more sexually than you wanted to?" (p. 12). The latter item was intended to reflect date rape. It is unfortunate, but the responses to this item were later discounted when it was found that 75% of the girls responded yes to it. In hindsight, Ageton herself identified several problems with her approach including the vagueness of the date-rape item, and the assumption inherent in the first screening item that girls who have had an experience that would legally qualify as rape will conceptualize their experience as a "sexual attack or rape." Nevertheless, Ageton developed estimated rape victimization rates for adolescent girls by extracting incidents involving violent force and/or the use of a weapon. The resultant estimates were 9.2 per 1,000 for 1978, 6.8 per 1,000 for 1979, and 12.7 per 1,000 for 1980. These are much higher than the rates reported in the NCS for girls age 13 to 19 for the years 1978 and 1979, which were 3.5 and 4.2 respectively. On a nationwide basis, Ageton's incidence rate for 1977 would translate into 540,000 sexual assaults of female teenagers. This rate alone is 7 times greater than the total number of rapes officially recorded for *all* women in that year by the *Uniform Crime Reports*.

Koss and colleagues (Koss et al., 1987) administered 10 sexual victimization screening questions to a nationwide sample of 3,187 women college students at 32 colleges and universities selected to represent the higher education enrollment in the United States. There were six questions pertaining to rape that described various behaviorally specific scenarios but did not use the word rape. Typical items included the following: "Have you had sexual intercourse with a man when you did not want to because he used some degree of force such as twisting your arm or holding you down to make you cooperate?" or "Have you had other sexual acts with a man such as oral or anal intercourse or penetration with objects when you did not want to because he used some degree of force . . . or threatened to harm you to make you cooperate?" In a 12-month period, 76 per 1,000 college women experienced one or more attempted or completed rapes defined according to the UCR definition. (The use of state reform definition of rape doubled the incidence figure to 166 per 1,000 women.)

It can be instructive to compare these incidence rates to NCS figures for the year in which that data were collected (1985). A direct comparison with the NCS must be viewed with caution, however, because there are several inherent limitations of the validity of this undertaking. The first limitation involves differences in the populations from which the data were obtained. Whereas the NCS involves a representative sample of all U.S. households, the present sample was restricted to college students who have a higher than average education level. Although common sense might suggest that less educated persons would be subject to more victimizations, in reality the reverse is often found on crime surveys and is explained by a phenomenon known as "differential productivity" (Sudman & Bradburn, 1974). College-educated respondents recall more crimes than others, particularly in the category of assaultive violence (Skogan, 1981). This tendency of educated respondents to evidence greater productivity is suspected of masking the negative association between social position and victimization.

There also is an important methodological difference between the survey of college students and the NCS that could affect the validity of the comparisons. The recall period in the NCS is limited to a six-month period, and the respondents' previous contact with the interviewer serves as a reference point for where to begin remembering. The college students were contacted only once and were asked subsequently to specify the number of victimizations that occurred in the previous year. A phenomenon known as "telescoping" may occur under these circumstances. Experiences may be recalled as having happened closer to the present than they actually did (forward telescoping), or further away from the present than they actually did (backward telescoping). Studies with NCS data have revealed that single, retrospective reports of victimization produce rates that are about one third higher than bounded recall. As the incidence data on college students were obtained from unbounded recall, they were reduced by one third to adjust for forward telescoping. The adjustment lowered the estimate of rape incidence among college women from 76 per 1,000 using the UCR definition to 50 per 1,000. Even after discounting the rate by one third, 1 in 20 college women experienced rape or attempted rape in a year as defined by the FBI (1 in 9 using a reform definition). This rate is still between 10 and 15 times larger than the 1985 NCS estimates for women age 16 to 19 (4.3 per 1,000) and age 20 to 24 (3.4 per 1,000).

Many people have trouble believing that this level of assault could exist without coming to the attention of police or institutional authorities. However, fewer than 5% of college student rape victims stated that they had reported their assault to the police; almost half told no one at all. Responses to follow-up questions revealed that 95% of the rapes involved one offender, and 84% of the incidents involved an offender known to the victim. In 57% of the rapes, the perpetrator was a date (Koss, 1988).

To generalize these results to a broader population base, a second study focused on more than 2,291 adult women in Cleveland, Ohio (Koss, Koss, & Woodruff, 1990). A mailed survey was sent to over 5,000 women and a 45% response rate was obtained. Whereas the college women averaged 21 years of age, these women averaged 36 years of age. A total of five questions were used to screen for rape and attempted rape, which were defined according to Ohio rape statutes (Ohio Revised Code for Rape, 1988). A typical item is the following: "Has a man made you have sex by using force or threatening to harm you? When we use the word sex we mean a man putting his penis in your vagina even if he did not ejaculate (come)." The incidence of rape in a 12-month period was 28 per 1,000 women based on the FBI definition (the rate was 62 per 1,000 using a reform definition). Even after reducing this rate to allow for telescoping, it is still 15 times larger than NCS estimates for the year 1986, which were 1.2 per 1,000 for women collapsed across all ages (BJS, 1988). These data mean that 1 adult woman in 55 experienced a rape as defined by the FBI during a one-year period (1 in 24 using a reform definition). Many of these assaults occurred in highly intimate contexts. Specifically, 39% of the rapes were perpetrated by husbands, partners, or relatives of the victim. Only 17% of the rapes were perpetrated by total strangers.

A concern that arises in some minds after reviewing rape incidence data is whether there is a "rape epidemic." An epidemic is defined as a dramatic increase in a phenomenon over previous levels. In the 40-year period from 1933 to 1973, the reported rape rate increased 557% (Hindelang & Davis, 1977). In the short period since 1984, the number of reported rapes has increased 10%, and the rate of rape per 100,000 women has increased 6% (FBI, 1989). It is important to focus on increases in the rate as opposed to increases in the total number of rapes because these latter increases could simply reflect population growth. Increases in rates per 100,000 women could be due to a true increase in the underlying number of crimes, or it could be accounted for by a growing tendency to report crime. Data from the NCS are designed to track changes in reporting; thus they should be able to resolve this ambiguity. Since 1984, the NCS rape victimization rate for women has been unchanged (1.3 per 1,000 in 1985; 1.2 per 1,000 in 1986; and 1.3 per 1,000 in 1987) according to BJS data (1987, 1988, 1989). Furthermore, the percentage of rapes that are reported to the police have not increased significantly (1984, 56%; 1986, 48%; 1987, 54%). However, as we will explain in the next section, the NCS approach to the measurement of rape is so flawed that little confidence can be placed in these data, and the question of whether the rape rate is increasing must be considered unanswered by current information.

NATIONAL CRIME SURVEY TECHNIQUES THAT UNDERMINE RAPE DISCLOSURE

All of the data from which generalizations about the scope of rape can be derived depend on information given by victims themselves (Hindelang & Davis, 1977). It is unfortunate but there are many reasons why rape victims cannot or will not reveal victimization by rape. Even in contemporary society, a rape victim often fears that she will not be believed, that she will be viewed as a precipitant or even as a participant in the crime (Burt & Katz, 1985). Additional hesitancy over public exposure can be traced to acceptance of traditional views of raped women as damaged goods that have lost their value (Taylor, Wood, & Lichtman, 1983). Thus, when a woman acknowledges her status as a victim, some degree of devaluation and stigmatization inevitably is incurred. As a result of these influences, there is considerable motivation to avoid identification with the role of "rape victim." The desire to withhold information about victimization often can be quite high. In one reverse records check, only 54% of acquaintance rape victims known to police would admit to an interviewer that they had been raped (Curtis, 1976). The compelling forces that actively oppose self-disclosure of victimization must be overcome in any data-collection effort that purports to describe rape incidence. Many experts who work closely with rape believe that NCS estimates of rape are low because of methods that undermine self-disclosure (Kilpatrick et al., 1985; Koss, 1990a; Koss, 1990b; Russell, 1984). There are at least six problems with the NCS handling of rape that could foster low disclosure rates.

Conditions of the Interview

The first problem involves the conditions under which the interviews are conducted. The compilers of the NCS acknowledge that "violence or attempted violence involving family members or close friends is underreported in the NCS . . . because some victims do not consider such events crimes or are reluctant to implicate family members or relatives, *who in some instances may be present during the interview*" (emphasis added, BJS, 1984, p. 10). It is obvious that some women may be reluctant to acknowledge a rape when other family members who do not know about the incident are present, particularly if the perpetrator of the rape is among those present. Independent research has repeatedly documented the large proportion of rapes that are committed by persons known to the victim. This criticism is further supported by the observation that police files contain approximately 3½ times more acquaintance violence than is revealed in the household interviews (Skogan, 1981).

Characteristics of Interviewers

The second problem involves the interviewers that are used, who do not have any special training to handle sensitive issues and who are not matched along gender or ethnic lines. Studies conducted as part of the NCS data-collection effort have suggested that interviewer effects are most substantial for sensitive topics—particularly rapes, intrafamilial disputes, and public brawling (Bailey, Moore, & Bailar, 1978). To the extent that rape is viewed as stigmatizing, many people are unlikely to disclose it to a stranger of the opposite sex. This methodology is especially detrimental among several major ethnic groups whose mores dictate that women do not speak to men about sexual matters.

The Rape Screening Questions

The third problem is the text of the questions that are used to screen for rape. Most of the NCS crime screening questions are behaviorally concrete and are written to specify the types of experiences that can qualify as a particular crime. An example is the following typical item: "Did anyone beat you up, attack you, or hit you with something, such as a rock or bottle?" The principal questions that elicit reports of rape are "Were you knifed, shot at, or attacked with some other weapon by anyone at all during the last six months?" and "Did anyone try to attack you *in some other way*?" (emphasis added, BJS, 1989, p. 100). Even those untrained in survey methodology will be surprised at the BJS explanation for their approach to screening for rape, which is the following: "In the National Crime Survey, each victim defines rape for herself . . . no one in the survey is ever asked directly if she has been raped. This response must come voluntarily in reply to a series of questions on bodily harm" (BJS, 1985, p. 2).

Even if the respondent replies affirmatively to the screening item, the follow-up items designed to obtain details of the crime also are vague and do not specifically mention rape either. The follow-up questions are the following: "How were you threatened?" and "How did the person attack you?" Among the choices that the interviewer can check on the basis of the participant's reply are the following: "verbal threat of rape" and "raped" (BJS, 1989, p. 104). Respondents are not told, however, that rape is to be considered as a form of attack for NCS purposes. It has been known since the inception of the NCS that the average person does not know the meaning of criminal justice terms such as burglary, larceny, robbery, and rape; yet the NCS uses the word "rape" as a response alternative without providing either interviewers or respondents with a definition.

How can the compilers of the NCS ensure that they have properly applied the FBI definition of rape if each respondent makes up his or her own definition for rape? This loose approach to the definition of a central concept is not seen in the remainder of the NCS, where screening questions clearly specify in concrete language the intended crime respondents might have experienced. Furthermore, it is very risky in a nationwide sample in which some persons can be expected to be nonnative speakers of English to employ a screening question that relies on nuance. Finally, the NCS practice of using one or two items to screen for rape must be questioned. Respondents need be queried about the variety of guises under which rape can occur. Specifically, women need to be asked about unwanted sex that occurred with a stranger or with someone they knew, was forced or involved only verbal threats of harm, was not forceful but occurred when incapacitated, entailed penile-vaginal intercourse or other forms of penetration (even if ejaculation did not occur), or was an attempt of rape characterized by a man getting on top of the respondent and trying to insert his penis when it was unwanted but penetration did not occur. One or two items cannot contain enough information to cue respondents adequately for recall of the range of experiences that qualify as rape under law.

Context of Questioning

The fourth problem is the context of questioning. The NCS is clearly presented to the respondent as a survey of crimes that have been personally experienced. A primary assumption of the victimization study is that a raped woman will conceptualize her experience as a crime. Much has been written about the existence of a rape-supportive belief system in Western industrialized societies (e.g., Burt, 1980; Weis & Borges, 1973). One component of the rape-supportive belief system is rape myths, which are widely accepted false beliefs about rape such as the following: "Rapists are mentally deranged strangers," "You cannot rape an unwilling woman," "You cannot 'thread a moving needle,' " and "You cannot be raped by someone you know." Assaults that go against these stereotypes of "real rape" often are not seen as rape, even by the victim (Estrich, 1987). Often when the offender was an acquaintance or date, victims falsely conclude that the label of rape is inapplicable to their experience. For example, one victim said, "I never consider it [rape] because in my mind rape was something that happened to a woman on the street, someone dragged her to an alley and they beat her up. It was a stranger. I never really thought that what happened to me was any of that" (quoted in Roth & Lebowitz, 1988, p. 97). Among college women who had had experiences that met legal requirements for rape, only one quarter labeled their experience as rape (Koss, 1988). Another quarter thought their experience was some kind of crime but not rape. The remaining half did not think their experience qualified as any type of crime. Placing rape in the context of other serious crimes is likely to trigger various myths about rape and reduce the chances that victims will report episodes that deviate from accepted stereotypes. Rapes involving acquaintances and minimal violence are particularly unlikely to be volunteered by respondents questioned in a context of crime.

The Definition of Rape

The fifth problem is the FBI definition of rape that serves as the foundation of the NCS (FBI, 1989, p. 15). Excluded from this definition are rapes where the offender was the legal or common-law spouse of the victim, rapes involving forms of penetration other than penile-vaginal intercourse, rapes of male victims, and rapes without actual force where the offender took advantage of a victim incapacitated by drugs, mental illness, or mental retardation. This traditional definition is too narrow and eliminates incidents that clearly are within the contemporary meaning of the term rape as reflected in both state laws and the federal rape law.

Handling of Repeated Assaults

A final problem with the NCS approach to rape is the handling of "series victimizations." The NCS uses this term to refer to three or more repeated victimizations that are similar or identical in nature where respondents are unable to identify separately the details of each act or to recount accurately the total number of such acts. Almost all series victimizations involve assaultive violence, and intimate violence is second only to occupationally related violence (such as experienced by police officers) in accounting for series incidents (Dodge & Lentzer, 1978). Series crimes presently are excluded from the calculation of victimization rates in the NCS. The elimination of series incidents distorts the picture that is painted of rape. For example, because acquaintance rape is more likely than stranger rape to involve multiple incidents, elimination of series incidents exaggerates the extent to which rape is a problem attributable to strangers. And, because people who are acquainted are likely to be of the same race, the elimination of series incidents exaggerates the incidence of interracial rape.

In 1985, then-director of the Bureau of Justice Statistics, Steven R. Schlesinger, stated, "Rape is a brutal and terrifying crime. It is especially important that our understanding of this crime is based on reliable information." (BJS, 1985, p. 1) It is indeed unfortunate that even with the benefits of the elegant and expensive survey technology employed in the NCS, an accurate picture of rape fails to emerge. Rather than being revealed, the true incidence of rape is covered up by these data. As a document on the vulnerability to victimization experienced by women, the NCS does a disservice to American women (Kilpatrick et al., 1985; Koss, 1990a; Koss et al., 1987; Russell, 1984). In August of 1990 the urgent need for redesign of the NCS measurement of rape was the subject of testimony before the United States Senate Judiciary Committee (Koss, 1990a). Redesign has been promised that will be phased in over a three-year period. Because publication of NCS results usually lags two years behind data collection, this plan could mean that better data on rape would not be seen until after 1995. It is important to keep up the critical pressure to obtain redesign as early as possible. The first step in facing the reality of sexual violence in the United States is to take the blinders off official data-collection activities.

A final limitation to all of the incidence data reviewed above is its reference period of just the previous 12 months. If a woman was raped 13 months ago, she would not be considered to have been victimized for purposes of incidence estimates. Because incidence rates indicate how many new cases of rape are likely to occur during a typical year, they may be useful for extrapolating the need for hospital emergency or victim-witness services. Incidence data fail to capture the full mental health burden of victimization by sexual violence, however, because the aftermath lingers for a considerable period. It is not unusual for the symptoms of posttraumatic stress disorder from which victims of violence suffer to emerge after a latency of months or years following the trauma (American Psychiatric Association, 1980).

PREVALENCE STUDIES OF RAPE

Prevalence figures attempt to estimate the number of women who have been victimized by rape ever in their lives. Thus these figures may be more broadly meaningful to clinicians. It is unfortunate, however, that the prevalence literature is difficult to integrate because of major differences in the methods used by various investigators. The most troublesome variability is in the definition of the construct that was measured. A number of studies measure "sexual assault." In legal usage this term is synonymous with rape. In the prevalence literature, however, the term sexual assault often is treated as a generic term that subsumes rape as well as lesser degrees of unwanted and pressured sexual contacts not involving penetration, and even subsumes child abuse and incest. Therefore one has to be very careful in reading this literature to examine not only the reported prevalence percentages but also the definition that was used to select incidents that were included.

Our review has been limited to those studies of rape prevalence that used probability sampling methods (as opposed to studying anyone who happened to be conveniently available) and involved U.S. samples. The literature includes studies that have focused on *adolescents* (Ageton, 1983; Hall & Flannery, 1984; Moore, Nord, & Peterson, 1989); *college students* (Koss et al., 1987; Miller & Marshall, 1987); *adult women* (Essock-Vitale & McGuire, 1985; Kilpatrick et al., 1987; Kilpatrick & Best, 1990; Koss, Woodruff, & Koss, in press-b; Russell, 1982, 1984; Sorenson, Stein, Siegel, Golding, & Burnam, 1987; Winfield, George, Smartz, & Blazer, 1991); *adult men* (George & Winfield-Laird, 1986; Sorenson et al., 1987); and *special populations* including the elderly, nursing home residents, psychiatric patients, and prisoners (George & Winfield-Laird, 1986; Jacobson & Richardson, 1987); and *ethnic groups* including Hispanics (Sorenson et al., 1987) and African-Americans (Wyatt, 1990). In the following sections, we will briefly review what the prevalence of rape and/or sexual assault is among these groups.

Adolescent Girls

The work by Ageton was discussed earlier. Her question to elicit sexual experiences was, "How many times in the last year have you been sexually attacked or raped or an attempt made to do so?" (Ageton, 1983). Between 5% and 11% of female adolescents reported affirmatively to this question across the several years of the study. Hall and Flannery (1984) used the telephone survey to ask 508 Milwaukee adolescents, "Has a guy ever used physical force or threatened you, to make you have sex when you didn't want to?" Among their respondents, 12% reported a sexual assault in their lifetime.

College Students

In their national sample of college students, Koss and colleagues found that 15% of the women respondents had had an experience which met the Ohio legal definition of rape (Koss et al., 1987). An additional 12% had experienced attempted rape. A total of 10 screening items were used to obtain the data (a typical screening item was presented previously). These findings mean that 1 in 3.6 college women has been a victim of rape or attempted rape in her lifetime. More than half (54%) of the women surveyed had been sexually victimized to some degree. Women reported that their rapes occurred on average 1 to 2 years previously. The typical victim was 18.5 years old. One offender was involved in 95% of the rapes. Just 16% of the rapes involved a perpetrator who was a complete stranger; 57% of the rapes involved a date. The rapes happened primarily off campus (86%), equally as often in the man's house or car as in the woman's house or car. Victims were using intoxicants in 55% of the episodes. Prior mutual intimacy had occurred with the offender to the level of petting above the waist. The victims believed, however, that they had made their nonconsent to have sexual intercourse quite clear. Typically, the victim perceived that the offender used quite a bit of force, often involving twisting her arm or holding her down. Only 9% of the rapes involved hitting or beating. Forms of resistance used by the victims in their attempts to escape were reasoning with the offender (84%) and physically struggling (70%). Many women were virgins prior to the rape. Almost half of the victims told no one about their rape; just 5% reported to the police, and only 5% visited a rape crisis center.

These findings differ greatly from the view of date rape that has sometimes been promulgated by the popular media. For example, note this case history presented in *Newsweek* magazine (Seligman, 1984).

> Colleen, 27, a San Francisco office manager, had been involved with her boyfriend for about a year when it happened. After a cozy dinner at her apartment, he suggested that she go to bed while he did the dishes. But a few moments later he stalked into Colleen's bedroom with a peculiar look on his face, brandishing a butcher knife and strips of cloth. After tying her, spread-eagled to the bed, the formerly tender lover raped her brutally for three hours using his fist, the knife, a shampoo bottle, and other household objects. (p. 91)

Adult Women

A number of prevalence estimates for rape are available for adult women. The earliest was Russell's work (1982, 1984). As indicated earlier, she defined rape according to California law, and 38 items were used to elicit information. Interviewers were matched for gender and ethnicity whenever possible. Russell (1982) found that 24% of her San Francisco sample had experienced completed rape, and 31% had experienced attempted rape. These categories were not mutually exclusive; when each respondent is counted only once, a total of 44% of the sample experienced a rape or attempted rape (Russell, 1984). Among the 644 women who had ever been married, 14% reported being physically forced by their husband to engage in penile-vaginal, oral, or anal intercourse.

Sorenson and colleagues (1987) administered the following question to 3,172 participants from the Los Angeles site of the Epidemiological Catchment Area Studies (ECA): "In your lifetime, has anyone ever tried to pressure or force you to have sexual contact? By sexual contact I mean their touching your sexual parts, your touching their sexual parts, or sexual intercourse." The interviewers were not gender- or ethnicity-matched and other family members were present for half of the interviews. The results indicated that 14% of the women respondents had experienced one or more sexual assaults since age 16. The rates of sexual assault were found to vary with ethnic status and with education. Thus the rate of assault was 7% for Hispanic women and 16% among nonhispanic white women. The rate of sexual assault among white women age 18 to 39 with college educations was 28%.

Winfield et al. (1991) interviewed 1,157 participants in the Durham, North Carolina, site of the Epidemiological Catchment Area Studies (ECA) and asked the following question: "Have you ever been in a situation in which you were pressured into doing more sexually than you wanted to do, that is, a situation in which someone pressured you against your will into forced contact with the sexual parts of your body or their body?" Interviewers were not gender-matched. The remainder of the ECA interview focused on symptoms of mental illness. No definition of sexual assault is found in their report, but examination of the screening question presented above suggests that a broad spectrum of incidents were included without the ability to break out a separate rate for rape and attempted rape. The prevalence percentage reported by Winfield and colleagues (1991) is 6% for adult women in their lifetime.

Kilpatrick et al. (1985) used random-digit dialing techniques to telephonically contact a sample of 2,004 women residents of Charleston County, South Carolina (Kilpatrick and colleagues recently have completed a national telephone survey, but the results are not yet available.) In the context of other questions about crime, two items about rape were included, of which the following is representative: "Has anyone ever tried to make you have sexual relations with them against your will?" A total of 9% of the respondents reported experiences of rape or attempted rape. In a later study, a subsample of 391 women in this sample agreed to report for a personal interview (Kilpatrick, Saunders, Veronen, Best, & Von, 1987). The actual text of screening items is not given in the report, but the definition of rape required nonconsent, threat or use of force, and one or more types of completed sexual penetration. Although questions about other crimes were included, the sexual assault items were administered separately from the other crime items with an introduction designed to dispel the notion that the incident had to be a crime and to counteract the tendency to conceptualize rape in narrow, stereotypic terms. The results indicated that 53% of the women had been a victim of at least one sexual assault including 23% who had experienced completed rape and 13% who had experienced attempted rape. Sexual assaults constituted half of the crimes recalled by participants; completed rapes alone accounted for 19% of the crime volume.

Special Populations

The focus of research by Gail Wyatt has been comparisons of African-American and white women. The data were collected by an extensive standardized interview using gender- and ethnicity-matched interviewers. Participants were a stratified random sample of 126 African-American and 122 white women residents of Los Angeles County. The questioning about rape came after a lengthy period of the interview had passed to allow rapport to be established. Then respondents were read the following definition of rape: "I will be asking you about sexual experiences which may have occurred without your consent. These experiences may have involved a friend, relative, or stranger. . . . Rape is involuntary penetration of the vagina or anus by the penis or another object. Since the age of 18 have you ever been raped?" (Wyatt, 1984). The results indicated that 1 in 4 African-American women and 1 in 5 white women reported at least one incident of an attempted or completed rape since the age of 18 (Wyatt, 1990).

Prevalence data for men are available from the two ECA sites that included questioning about sexual assault. The prevalence rates reported for adult men vary from 0.6% (George & Winfield-Laird, 1986) to 7% (Sorenson et al., 1987). Prevalence rates

in special populations are 49% among female psychiatric inpatients and 0% among male patients, 100% among female
prisoners and 8% among male prisoners (George & Winfield-
Laird, 1986).

As the volume of research on rape prevalence has grown, it
is disconcerting to note that published prevalence rates have
tended to decrease dramatically. Accompanying these low rates
have sometimes been assertions that the figures are more accurate reflections of the extent of rape than earlier work. For example, in reference to a 6% lifetime prevalence rate for sexual
assault, George and Winfield-Laird (1986) concluded, "we believe the relatively low prevalence of sexual assault reported by
respondents to be a reasonable estimate of the population and
not an artifact of sampling or methodology" (p. 39). One could
accept such an assessment had it been demonstrated in recent
work that a large body of sexual experiences were identified,
but many cases were eliminated from the rate calculations because the reported incidents did not meet legal qualifications for
rape or were found to be exaggerated. This has not been the
case. In fact, several recent studies that have obtained low prevalence rates involved vague, imprecise definitions of rape applicable to many incidents that would fail legal standards for rape.
Yet, in the absence of any evidence, either compelling or suggestive, that respondents have fabricated reports, an alternative
explanation of the low prevalence rates must be considered.
Rather than reflecting accurately rape prevalence in the community, the possibility arises that choices of methods were made in
some studies that resulted in a relative lack of success in identifying eligible respondents. Among the methods that appear to
be associated with finding low prevalence rates are using just
one or two very global screening questions, failing to match
interviewers to participants on gender and ethnicity, conducting
the data collection in the presence of other family members, and
ignoring the need to dispel context effects due to the placement
of sexual assault screening questions in a crime or psychiatric
illness context.

There does seem to be some consistency among those studies
of adult women that have avoided the problems noted above.

Thus rape prevalence of approximately 20% for adult women has been reported by four separate groups of investigators working in different regions of the United States, who have all modeled their definition of rape on legal standards (Kilpatrick et al., 1987; Koss et al., in press-b; Russell, 1982, 1984; and Wyatt, 1990). These cumulative findings suggest that 1 in 5 adult women has experienced a completed rape up to that point in her life (i.e., the time of the survey). If more extensive data existed it would be possible to project the lifetime chances of being raped, and they would present an even more devastating picture. These findings transform rape from a heinous but rare event into a common experience in women's lives.

THE CAUSES OF RAPE

Of course the primary cause of rape is the rapist, but there is no simple answer to the question, "Why do men rape?" Multiple influences determine the expression of sexually assaultive behavior (for recent reviews see Craig, 1990; Malamuth & Dean, in press; and White & Koss, in press). In the material presented below, evidence from research on acquaintance rape as presented in White and Koss (in press) is emphasized. It has been our experience that these are the rapes that most plague victims with repeated, fruitless search for answers to the question, "Why me?" The model presented in the following material is a four-level hierarchical organization of the factors that support rape. The top of the hierarchy is the level of the broader society and the bottom is the characteristics of the individual potential offender.

Societal-Level Supports for Rape

At the societal level, rape can be seen as a manifestation of gender inequality and as a mechanism for the subordination of women. A number of macroanalytic studies have found relationships among indices of societal values and rape rates, such as between policies controlling gun ownership and hunting, and between subscription rates for pornographic magazines and reported rape rates (Baron & Strauss, 1989; Linsky, Straus, & Backman-Prehn, 1990).

Cultural Values

Sexist attitudes and values, in conjunction with a general acceptance of violence, contribute to rape (Brownmiller, 1975; Clark & Lewis, 1977; Muehlenhard & Shrag, 1990). Rape-supportive attitudes are socially acquired beliefs that function as releasers and can increase the likelihood of sexually aggressive actions (Mahoney, Shively, & Traw, 1986). Acceptance of beliefs that foster rape has been demonstrated among a variety of groups including typical citizens, police officers, and judges (Burt, 1980; Feild, 1978). Examples of rape myths include the following:

• *No really means yes.* Since women who give in to sex too easily or act like they really enjoy sex appear to be of low moral character (according to this myth), *"all* women *always* make initial protests, although they *never* really mean it."

• *Women love to be swept off their feet and taken by force.* We are often asked if it is not true that many women secretly fantasize about being raped. There is a big difference between dreaming about a commanding, handsome, and powerful man whose degree of forcefulness is at the control of the dreamer and facing a real-life rape.

• *Nice girls do not get raped.* This myth encourages a woman to feel guilty about being raped and may lead her to keep her experience secret for fear that it would degrade her reputation.

• *The typical rape involves a stranger in a dark alley.*

• *The typical rape is a violent crime.* As we have seen, the violent, stranger rape is the exception, not the rule.

• *It is impossible to rape an unwilling woman.* This myth supports the prejudice that a woman consented unless there are obvious signs of injury.

Sexual Scripts

A second societal-level variable that influences sexual aggression is a society's expectations about adolescent dating rituals.

Scripts about sexual expression can support rape when they deprive a woman of her right to say "no" to further sexual advances, encourage the man to be a sexual stalker and the woman his prey, and hold a woman responsible for the extent of sexual involvement. Evidence suggests that teenagers in the United States accept sexual scripts that dictate that men should use any strategy to induce dates to have sex, and that women either should passively acquiesce or use any strategy to avoid sex. Furthermore, many young women and men are taught that a woman should pretend she means "no," even when she means "yes" (Muehlenhard & Hollabaugh, 1988). Thus young men are socialized to believe in "male sexual access rights" (Mahoney et al., 1986). In fact, many date rapists report that they did not realize that what they had done was wrong (Parrot, 1989). Research conducted by the Rhode Island Rape Crisis Center (Teens express themselves, 1988) on 1,700 middle-school children indicated that 65% of the boys and 57% of the girls said that it was acceptable for a man to force a woman to have sex if they had been dating for more than six months. Approximately 25% of the boys said that it was acceptable for a man to force sex on a woman if he had spent money on her. Craig and Kalichman (1988) found that college students rated forced sex as being acceptable under the following conditions: when a woman has agreed to have sex with a man and then changed her mind (13%); when they have been dating exclusively (24%); when she has allowed him to touch her genitals (24%); when she has touched his genitals (29%); and when they have both willingly had their clothes off (35%).

Institutional Influences

Individual interpersonal interactions are embedded in social structures that define and direct the meaning of sex and violence. Social structures that directly encroach upon a young man's daily life include family, peer relationships, school, and religion.

Early Family Experiences

It has been hypothesized that male aggression toward women is highly likely for young men reared in families where female family members were the targets of male aggression and where attitudes that devalue women prevailed. Witnessing or experiencing family violence has been related to sexually aggressive behavior among college men (Koss & Dinero, 1989b).

Family attitudes toward sexuality and male-female roles also have been implicated. Ross (1977) suggested that parents socialize sons to initiate sexual activity and daughters to resist sexual advances. Sexually assaultive behavior in young men has been related to fathers' attitudes towards sexual aggression (Kanin, 1985), as well as fathers' sexual behaviors toward their wives (White & Shuntich, 1990).

Early sexual experiences, including sexual abuse, have been correlated with sexual aggression (Koss & Dinero, 1989b; White & Humphrey, 1990). In a series of longitudinal investigations of sexually abused children, Friedrich and colleagues observed a significant relationship between sexual victimization and subsequent sexual aggression in boys (Friedrich, Beilke, & Urquiza, 1988). Early sexual experiences, especially abusive ones, may alter a young man's notion of what normal sex is. Furthermore, the psychological consequences of abuse may play a role in lowering self-esteem, another factor predictive of assaultive behavior (White & Humphrey, 1990). In addition to possible alterations in the meaning of sexual relations associated with sexual abuse, the early initiation into sexual activity created by the abuse increases the opportunity for sexual assault to occur. The greater number of sexual partners a man has had, the greater the likelihood that he will have been sexually assaultive at least once (Kanin, 1967; Koss & Dinero, 1989a; Mahoney et al., 1986; Malamuth, 1986; White & Humphrey, 1990).

Peer-Group Influences

Peer-group socialization has been identified as a powerful predictor of sexually assaultive behavior (Koss & Dinero, 1989a; White & Humphrey, 1990). Ageton (1983) found that delinquent peer-group association was the single best predictor of sexual assault.

Other Social Institutions

Other social institutions that are less studied also influence the likelihood of sexual aggression. Ageton (1983) reported that several indices of school-related functioning were significantly related to the probability of sexual aggression, including lower academic aspirations, poorer current school success, and school normlessness. In addition, lower scores on religious commitment also have been found to predict sexual aggression (White & Humphrey, 1990).

Dyadic Interpersonal Context

An individual performs a sexually assaultive act in a microsystem, which is the dyadic interpersonal context and includes features of the relationship and situation.

The Relationship

The degree of acquaintanceship between a young man and his potential victim appears to contribute to the prediction of whether or not a sexual assault will occur, the type of coercion he will use, and the likelihood that the assault will end in a completed rape. Research on the question of whether first dates are riskier than later dates is inconclusive; some suggest that early dates are more dangerous (Muehlenhard & Linton, 1987), others implicate longer relationships (Kirkpatrick & Kanin, 1957; Russell, 1984; Weis & Borges, 1973). It is known that completed rape is more likely in couples who know each other well than among persons who are acquaintances (Belnap, 1989). The degree of relationship also affects perceptions of the assault. The greater the acquaintanceship, the less likely people are to judge an instance of forced sexual intercourse to be rape (Goodchilds, Zellman, Johnson, & Giarrusso, 1988). Prior intimacy may also increase the likelihood of a sexual assault (Kanin, 1970). Prior intimacy may increase the man's belief that he has a right to sex any time he desires and that rape will not really hurt the woman with whom he previously had been intimate (Johnson & Jackson, 1988).

Victim Characteristics

Amir (1971), who has published several papers on "victim precipitation of rape," observed from police records that rape victims often were described by police officers as "a woman with a bad reputation in the neighborhood." Therefore he reasoned that the woman could be held partially responsible for her rape. The observation that highly sexually aggressive men often justify their behavior by stating that "she deserved it" or "she dressed like that kind of woman" was offered as support for victim precipitation of rape by Kanin (1957).

A vulnerability model of rape has been explored in several studies (e.g., Myers, Templer, & Brown, 1984; Selkin, 1978). For example, Selkin compared the California Psychological Inventory (CPI) responses of "rape resistors" (i.e., attempted rape victims) and rape victims. He reported that successful resistors scored higher on several scales: Dominance, Social Presence, Sociability, and Communality. He concluded that the victims' likelihood of being raped had been increased by their personality characteristics including greater passivity and lower social poise.

The conclusions of vulnerability studies can be challenged on methodological and theoretical grounds. For example, Myers et al. (1984) employed different recruitment techniques for their rape victims and nonvictimized women. Victims were some subgroup of the women who had reported to three rape crisis centers, many of whom came on their physician's orders. They were compared to a group of women recruited on or near a college campus through handbills announcing "psychosocial assessments." The first technique seems likely to obtain women biased toward compliance with doctors' orders and reliance on social services. The second procedure would likely result in a group of assertive, adventuresome, extroverted women. Thus the very differences Myers et al. (1984) report (i.e., victims scored lower on CPI scales for Dominance, Social Presence, and so forth) could easily be supported by the biases built into the groups by the selection procedures. When identical sample selection procedures have been used to select victims of rape, victims of attempted rape, victims of sexual coercion, and nonvictimized women (Koss, 1985), no differences were found between the groups on the personality characteristics measured by the CPI.

Vulnerability studies such as that conducted by Myers et al. (1984) involve psychological assessment administered postrape but advance the view that the differences obtained actually predated the rape. It is difficult to substantiate the validity of this assumption. Because the significant impact of rape victimization on psychological functioning is so well documented by a number of excellent studies (see Chapter 2), it is much more logical to view differences between raped and nonraped women as reflective of the impact of rape, not as evidence of preexisting personality differences. In conclusion, no uncontested evidence supportive of victim precipitation or victim vulnerability to rape currently is available.

There exists a large number of studies in social psychology that have used made-up scenarios about rape in which various victim characteristics are altered, including her character, past sexual history, attractiveness, style of dress, and provocativeness of behavior. Two tacit assumptions appear to underlie such research. First is the assumption that these factors inform one about the woman's interest and consent to engage in sexual activities. The second assumption is that the characteristics are responsible for the perpetrator's behavior. In a recent paper, Koss and Dinero (1989b) compared the relative predictive power of three major theories of rape victimization: vulnerability-creating early experiences, social-psychological vulnerability, and vulnerability-enhancing situations. A total of 13 risk factors were chosen to operationalize these vulnerability theories. Participants were an approximately representative national sample of 2,723 female college students. A risk profile emerged that characterized just 10% of the women, but among them the risk of rape was twice the rate for women without the profile. A major contributor to the risk profile for rape was having been sexually abused as a child. The most important finding, however, was that the vast majority of sexually victimized women could not be differentiated from nonvictims (between 75% and 91% were undetected across four different levels of victimization severity). It was concluded that rape either was predicted by circumstances in a victim's past beyond her control, or it was not predictable. The study offered no support for assertions that some women are uniquely vulnerable to rape by virtue of their personality characteristics, assertiveness, or degree of identification with feminine stereotyped behavior. The important implication of the research is the urgent need for research directed at understanding the mechanisms by which childhood sexual experiences can create lifetime legacies of increased risks for sexual assault.

Another group of studies that should be mentioned briefly are those that examined "rape avoidance." In these studies the resistance strategies of women who were raped are compared to the strategies that were used by women who "avoided rape," which is simply another way of saying they were victims of attempted rape but penetration did not occur. Javorek (1979) found that whether the potential victim screamed for help or not was the most useful predictor of whether a rape attempt was completed. Bart (1981) found that fleeing or attempting to flee was associated with the highest rates of rape avoidance (81% of the women who used this tactic avoided being raped). Two recent studies have cautioned, however, that it is the offender's behavior that largely determines the outcome of a sexual assault, not the victim's resistance (Levine-MacCombie & Koss, 1986; Siegel, Sorenson, Golding, Burnam, & Stein, 1989).

Miscommunication

Sexual scripts for sexual relationships, described above, contain an inherent tension between the man and woman and create the opportunity for miscommunication (Goodchilds et al., 1988; Lundberg-Love & Geffner, 1989; Muehlenhard & Linton,

1987). It has been observed that many people feel uncomfortable discussing sexual intentions and desires. As a result, people attempt to infer sexual intent from indirect and nonverbal cues, a strategy that is bound to produce frequent errors (Abbey, 1990, p. 2). A man may interpret a woman's friendly behavior in a more sexualized way than she intends (Abbey, 1990); may not take a woman's objections to sexual contact seriously (Check & Malamuth, 1983); and may perceive refusal as a threat to his manhood (Beneke, 1982). Abbey (1987) found that two thirds of the students she surveyed believed that on various occasions their friendliness had been perceived as a sexual invitation. Koss (1988) found that 75% of the men who had raped believed that the victim's nonconsent to have sexual intercourse was "not at all clear," while most of the raped women believed that their nonconsent was "extremely clear."

The Situation

Situational characteristics that affect the likelihood of a sexual assault are those that create the opportunity and contribute to the ambiguity of cues. Victims in Ageton's (1983) adolescent sample cited the time of day, the location, and the offender's being drunk and sexually excited as the major precipitants of the assault. According to Belnap (1989), the riskiest season for acquaintance rape is summer and the riskiest time of day is between 6:00 p.m. and midnight. Assaults occur as frequently in the victim's home or car as in the offender's home or car (Koss, 1988). In fact, any secluded place that allows for privacy fosters rape (Ageton, 1983; Goodchilds et al., 1988; Lott, Reilly, & Howard, 1982; Muehlenhard & Linton, 1987). Women have reported that rapes also occur at parties, especially when alcohol is involved (Muehlenhard & Linton, 1987).

Alcohol and drugs have been implicated frequently in sexual assaults. It is likely that alcohol may serve multiple functions— as a disinhibitor for the male, as an excuse for the male after the fact, and as a strategy to reduce victim resistance (Richardson & Hammock, 1990). Furthermore, alcohol may function as a cue; women who drink might be perceived as "loose" or more interested in sex. One third to two thirds of rapists and approximately half of rape victims have consumed alcohol prior to the rape (Lott et al., 1982; Wilson & Durrenberger, 1982; Wolfe & Baker, 1984). Many young men feel that rape is more justifiable if the woman is drunk or "stoned" (Goodchilds et al., 1988).

Other situations that have been linked to the likelihood of rape involve the circumstances of the date. It is well documented that many high school and college students think forced sex is acceptable when the man spends a lot of money on the woman (Goodchilds et al., 1988; Muehlenhard, Friedman, & Thomas, 1985). Men who initiate the date, pay all expenses, and drive the car are more likely to be sexually aggressive than other men. Apparently, a man may feel justified in using force if necessary to obtain sex because of his "investment."

Individual Determinants

Individual determinants are the individual characteristics of the potential perpetrator. Kanin has suggested that "the orientation to sexually exploit was acquired at a previous period—high school or perhaps earlier—and the choice of sympathetic membership groups at college largely represents a selective attempt to sustain and receive support for the earlier acquired values" (1967, p. 501). The connections between the individual level and the interpersonal context have been discussed extensively by Craig (1990).

Demographic Characteristics

The typical image of a rapist, derived primarily from crime statistics, is that of a young, black, urban male, often of lower class status. However, other information suggests that this image is incorrect. Several investigators have found no significant differences in the incidence or prevalence of sexual assault as a function of race, social class, or place of residence (Ageton, 1983; Hall & Flannery, 1984; Rouse, 1988). Koss et al. (1987) found that the rate of self-reported rape was related to ethnic group and region of the country where attending school, but not to religion or family income. The magnitude of the differences was so small, however, that they concluded that sexual assault was ubiquitous.

Attitudes

Sexually aggressive men more strongly subscribe to traditional gender-role stereotypes than nonsexually aggressive men (Burt, 1980; Malamuth, 1988; Mosher & Anderson, 1986; Rapaport & Burkhart, 1984). The two groups of men differ most strongly in their attitudes regarding the acceptance of male dominance, acceptance of rape-supportive myths, acceptance of interpersonal violence as a strategy for resolving conflicts, and hostility toward women (Koss & Dinero, 1989a; Malamuth, 1986, 1988; Malamuth & Ceniti, 1986; Rapaport & Burkhart, 1984; 1987). Sexually aggressive men are less reluctant to view forced sexual relations on a date as rape; rather, rape is judged to be normal and acceptable. These men are more likely to perceive a rape victim as seductive and desiring of sexual relations (Jenkins & Dambrot, 1985; Koss & Dinero, 1989a; Muehlenhard et al., 1985; Muehlenhard & Linton, 1987). The amount of predictive power contributed by attitudes, however, is smaller than that of personality characteristics, needs, motives, and situational features (Niles & White, 1989).

Personality Characteristics

A range of men's personality characteristics have been linked with sexual aggression including antisocial tendencies (Calhoun, Kelley, Amick, & Gardner, 1986; Malamuth, 1986); low socialization and responsibility (Rapaport & Burkhart, 1984); nonconformity (Rapaport & Burkhart, 1987); impulsivity (Calhoun, 1990); and deficient self-monitoring (Yescavage & White, 1989). Of particular interest are associations between scores on a hypermasculinity scale and sexual aggression (Mosher & Anderson, 1986), self-reported drug use, aggressive behavior, dangerous driving, and delinquent behavior (Mosher & Sirkin, 1984).

Masculinity and Gender Schema

Sexually aggressive men generally describe themselves in more traditional masculine terms than do sexually nonaggressive men (Koss & Dinero, 1989a; Tieger, 1981; White & Humphrey, 1990). Recent conceptualizations of gender schemas have suggested that they serve as expectancies that selectively organize and even bias perceptions of the world. Quackenbush (1989) found that men who lacked the feminine gender schema were more sexually aggressive than those who had it. Men who lack feminine gender schema lack the social skills of femininity, which include concern for and ability to empathize with others (Dietz, Blackwell, Daley, & Bentley, 1982; Quackenbush, 1989). Instead they rely on social myths to negotiate social interactions. Once men develop a schema about women, they are likely to (mis)interpret ambiguous evidence as confirming their beliefs (Abbey, 1990).

Attraction to Sexual Aggression

Sexually aggressive men are likely to find aspects of sexual aggression attractive, are more likely to report a likelihood of raping a woman in the future (Malamuth, 1989a, 1989b), and more likely to engage in coercive sexual fantasies (Greendlinger & Byrne, 1987). Malamuth developed an Attraction to Sexual Aggression scale, which is thought to reflect tendencies to believe that sexual aggression is an arousing experience for both the man and the woman. He demonstrated that men high on this measure were likely to say that they would aggress sexually if the fear of punishment and other inhibitory factors were absent.

Sex and Power Motives

Although rape is widely viewed by the public as a violent act motivated by needs to dominate the woman, the academic community has not been converted to this view (Palmer, 1988). Some argue that sexual assault is fulfillment of sexual needs via violent behavior (Ellis, 1989; Shields & Shields, 1983). Others see sexually aggressive actions as extreme acts but ones that are extensions of normative heterosexual practices (Jackson, 1978; Russell, 1982, 1984; Weis & Borges, 1973). Those who have actually tried to measure these two motives found that motives other than sex, including power and anger, were stronger (Lisak & Roth, 1988). Other attempts to resolve this question have focused on patterns of sexual arousal to depictions of pure violence, pure consensual sex, and nonconsensual sex (which includes violence). This research has shown consistently that some "normal" males, with no known history of sexual aggression, may be aroused by rape stimuli involving adults. This line of research has led to the conclusion that diagnosis of sexual deviance solely on the basis of physiological arousal is unacceptable (Hall, 1990). It has been shown consistently, however, that sexually aggressive males appear to be generally more sexually aroused to both consenting sexual stimuli and rape stimuli (Rapaport & Posey, 1990). Date rapists have been found to have higher sexual expectations than nonsexually aggressive peers (Kanin, 1985). Thus even though they are sexually active, they remain chronically frustrated. This frustration may serve to disinhibit aggression as a tactic to achieve sexual fulfillment.

Cognitive Restructuring

Studies have suggested that sexually aggressive men engage in cognitive restructuring that allows them to interpret as seduction behavior that was seen by the woman as rape or sexual assault. Men who were consuming alcohol or drugs when they raped may convince themselves that the alcohol promoted the violence (George & Marlatt, 1986). They may perceive the victim's struggles and verbal protests as consistent with their beliefs about what women want sexually (Koss & Dinero, 1989b). Finally, they may blame the victim—stating that she was asking for it or deserved it (Kanin, 1957; Scully & Marolla, 1984). Because men who have raped acquaintances see what they have done as consistent with seduction and with what the victim wanted, they almost always can "pass" a polygraph test.

TWO

The Trauma of Rape

Nothing that can be said about the trauma of rape is more poignant than victims' testimony: "It's the worst thing I have ever gone through. I wouldn't wish it on my worst enemy. [The counselor asked, "How about your father's death?"] I remember my father and I remember the good and happy times. There are good memories from that but this just has horrors. Nothing can top this." Other victims described their experience with the following comments: "I'd rank it a 10 . . . or even higher than your top number, a 12 or a 15"; "Worst thing that ever happened"; "Equal to the death of a spouse . . . takes away all security" (quoted in Burgess & Holmstrom, 1979). The focus of this chapter is the symptomatic impact of rape. We begin with an ecological model of the response and resolution of rape. The model schematizes the features that determine the distress a victim experiences and delineates several long-term outcomes of rape. Following presentation of the model, the symptoms seen in the aftermath of rape are examined, beginning with clinical observations of the patterns of recovery and progressing to the empirical studies of emotional distress, cognitive patterns, physical symptoms, sexual dysfunctions, and social disruptions. Because the vast majority of rape victims are women, both the clinical and empirical literature have focused on them. Little information is available on the male rape victim. We include a short section about the male rape victim, although most clinicians have concluded that the impact of rape is very similar regardless of gender. While the recovery environment faced by the male victim may be somewhat different from that faced by the female victim, the bottom line is that both are unsupportive in their own ways.

The complex of symptoms seen in the aftermath of rape often meet the criteria for the diagnosis of posttraumatic stress disorder (American Psychiatric Association, 1987). Therefore requirements for formal diagnosis are reviewed briefly in this chapter and contemporary models of the psychological processes that create and maintain posttraumatic stress disorder (PTSD) symptoms are summarized. The chapter concludes with suggestions for clinical screening to identify the history of sexual assault and suggestions for the psychometric assessment of the severity of symptomatology.

AN ECOLOGICAL MODEL OF
RAPE TRAUMA

"Ecology" is the science concerned with the interrelationship of organisms and their environments (Webster's Ninth New Collegiate Dictionary, 1985). An ecological model of rape trauma is concerned with the interrelationships among the characteristics of the person who has been victimized, the rape event that has occurred, and the social environment in which recovery must take place (Green, Wilson, & Lindy, 1985; Harvey, 1990). Such a model is presented in Figure 2.1.

Assumptions

Three assumptions underlie the model in Figure 2.1. The first assumption is that not all potentially traumatizing events are traumatic (or equally traumatic) for all individuals. The second assumption is that the individual's posttraumatic response is multiply determined. The final assumption is that clinical and community interventions, or the lack thereof, will interact with

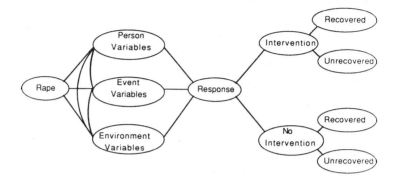

Figure 2.1 An Ecological Model of Rape Response and Recovery
Adapted from Harvey (1990).

these same multiple determinants to aid or impede recovery. Consider the following examples. A middle-class college student who has been raised in a family that values daughters as much as sons and who is well informed about rape and able to avail herself of the supportive resources of an active feminist community will respond to sexual assault quite differently than will a teenage girl whose prerape beliefs were basically victim blaming and whose key support figures continue to believe that "an unwilling woman can't really be raped." Similarly, individuals who experience violence and abuse in isolation from others and who feel obliged to recover from their experience in continued isolation will adjust differently over time than will those individuals whose suffering has been shared and/or those who have access to and are able to make use of helpful support figures. There is nothing in any of these examples that in and of itself would inoculate against a difficult posttraumatic response and/or guarantee rapid recovery. Nevertheless, it is possible to predict quite varied posttraumatic response and recovery outcomes and it is likely that certain aspects of each situation will exert significant influence toward the determination of these outcomes.

Determinants of Posttraumatic Response and Recovery

A variety of personal, event, and environmental factors have the potential to influence individual response to and recovery from sexual assault. Examples of these influences are summarized in Table 2.1. Person variables of particular relevance include the age and developmental stage of the victim; her or his relationship to the offender; the ability of the victim to identify and make use of available social support; and the meaning that is assigned to the traumatic event by the victim, by family and friends, and by others including police, medical personnel, and victim advocates with whom the victim has contact in the immediate aftermath of trauma. Relevant event variables include the frequency, the severity, and the duration of the traumatic event(s) and the degree of physical violence, personal violation, and life-threat endured by the victim. Environmental variables involve the setting where the victimization occurred, including home, school, workplace, or street. Other environmental variables are the degree of safety and control that are afforded to victims posttrauma; prevailing community attitudes and values about sexual assault; and the availability, quality, accessibility, and diversity of victim care and victim advocacy services.

Recovery Outcomes

An ecological view of rape proposes that in the aftermath of rape, victims can be conceptually grouped into those who do and those who do not become recipients of clinical and community services. Each of these groups can be further divided into those who recover from and resolve the rape and those who do not achieve resolution. Resolution and recovery are defined in Chapter 5. At this point, we simply examine four logical outcomes of rape and intervention.

Table 2.1 Factors Affecting Responses to Trauma and
Recovery from Trauma

Person	Age/development stage
	Relationship to offender(s)
	Pretrauma personality, functioning, and coping capabilities
	Ability to utilize social support and to perceive help as helpful
	Immediate response/subsequent response
	Perceptions of and meaning ascribed to trauma
	Qualities assigned to self and others posttrauma
Event	Severity, duration, frequency
	Degree of physical violence/personal violation
	Shared with others or suffered alone
	"Power politics"
Environment	Quality and continuity of social supports
	Immediate response of the "recovery environment"
	Community attitudes and values
	Quality, availability, and diversity of community resources
	Measure of physical and emotional safety ensured posttrauma
Intervention	Timing/appropriateness of timing
	Setting/appropriateness of setting
	Competence versus deficit orientation
	Aims, methodologies, and "empowering" aspects
	Nature of intervention/relationship of victim to providers
	Locus of control

Recovered With Intervention

These are victims who receive clinical care in the aftermath of rape and who have recovered. This is the group in which clinicians are understandably the most interested. It comprises those who seek out and apparently benefit from clinical care. Future study of this group can confirm and assess the benefits of intervention and document those interventions that work.

Symptomatic Despite Intervention

These are victims who have received clinical care and have not (or not yet) recovered. As important as the documentation of successful outcomes is the understanding of negative outcomes.

The search for new strategies can only be aided by an open sharing of the setbacks.

Recovered Without Intervention

Victims in this group are resilient individuals. They have either inner or outside resources (probably both) upon which they can call in times of crisis. Study of this group can reveal whether there are identifiable characteristics of the "spontaneously resolvable" sexual assault or particular resistances to trauma that some individuals possess that in effect protect them against posttraumatic distress. Or, do these victims possess specific recovery skills and resources that could be transmitted to others through intervention?

Unrecovered and Isolated

These are trauma victims who have not received care and who remain traumatized and distressed. They traditionally elude both the researcher and clinician. They live in relative isolation from others in the community and they do not seek or receive clinical care. Study of this group can lead to the development of alternate, nonclinical modes of intervention including public education programs and outreach efforts that could foster recovery. We have used the ecological model of trauma to organize the remaining chapters of the book. Person and event characteristics that predict response and recovery will be addressed in this chapter. Environmental influences are considered in Chapters 3 and 4. The delivery of clinical interventions is the subject of Chapters 5 and 6. Prevention efforts to reduce the likelihood of rape and to reach the untreated victim of assault are considered in the final chapter.

PHASES OF RESPONSE TO RAPE

Several clinicians have described their observations of the phases of response seen in victims of rape (e.g., Burgess & Holmstrom, 1974a; Forman, 1980; Sutherland & Scherl, 1970).

Another contribution to this section is the qualitative study of women's experience of sexual trauma by Roth and Lebowitz (1988). The following material has drawn from these four sources.

Anticipatory Phase

The response to rape begins with an anticipatory phase during which the victim's earliest recognition develops into a situation that is potentially dangerous. During this stage victims report the use of defense mechanisms such as dissociation, suppression, and rationalization to preserve their illusion of invulnerability. For example, they may say to themselves, "This man would never rape me. How stupid to be scared."

Victim behaviors during the assault include thinking about how to get away, verbally reasoning or arguing with the offender, taking physical action, mentally focusing and directing attention toward survival, remaining calm so as not to provoke additional violence, memorizing details, recalling advice people had given on rape, picturing previous violent situations, and praying for help (Burgess & Holmstrom, 1976).

Impact Phase

The impact phase describes the time period of the actual crime and its immediate aftermath. Intense fear of death or serious bodily harm was usually experienced during the rape by the victims interviewed by Burgess and Holmstrom (1974a). The high level of fear resulted in varying degrees of disintegration and disorganization in the ability to appraise and respond to the situation. Learned behavior seemed to disappear under stress and major physiological reactions such as vomiting sometimes occurred. "The object of a sudden, unexpected attack of violence will initially respond with shock, numbness, and disbelief. The reaction of fear is so profound and overwhelming that the victim feels hopeless about getting away" (Symonds, 1975,

p. 22). When the victim later recalls her behavior during the impact phase, she often feels intense guilt over what she perceives as her inefficient handling of the assault.

The following violent and graphic case may help the clinician to connect with the immediate impact of rape:

[Sandy, age 35, recounts walking at a swift pace muttering to herself.] Only two miles from home and my car had suddenly quit on me on a country road that is a scenic shortcut home from work. A blue van drove by, stopped, turned around, and came to a stop. "Need a ride?" asked a nice looking man in his twenties. I noticed a couple of other men in the van, hesitated for a moment, and then said, "Sure—can you take me into town?"

As I climbed into the van, I began to feel anxious. I saw empty beer bottles strewn all over the floor of the van and the men were swearing, laughing, and leering at me. Before I knew what was happening, the van turned sharply off onto a dirt road, pulled over and stopped. "What's going on?" I demanded. "I think I'll just get out and walk the rest of the way." "You're not going anywhere," the driver replied. "But you are gonna give us a little payback for the lift."

Before I could scream, one of the men clamped his hand over my mouth so hard that I could hardly breathe. A second man unzipped his pants, pulled them down, and pushed me onto the floor. He ripped off my skirt and forced himself inside. All I felt was terror and pain. The other men stood around stinking of sweat and beer. When the first man was finished the driver ordered me to suck him. I complied only after he socked me so hard in the face that I felt numb. As he forced his penis further into my mouth and throat I began to gag. He came in my mouth and roared with laughter, "Wasn't that sweet?"

I began to whimper. The third man, a short, fat man, now demanded, "Get on your hand and knees, honey—you're really gonna love this." He pulled me up and forcefully thrust his penis into my anus. I screamed and felt tearing in my rectum.

Finally, it was over. The driver grunted, "Get out." The door of the van was opened and I was pushed out into a ditch. I was half dressed with bruises coming out all over my body and aching with pain. I couldn't even cry. . . .

Expressive Styles

Once a victim arrives at the emergency room, two emotional styles are noted. An expressed style is characterized by open expression of feelings of fear and anxiety through crying, sobbing, and restlessness. Alternately, some victims appear to mask their feelings by a calm, subdued affect which Burgess and Holmstrom label the controlled style. The following case describes a client who presented the counselor with a controlled reaction to rape:

> Karen is a young woman in her early twenties who was at a friend's house with a group of her friends. There were three men, one other woman, and herself present. They were kidding around and watching television for the evening. Eventually the other woman asked to be taken home and one of the men drove her. When the man who had brought her home came back, the three men raped Karen.
> She was aghast and could not believe that these men, whom she had known from high school, had raped her. She went home in a dazed state. She is married and felt she could not tell her husband as he would think that she had been fooling around or flirting. She did nothing, and told no one about her rape for a few days. Then she called a rape crisis center and requested information on how to file a report. She said over and over again that she was fine, that she could handle everything herself, and she simply wanted someone to have the men's names on record.
> The volunteer counselor encouraged Karen to go to the hospital and see a physician and gave her information on how to file a police report. The volunteer conveyed to Karen that although she may be feeling no repercussions currently it was possible, and indeed was likely, that there would be aftereffects that she would feel with the passage of time. She was counseled that it would be best to find

someone to talk to at that time. She was encouraged to seek support by telling a member of her family and her friends about the rape. Karen responded positively to the suggestion of calling the police but responded tentatively to the suggestion that she share her rape experience with others.

Occasionally a compounded reaction is seen in the immediate aftermath (Burgess & Holmstrom, 1974a). In a compounded reaction, the victim experiences not only the symptoms related to rape trauma, but also experiences reactivated symptoms of previous conditions such as physical illness, psychiatric, or social difficulties. This group was observed to develop additional symptoms such as depression; psychotic behavior; psychosomatic disorders; suicidal behavior; and acting-out behavior associated with alcoholism, drug use, or sexual activity. The following case describes a victim whose response to rape is heavily colored by her past social and emotional difficulties:

Sandra was in a bar drinking and left the bar with two men, whom she alternately says were her buddies or new acquaintances. They drove her to a rural location and raped her. They treated her roughly—pushing and shoving her, but no weapons were used. When they were finished assaulting her, they left her and drove away.

She was drunk at the time of the rape and was intoxicated when she found her way to a Catholic hospital. The hospital staff found her obnoxious and difficult to handle. She requested to see a priest, although she was not a Catholic. She spoke with the priest, but did not become calmer. At that time the rape crisis center was called and a counselor went to the hospital.

The counselor attempted to mediate between the hospital staff who were annoyed and believed that Sandra had "asked for it," and Sandra, who was upset and irrational. Sandra immediately accepted the counselor as someone who was on her side and who would help her. She cooperated with the medical procedures and filed a report with the police while the counselor acted as an intermediary.

Following these procedures, the counselor worked for a brief period on clarifying with Sandra what had happened, her feelings about the rape, and her reaction to her treatment at the hospital. Sandra was most upset by the fact that "her friends" had betrayed her. She gave a childlike appearance of not understanding why those nice people would hurt her.

During this period a bit of history was obtained. Sandra is married and has two children. She did not want to tell her husband as he would accuse her of running around without him. This was a habit of hers; frequently she went to bars without him and picked up men. There was a good probability that she had been raped before, although she was not clear on this point.

Additionally, she had an extensive psychiatric record, a poor prerape functioning level, and a history of alcohol abuse. After a 3½-hour session, Sandra went home. She was under the care of a community mental health center's psychiatrist, and she was encouraged to contact him or the rape center. Future contacts were sporadic. She would call the center seeking her initial counselor and would be upset when she was not available. She did not inform her psychiatrist of the rape, and at her last contact her multiple problems remained unattended to in any systematic fashion.

Another type of compounded reaction may occur when a woman is raped and feelings are triggered from an earlier sexual assault or molestation about which the victim has not settled her feelings. In these instances, victims may talk as much about their past experience as about the present one. The following victim sought help after a relatively minor sexual experience compared to her earlier rape:

Norma, a 19-year-old college student, was referred for treatment at a university counseling center by the police following an incident of "sexual harassment" on campus. Two drunk college men were standing outside a bar and made some passes at Norma. She ignored them. Then one of the men picked her up and started tossing her around. He bounced her off a wall before someone called the police, who arrested the men.

During her intake interview she described an experience that had occurred two years before: "I was downtown doing some shopping when these guys jumped out of a van and dragged me into it. They drove around and I fought them. But there were more of them than of me. They got me down for awhile and fucked me. One of them made me suck his cock. I kept on fighting whenever they eased up and I finally got away. I had bruises all over me. I went into a K mart and was wandering around without all of my clothes on right. A policeman arrested me for shoplifting.

They brought me to jail and booked me, then put me into a cell. They thought I was on drugs. Finally my uncle got there and knew something was wrong. He made them take me to the ER. The doctors there said I had a concussion. They did all sorts of medical tests and did all of the stuff about the rape. And that was that. Even though I couldn't remember all of the details, I knew what I've told you. But, no one paid any attention to the rape. No one ever mentioned it. My family is Catholic and I guess that might have something to do with it. I went north to college to get away. But it wasn't until two years later that all of this really began to bother me.

Somatic Reactions

Somatic symptoms during the impact phase included the direct effects of physical trauma—general soreness, bruising, irritation, and other injuries. Skeletal muscle tension as manifested in tension headaches, fatigue, and sleep pattern disturbances was seen. Victims were edgy, jumpy over minor incidents, and showed startle reactions similar to those seen in combat veterans. Gastrointestinal irritability was another frequent category of complaint including stomach pains, nausea, no appetite, and inability to taste food. Women who were attacked in their own beds were particularly troubled with insomnia (Burge, 1988). Finally, genitourinary symptoms such as vaginal discharge, itching, burning on urination, generalized pain, chronic vaginal infections, and rectal bleeding and pain were seen.

Reconstitution Phase

Reconstitution begins with the victim attending to basic living considerations such as changing her telephone number, moving to a different residence if necessary, and turning to family for support. Immediately after the initial impact of rape has occurred, a denial phase often is seen (Forman, 1980). Characteristic of this phase is an outward appearance of adjustment. The victim may express many concerns but seems to disregard the sexual assault. Life activities are resumed but undertaken superficially and mechanically. "In some respects, this phase resembles the denial encountered by an individual going through the grieving process. It is not unhealthy, but reflects attempts to actively cope with the trauma and restore equilibrium" (Forman, 1980, p. 307). Denial may reflect the victim's need to take more time before she is ready to deal with issues any further.

Sometime between two weeks and several months later, the feelings experienced at the time of the assault return. This phase may be short and its disruptive effects minimal, or it may be lengthy and have serious debilitating effects (Forman, 1980). Common experiences at this time include specific anxiety, nightmares, and fears; depression, guilt, or shame; catastrophic fantasies; feelings of vulnerability, helplessness, dirtiness, alienation, and isolation; sexual dysfunctions and physical symptoms.

A major factor in determining the length of the reconstitution phase is whether the victim chooses to press charges against her offender. While a victim has a right to expect that prosecution will result in punishment of the offender and validation of her violation, the opposite often is the case. McCahill, Meyer, and Fischman (1979) write,

> Many victims are upset by the discovery that they must publicly testify about something that is to them a very private matter. There is often standing room only in the section of seats reserved for the public in courtrooms where sex offenses are tried. The bulk of the observers in these cases are retired men, the unemployed, school children, and policemen in training. Victims may also be bothered by the

lack of seriousness in the proceedings, defense arguments containing myths about women, and isolation from her support system. It is clear from the description . . . that the trial meets all . . . conditions of successful degradation ceremonies. (p. 211)

Each new stage of the litigation process reawakens the rape for the victim and reinstitutes the symptoms of the impact phase. Reconstitution cannot take place until the prosecution process has been completed.

Resolution Phase

Subsequent to the symptomatic phase, many victims experience an anger phase. These feelings may be directed at the assailant, society, the courts, police, or men. Victims sometime direct their anger at their therapists or the medical and psychological agencies who cared for them. Underlying the anger appears to be deep feelings of despair, hopelessness, and shame that psychotherapeutic intervention can help direct away from the self (Forman, 1980). Burgess and Holmstrom (1979) interviewed rape victims four to six years after being raped. Victims were asked if they "felt back to normal, that is, the way you felt prior to the rape." Their responses indicated that 37% had felt recovered from the rape within months; 37% felt recovered, but the process had taken several years; and 26% still did not feel recovered four to six years after the rape. In a second study, more than 40% of rape victims between one and 2½ years postrape still experienced sexual difficulties, restricted going out, and experienced suspiciousness, fear of being alone, and depression (Nadelson, Notman, Zackson, & Gornich, 1982).

THE MALE VICTIM

Male rape victims represented 10% of the volume at a university-affiliated facility (Kaufman, DiVasto, Jackson, Voorhees, &

Christy, 1980), and 6% of the reported rape volume in the city of Columbia, SC (Forman, 1983). Most of these rapes were by other men, and the victims often sustained more injuries than is typical for female victims (Calderwood, 1987). Treatment of male victims is hampered by lack of knowledge about their experiences and male support groups. In one series of male rape victims who were serving in the military, 85% were assaulted by more than one offender (Goyer & Eddleman, 1984). Clinical evaluations of these men indicated similar clusters of symptoms to those observed among female victims, including fear (the most commonly reported sequelae), depression and suicidal ideation, anger, somatic problems, sexual dysfunctions, and disturbances in peer relationships. The following case report was typical of the gang violence involved in these male rapes:

Mr. A, for example, was referred for a psychiatric evaluation two weeks after being physically and sexually abused when he was given a "blanket party" the first day he reported on board his ship. A blanket party consists of several men forcibly wrapping the victim in blankets so that he is unable to determine exactly who is physically or sexually abusing him. One week later he was given a "greasing" by three shipmates. A greasing involves stripping the individual naked and massaging him with a thick black grease used to lubricate heavy machinery. In some cases a flexible tube is forced through the victim's anus and into his rectum. The tube is connected to a cylindrical reservoir filled with the lubricating grease. The reservoir and tube resemble a large hand-driven tire pump. The contents of the piston-driven reservoir are then pumped into the victim. When Mr. A reported the greasing, judicial action was taken against the three sailors who assaulted him. Following the judicial action, he became fearful of threats some of his shipmates subsequently made to physically hurt him, throw him overboard, or sexually abuse him again. The fears became more troublesome to Mr. A as the ship's deployment date approached, so he sought assistance from the on-board physician. In his referral, the doctor stated that Mr. A "lives in constant fear and anxiety." In his response to how the psychiatrist might be able to help him, he replied, "get me to my

dad and out of here, away from this; my dad can help me."
(Goyer & Eddleman, 1984, pp. 576-577)

SYMPTOMATIC RESPONSES TO RAPE

Empirical studies are the focus of this section, including research on anxiety/fears, depression, social adjustment, sexual functioning, physical health, and cognitive processes.
Extensive reviews of this literature are available (Ellis, 1983;
Holmes & Lawrence, 1983; McCann, Sakheim, & Abrahamson,
1988; Resick, 1987; Roth & Lebowitz, 1988). An important methodological issue in this literature is the use of cross-sectional
versus prospective measurement. A prospective study involves
the same group of victims who are followed from their rape
forward and assessed on repeated occasions. Prospective studies of rape aftereffects are quite consistent in the pattern of
recovery that is seen. Victims typically show very high distress
levels within the first week that peak in severity by approximately 3 weeks postassault. The distress then continues at a
high level for the next month but begins to improve by 2 to 3
months postassault. After 3 months rape victims do not differ
from nonvictims on most symptom scales except fear, anxiety,
self-esteem, and sexual dysfunction scores, which may remain
elevated for up to a year (Resick, 1987).

In contrast to the repeated assessments in a prospective design, a cross-sectional design involves just a single assessment
of a large group of rape victims who are recruited to represent
all of the possible lengths of elapsed time since rape. Cross-
sectional comparisons *always* reveal elevated psychological distress in rape victims compared to nonvictims even though some
victims in the sample may have lived 20 or more years since
victimization (Burnam et al., 1988; Ellis, Atkeson, & Calhoun,
1981; Kilpatrick et al., 1987.) For example, analysis of the ECA
data for Los Angeles revealed that women with histories of
sexual assault (defined broadly) were significantly more likely
than nonvictims to qualify for psychiatric diagnoses including major depression, alcohol abuse/dependence, drug

abuse/dependence, generalized anxiety, obsessive-compulsive disorder, and posttraumatic stress disorder (Burnam et al. 1988). Likewise, in a community sample of women residing in Charleston County, South Carolina, increased psychological distress among victims of completed rape and aggravated assault, compared to nonvictims, was found on several scales of the Symptom Checklist-90-R (Derogatis, 1977) including Hostility, Depression, Paranoid Ideation, Psychoticism, Anxiety, and Obsessive-Compulsive symptoms (Kilpatrick et al., 1987).

In short, the picture of rape aftereffects that emerges from cross-sectional studies suggests much longer lasting distress than the evidence from prospective studies. The discrepancy need not be disconcerting because there are several explanations for it. Victims who are followed prospectively may have a sense that they are improving and could alter their responses somewhat over repeated occasions to reflect better their perceptions of positive change. It is also possible that interaction over multiple occasions with a concerned group of researchers has a therapeutic effect. Additionally, the very fact of participation in the research might increase the legitimacy of the experience and alter the reactions of the victims' environments and support networks. Finally, it could be that only rape victims with the best prognosis for recovery possess the ability to remain reachable by research staff and to show up for a series of assessments separated by several months and even years. For all these reasons, prospective data may reflect the best possible outcomes that are seen among rape victims. In cross-sectional data, respondents are assessed only once and they may shade their responses somewhat to reflect their beliefs that the rape was traumatic, or to please the researcher whom they believe must think rape was traumatic. A one-shot data collection demands less from a respondent and thus cross-sectional samples often contain a wider variety of raped women than prospective studies (including women who have had minimal therapeutic contacts since their assaults and who have faced malevolent recovery environments). For these reasons, cross-sectional data may be more reflective of the worst possible outcomes of rape. It

is hoped that this short overview will reduce the sense of incon-
sistency readers may have about the rape impact literature.

Anxiety/Fears

   Symptoms of fear and anxiety predominate in the immediate
postrape clinical picture (Kilpatrick, Veronen, & Resick, 1979a;
Ruch, Gartrell, Amedeo, & Coyne, in press). Victims identified
the following symptoms they experienced during the rape itself
and two to three hours afterward (the percentage of victims who
experienced the symptom is given in parentheses): feeling
scared (96%); worried (96%); shaking or trembling (96%); terrified (92%); confused (92%); helpless (88%); racing thoughts
(80%); racing heart (80%); pain (72%); tight muscles (68%); rapid
breathing (64%); and numbness (60%) (Kilpatrick et al., 1979a).
Within 72 hours of the assault, 86% of the victims reported
intense fear of the assailant and fear for their personal safety,
and expressed "disclosure anxiety," which was heightened concern about others' reactions to the assault (Ruch et al., in press).
Clinical experience suggests to us that in recent years fear of
AIDS has also become a primary concern of victims, particularly
those raped by strangers.
   Three areas of rape-related fears have been identified: (a) fears
of stimuli or items that were directly associated with the attack
itself such as a man's penis, anal intercourse, tough-looking
people; (b) fears of rape consequences including testifying in
court, venereal disease, or talking to police; and (c) fears of
future attack including being alone, having people behind you,
or being in a strange place (Kilpatrick, Resick, & Veronen, 1981).
Approximately 90% or more of all rape victims studied feared
being alone, going out alone, night or darkness, and sleeping
alone. The anxiety induced by sexual assault reaches maximum
levels in the third week (Peterson, Olasov, & Foa, 1987). After
this point there are no further increases in fear levels, but significant decrements in fear may not begin for a long time. Rape
victims, compared to nonvictims, have been found to receive
elevated scores on seven of the eight Modified Fear Survey

scales (MFS) and the Phobix Anxiety scale of the Symptom Checklist-90-R not only immediately but at 1, 3, 6, and 12 months after assault (Kilpatrick & Veronen, 1984). Fear decreased at 18 months but reemerged at 2 and 3 years postcrime. The degrees of anxiety, fear, and stress experienced by victims of assaultive crime (including rape and physical assault victims) has been found to be significantly higher than the levels experienced by nonassaultive crime victims at both 1 and 6 months postattack (Wirtz & Harrell, 1987).

The following case demonstrates the development of rape-related fears:

Kathy, a 47-year-old married woman related the following assault: "My daughter and I usually run together in the early evening. On that day, at about 5:30, she called to say that her husband had just called and he was held up at work, and as she couldn't leave Jesse alone, she wouldn't be able to join me. I was a bit leery of going alone as by 5:30 it was already getting dark and I knew that the area wasn't the safest place for women. But I was in a good routine and I wanted to keep up my momentum so that I'd be in form for the Bonnie Bell race. I left a note for my husband, and drove over to the jogging track. There was hardly anyone in the parking lot, and I thought that maybe I should just not go, but I thought to myself that I was just being an old fogey. So I warmed up and went down the open stretch at the beginning of the track where the street lights flooded the path. Then I turned the curve. I saw the outline of the woman's form painted on the path, which was the place where a woman was raped, and which the Women's Center had painted there as a reminder.

"I was a bit taken aback, more so than usual. But again I chided myself for being silly. I ran a bit faster. It's a 5-mile course, and as I passed the 3-mile marker I felt that I'd have been foolish to have stayed home. It felt good to be moving. That's when he got me. He must have been hiding in the bushes by the golf course, as all of a sudden he was in front of me. He pulled me off the path and as I began to yell he clamped a hand over my mouth and told me he had a knife. He said that I had better do what he wanted. I did. I lay down. He raped me. I was sobbing. My eyes were wide open—startled. Finally, he let me go. I was terrified!

"I ran away for a few minutes and then I stopped. I was too frightened to go on, thinking someone else was waiting for me further ahead. I stood there immobile. Finally another runner appeared—a woman, and I started wailing. She walked me the rest of the way back to the parking lot and drove me to the hospital. She called the rape crisis center, and I called my husband. He came right away, as did a woman from the center. She stayed with me throughout all of the tests they did. My husband was gentle but confused.

"Now I have stopped running—there is nowhere safe in the city to run. I'm seeing a woman counselor in an attempt to overcome my fears of being alone outside at night. It's even hard to go for an evening stroll with my family."

Depression

Although symptoms of anxiety predominate in the majority of victims within a few hours to a few days of the assault, some precursors to depression can be seen immediately including sad feelings about the assault, apathetic feelings about life, and suicidal thoughts (Ruch et al., in press). Within a few weeks of rape, depressive symptoms and frequently a full-blown depressive syndrome becomes apparent (Frank & Stewart, 1983). Frank, Turner, and Duffy (1979) and Frank & Stewart (1984) used the Beck Depression Inventory (BDI) and the Research Diagnostic Criteria (a standardized interview procedure) to assess major depressive disorder. On the BDI, nearly half (44%) of the victims received scores within the moderately or severely depressed range; 38% met the criteria for major depressive disorder. Rape victims' scores on the BDI were significantly higher than nonvictims at 1 and 2 months postassault but the depression diminished by 3 months postassault. Postvictimization depression has been found consistently to last approximately 3 months (Atkeson, Calhoun, Resick, & Ellis, 1982; Peterson et al., 1987; Resick, 1987). Only a single prospective study reported that rape victims were still significantly depressed at one year after the assault (Kilpatrick & Veronen, 1984).

In addition to depression, the frequency of suicidal ideation is notable among rape victims. In the first month after victimization, the reported rates of suicidal behavior have varied between 3% and 27% (Frank et al., 1979; Frank & Stewart, 1984). Suicidal ideation is reported by between 33% and 50% of rape victims examined in cross-sectional studies (Ellis et al., 1981; Koss, 1988; Resick, Jordan, Girelli, Hutter, & Marhoefer-Dvorak, 1989). Suicide attempts had been made by 17% to 19% of rape victims, the latter figure stemming from a community sample of women who were not seeking treatment (Kilpatrick et al., 1985; Resick et al., 1989).

Social Adjustment

The impact of rape on a victim's ability to carry out major social roles has been investigated in a prospective study by Calhoun, Atkeson, and Ellis (1981). The self-report form of the Social Adjustment Survey was administered at 2, 4, 8, and 12 months postrape. This survey consists of subscales that reflect the respondent's ability to function effectively at work, financially, in social and leisure activities, within the marriage and nuclear family, as well as within the extended family. The investigators found that rape victims differed from nonvictims:

- in work functioning for the first 8 months;
- in economic functioning for the first 2 months;
- in social and leisure functioning for the first 2 months; and
- in extended family functioning for the first month.

In contrast, marital, parental, and family-unit adjustment were not impaired at all. The investigators suggested, however, that these are the primary social networks whose behavior toward the victim could have been altered by the validation that stemmed from her participation in ongoing research. Among a group of rape victims who lacked extensive contact with researchers, Kilpatrick and colleagues (1987) demonstrated long-term effects of rape in the family unit and in marital adjustment, as well as in areas of social and leisure functioning. At work, rape victims are found to be no more severely affected than robbery victims (Resick, 1986). Difficulties in social functioning as well as signs of depression are seen in the following description of one victim's experience:

> The victim is a 20-year-old, single black female living with her grandmother, aunt, uncle, and three younger male cousins. One night, while accompanying her aunt's ex-boyfriend to a neighborhood Chinese restaurant, she was told by him that he had to pick up something at his apartment. Once there, he injected heroin into his own arm and then forced the victim, at the point of a gun, to take heroin herself. Feeling dizzy and weak, she was led into another room where, over a 3-hour period, she was forced to engage in cunnilingus, fellatio, and repeated intercourse. When, at one point, the victim attempted to leap from a window, the offender grabbed her and injected more heroin into her arm.
>
> As a result of the assault, the victim's behavior changed dramatically. Her once active social life came to a complete halt, she lost her job because she would not venture far from home, became upset whenever a family member left the house, and, by her own admission, wore out her family and friends by constantly talking about the rape. When she was first interviewed, the assigned social worker noted that the victim's food consumption had decreased markedly. Over the course of 1 year, a substantial weight loss was noticed in the victim. (McCahill et al., 1979, p. 24)

Sexual Functioning

Sexual dysfunctions are among the most long-lasting problems experienced by rape victims (Becker, Abel, & Skinner, 1979; Becker, Skinner, Abel, & Cichon, 1986; Becker, Skinner, Abel, & Treacy, 1982; Burgess & Holmstrom, 1979; Ellis, Calhoun, &

Atkeson, 1980; Feldman-Summers, Gordon, & Meagher, 1979; Miller, Williams, & Bernstein, 1982). Ellis and colleagues (1980) found that 61% of rape victims noted disruption in sexual functioning immediately postrape. The most immediate reaction was avoidance of sex. Among women who had been sexually active before the rape, 29% stopped having sex with their partner completely, and 32% reduced frequency. One year later, 21% were still reporting some sexual problems, but the frequency of sexual activity had returned to normal levels for those women who were sexually active before the crime. At least one problem in sexual functioning was reported by 58% of rape victims compared to 17% of nonvictims (Becker et al., 1986). Even 4 to 6 years after sexual assault, 30% of raped women still did not feel their sexual functioning had returned to prerape levels (Burgess & Holmstrom, 1979).

Studies of sexual satisfaction ask victims to rate the frequency with which they engage in a number of different sexual activities and the pleasure they obtain from them (Feldman-Summers et al., 1979; Orlando & Koss, 1983; Resick, 1986). Once out of the immediate postrape period, victims and nonvictims do not differ in the reported frequency of oral sex, sexual intercourse, masturbation, or orgasms. Sexual satisfaction is affected in the immediate postrape period but as early as three months later it returns to prerape levels. It is notable that declines in sexual satisfaction are seen even when the assault was not conceptualized as rape (Orlando & Koss, 1983).

The largest study of sexual functioning involved assessment of 372 victims (including rape, attempted rape, incest, and child molestation) compared to 99 nonvictim controls (Becker et al., 1986). More than half (59%) of the sexual assault victims had at least one sexual dysfunction compared to 17% of the nonvictims. Two thirds (69%) of victims with dysfunctions directly related the onset of their problems to the assault. The most prevalent sexual dysfunction among assaulted women was response inhibitory problems, which are difficulties that interfere with early sexual responsiveness (Becker & Skinner, 1983). In comparison, nonassaulted women complained of less frequent or less intense orgasms, and/or increased boredom with sex in general or with their sexual partners. The groups of women did not differ significantly in the incidence of orgasmic problems (including primary, secondary, and situational secondary non-orgasmia) or the incidence of intromission problems (vaginismus and dyspareunia).

The following case illustrates the development subsequent to sexual assault of difficulties in the earliest stages of approach to sexual situations:

Michele is a college senior. She relates, "I was walking home, up the road to our house. Some friends had dropped me off at the foot of the road as it was winter, and snowing. . . . It was dusk. As I walked along I thought I heard someone behind me. I wasn't real worried because I was in real good shape from playing varsity basketball, and being athletic in general. Again, I thought I heard someone and turned around . . . and there was a man there.

I took off running. He caught me, and dragged me off the road. I was fighting real hard, but could not get away. He tied me down with rope to the trees so that I was lying on the snow. He taunted me as he undressed me, telling me that I was helpless, and that I couldn't stop him. Then he raped me. I didn't say anything to my mother or father then, but a few days later I told my mother. She responded, 'Did you say anything to your father?' When I said no, she told me not to, as it would only upset him. That's all she said.

"About a month later I went to the police to report it. They asked what I'd done to entice him and told me I was too big (I'm 5'10") to have been raped! I didn't tell anyone else until May when I was raped a second time. A friend had left basketball practice really upset, and I went off to find her. I was walking through the parking lot, and heard something by the side near the bushes. I thought maybe it was my friend so I went over. Two men came out and grabbed me and pinned me to the ground. They raped me.

"Now I sleep with a hockey stick and feel as though my previous sense of confidence has been replaced with an overwhelming feeling of helplessness. I'm scared of men and have never had a relationship with either a man or a woman. I'm pretty confused about sexual relationships now. . . . "

Effects on Health and Medical Service Utilization

Victimization is clearly a major life stressor outside the realm of ordinary experience. Several potential pathways exist by which victimization-induced stress could lead to ill health. First, emotional responses to rape might be perceived by the patient as physical disease. Second, preexisting symptoms could be exacerbated, or the tolerance for them lowered, by victimization-induced distress. Third, resistance might be taxed by the stress of victimization, thereby inducing disease. Several studies have reported that rape victims, regardless of the length of time that has elapsed since assault, perceive their current health less favorably and report using physician services more often compared to nonvictims (Golding, Stein, Siegel, Burnam, & Sorenson, 1988; Koss et al., in press-a; Koss et al., in press-b). Women victimized by rape and physical assault were more likely than nonvictims to report symptoms in every body system except dermatology and eyes (Koss et al., in press). The most sizable effect was seen for gynecologic complaints and sexual dysfunction. In addition, victimized women compared to nonvictims reported more injurious health habits including smoking, drinking alcohol, overeating, and failing to use seatbelts.

Victimization by rape as well as other serious crimes has also been found to affect objective indexes of health and medical service utilization. Women who had experienced both a rape and a physical assault in their past made physician visits twice as frequently in the current year, and had outpatient medical expenses that were 2½ times higher than those of nonvictims (Koss et al., in press-b). In addition, utilization data across the five years preceding and following crime were compared to that of nonvictims. Rape victims' number of physician visits increased 18% in the year of the crime, 56% in the year following the crime, and 31% in the second year following crime compared to their previctimization levels. The changes observed among nonvictims across these years were –13%, 2%, and 1%.

The most notable aspect of these findings was that impacts on health endured throughout the entire length of the study. Whereas the medical profession is traditionally seen as offering emergency services to victims, the present results dramatized the long-term health care implications of victimization. Yet, it is very unlikely that the medical establishment realizes their potential to initiate service provision for traumatized crime victims. All the evidence suggests that physicians rarely screen for exposure to violence—even in psychiatric settings, emergency rooms, or when taking a sexual history (Jacobson & Richardson, 1987; Liese, Larson, Johnson, & Hourgan, 1989; Stark et al., 1981). Failure to screen for victimization in the medical setting communicates a lack of permission to discuss these issues. When psychosocial variables are ignored in diagnosis, somatic complaints may be inaccurately and inappropriately diagnosed and treated as organic pathology (Katon, Ries, & Kleinman, 1984).

Studies are beginning to appear in the literature that document the frequency of sexual victimization in the past lives of women who currently are diagnosed with somatization disorder. Physicians privately refer to persons with this diagnosis as "crocks." They are people who come back to the physician for repeated complaints, utilize a lot of medical resources, but are never made well. It is entirely possible that these somatizers were created in the first place by the medical profession's failure to elicit relevant life experiences in their rush to seize on organic pathology. Then, in subsequent visits, the organic pathology becomes the ticket of admission to the physician's office. Both patients and physicians must be educated that victimization has demonstrated effects on health and should not be ignored in the diagnostic process. Future work must determine whether these deleterious effects can be partially alleviated by physicians facilitating victims to confide in a caring person, providing validation of the experience, and giving encouragement to use victim-assistance services.

COGNITIVE IMPACT OF RAPE

Cognitive processes include perceiving, thinking, and remembering. Social cognitions involve how people think about themselves and others. Clinical work with victims has revealed the "overwhelming assault that victimization is to the child's and adult survivor's world of meaning" (Conte, 1988, p. 325). In the words of one victim, "I felt different from other people" (quoted in Roth & Lebowitz, 1988, p. 97).

Traumatic Memories

One of the most painful experiences of the trauma survivor is finding themselves "constantly haunted" by vivid, traumatic memories (Neiderland, 1982, p. 414). As one woman said, "I can't stop crying . . . and sometimes I feel a little bit overwhelmed. All these things flashing, all these memories" (quoted in Roth & Lebowitz, 1988, p. 90). Many incest victims say that they still regularly experience vivid memories of their past (Silver, Boon, & Stones, 1983). Trauma victims can avoid emotional involvement, but they cannot avoid traumatic memories (van der Kolk, 1987a). Even when pushed out of consciousness, traumatic memories come back as reenactments, nightmares, or feelings related to the trauma. Posttraumatic dreams often are exact replicas of the traumatic event. They appear more like a memory than a dream or fantasy and are replayed over and over with recurrences throughout life during periods of stress (Ross, Ball, Sullivan, & Caroff, 1989; van der Kolk, 1987a).

Causal Explanations

The bulk of cognitive activity that occurs in the midst of life crises appears to involve attempts to understand the causes of an outcome, to evaluate its inevitability, and to reconstruct alternative scenarios for how things could have gone differently (Drauker, 1989; Janoff-Bulman, 1985b; Silver et al., 1983; Taylor,

1983; Wortman & Silver, 1989). Among the questions to which victims seek answers are "Why me?" and "How could it have turned out differently?" Unexpected events like rape are especially likely to elicit causal attribution judgments, which are attempts to understand the factors responsible for causing the event.

Many attributions appear to be self-blaming, but in theory even self-blame has been viewed as functional. First, self-blame may satisfy needs to impose meaning on life. Second, self-blame may allow victims to preserve beliefs in a "just" world where bad things only happen to bad people (Lerner, 1980). Finally, self-blame may enhance illusions of control over life outcomes (Taylor & Brown, 1988; Wortman & Silver, 1989). Two types of self-blame have been distinguished: characterological self-blame and behavioral self-blame (Janoff-Bulman, 1979). Characterological self-blame—that is, blaming enduring features of yourself—is thought to be maladaptive. An example of characterological blame is the following, "I guess I must have believed, on some level, that I deserved this, or it was my fault or now I'm an awful person" (quoted in Roth & Lebowitz, 1988, p. 93). Behavioral self-blame involves blaming your own actions. For example, "I felt like it was my fault . . . 'cause I had disobeyed my parents. . . . I blame myself for lying to my parents. I was in a place I shouldn't have been. . . . I had lied to my parents and it just felt like I had brought this on myself. . . . I felt like it was my fault" (quoted in Roth & Lebowitz, 1988, p. 93). Behavioral self-blame is theorized to promote adjustment by enhancing feelings of control. At least the event gets a predictable cause, even if it must be secured at the expense of denigrating one's own actions.

Several studies have suggested that those who blame their actions are better adjusted than those who do not feel responsible. For example, accident victims with spinal cord injuries, who believed that some action on their part caused their near-fatal accident, were less psychologically distressed than those who took no responsibility for the accident (Bulman & Wortman, 1977). These findings *do not* characterize rape victims, however, who appear to be an *exception* to the self-blame model. Although self-blame is frequently seen among victims, neither form of self-blame has been associated with good adjustment either among incest victims (Gold, 1986; Silver et al., 1983) or rape victims (Abbey, 1987; Meyer & Taylor, 1986).

Altered Schemas

Schemas are the organizing structures of the information that is stored in the central nervous system. They encode and represent a wide range of knowledge including self-representations. Schema are modifiable by experience; they accept information and are changed by it (Neisser, 1976). Schema direct movement and activities to make more information available by which they are further modified. The effect of environmental input on cognitive schema typically is either assimilation or accommodation. In assimilation, the input is changed or distorted to be consistent with internal models. In accommodation, the schema is altered to account for the input. When bombarded with disconfirming and threatening input that contradicts deeply held beliefs, self-protective distortions typically emerge and are adaptive in many situations (Taylor & Brown, 1988). The greater the contradiction between an experience and existing schemas, the more attention that must be directed towards emotionally processing it.

People untouched by victimization often maintain beliefs (or cognitive schema) that are incompatible with the experience of sexual assault. "The trauma of rape is indeed extremely difficult to assimilate. It is a devastating event, which violates basic human assumptions of personal integrity and control of a just and safe world" (Roth & Cohen, 1987, p. 533). A great deal of the work that occurs in the aftermath of victimization is the struggle to process the experience and make necessary alterations, including changing the way the experience is remembered (assimilation) and changing inner models to fit the experience (accommodation). In the words of one victim, "I really do think that I started to question the basic assumptions that I had been operating on all of my life" (quoted in Roth & Lebowitz, 1988, p. 95).

McCann and colleagues (1988) have suggested that the emotional processing of traumatic experiences may engage schemas about safety, power, trust, esteem, and intimacy. In each of these areas schemas exist concerning the self and concerning the behavior of others (McCann et al., 1988). Each of these types of schemas is described below and is followed by a brief comment on the likely effects of victimization-induced negative alterations in the schema. The reader is, however, encouraged to read the original report which is rich in examples.

Safety

Self-safety schemas involve expectations that one is capable of protecting oneself from harm and is uniquely invulnerable to negative consequences. A negative alteration in this schema that could be associated with victimization is the belief that one is unable to protect oneself in the future. If such a schema existed, it would tend to influence the interpretation of ongoing behavior. Intrusive thoughts about danger, intense fears about future victimization, and the physiologic arousal associated with these cognitions might be expected. Because schemas also govern choices about future behavior, a negative safety schema could lead to behaviors that tend to confirm and reinforce the victimization-induced negative alterations in the schema. Safety schemas about others involve beliefs that people are basically good and are not expected to cause harm, injury, or loss. Victimization-induced negative alterations in these schemas could be associated with self-protective social withdrawal and phobic avoidance.

Trust

Self-trust involves beliefs that one's perceptions and judgments can be relied on. Negative alterations in this schema may be associated with confusion, overcaution, or paralysis when confronted with important life decisions. Two studies have suggested that rape victims who were following their personal safety rules at the time of the rape, thereby judging themselves to be safe, experienced greater fear and depressive reactions than women who had perceived that they were in a dangerous situation (Frank & Stewart, 1984; Schepple & Bart, 1983). Trust schemas about others involve expectations that people can be relied upon not to betray or disillusion those they care about. Negative alterations in this schema may be associated with pervasive disillusionment and disappointment in others, fear of betrayal or abandonment, or anger and rage toward betrayers.

Power

Self-efficacy is a more common term for self-schemas related to power. They are beliefs in one's capacity to solve problems and meet new challenges. Negative schemas may involve either unrealistically high or unrealistically low expectations about personal power. If the schema is altered to accommodate views of the self as weak, needy, and helpless, it may be manifested by actions consistent with beliefs that one is helpless to control forces both within and outside of the self. Power schemas related to others are beliefs that one can be a partner in relationships and can exert control over the outcome of the relationship. Negative alterations in these schemas may be seen in patterns of passivity, submission, and lack of assertiveness in some, or even generalized to all, interpersonal relationships.

Esteem

Self-esteem is understood to involve beliefs in one's worth or value. If some beliefs already exist about badness or unworthiness, victimization will confirm and strengthen them. Negative alterations in these schemas may include beliefs that one is bad, evil, destructive, and even that one is responsible for bad outcomes. As one victim said, "I just believed there was some flaw in me. . . . I was always convinced I was a horrible person. Really rotten, because of [the perpetrator]" (quoted in Roth & Lebowitz, 1988, p. 95). Decreased self-esteem in comparison with nonvictims has been demonstrated in rape victims at 6 to 21 days, 1, 3, 6, 12, and 18 months after the incident (Murphy et al., 1988). Esteem schemas about others involve basic assumptions about the worth and true nature of people. Profound alterations in basic assumptions about others may be triggered by violation sustained at the hands of another human being. Negative schemas could include beliefs that people are basically uncaring, evil, or bad. The result may be experiences of chronic anger, bitterness, or cynicism toward other people.

Intimacy

Self-schemas about intimacy are internalizations of images of loving parental figures, and they drive our capacities to nurture and care for the self. A negative alteration in this schema would be reflected in beliefs that one is unable to comfort or nurture the self. The result is overwhelming anxiety in the face of demands, fear of being alone, or even a feeling of inner deadness. Upsurges in memories about trauma when alone may result in devastating panic. Desperate attempts may be seen to obtain comfort via alcohol, pills, excessive spending, or superficial sexual encounters. Other-directed intimacy schemas are expectations about human connections and needs for relatedness to others. Negative alterations include expectations that one will be alienated from other people. Rape victims often say that they feel they trust men less and have greater fears of getting close than they did before the rape (Ellis et al., 1981; Koss, 1988).

Much of the depression seen among victims may be attributed to the loss of illusions (Janoff-Bulman & Frieze, 1983), loss of former images of the self (Horowitz, Wilner, Marmar, & Krupnick, 1980), and the loss of self-efficacy. "[The rapists] had taken one thing, they had taken something away from me that wasn't theirs. When they raped me they had taken something of mine. They forcefully took it. They took it all away . . . " (quoted in Roth & Lebowitz, 1988, p. 93).

A primary choice of action after a threatening experience is to reaffirm the self by seeking validation from others. Yet two factors have dramatically altered the potential for cognitive adaptation to violent victimization: (a) the interpersonal nature of the victimization, and (b) the pervasive, malevolent social environment (Burt & Katz, 1985). Many acts of violence involve the most private interpersonal acts and have a direct focus of intentional harm. Further, victims of violence must contend with a culture in which socially transmitted beliefs support women's responsibility for provocation of sexual assault (Burt, 1980). In addition, many victims learn painfully that people are not as supportive to victims as might be expected given our Judeo-Christian ethics and general tendency to help the powerless (Janoff-Bulman & Frieze, 1983). Acquaintance rape, in particular, places these factors in bold relief. The victim, participating in a social context assumed to be at least benign, is suddenly exposed to a hateful, personally directed experience. Moreover, the social response does not affirm the victim's emotional experience in that her assailant as well as others in the social environment are likely to interpret the outcome as "no big deal." One woman, after her companion had sexually assaulted her, reported that her assailant asked if he should walk her back to her apartment for her protection (Koss & Burkhart, 1989).

PERSON CHARACTERISTICS THAT AFFECT RAPE RESPONSE

Demonstration of suspected relationships among various person or event characteristics and the amount of trauma experienced as a result of rape is a difficult challenge. The difficulty stems in large part from the small size of most samples in studies of rape victims. With a small sample, statistical power is insufficient to detect even weak relationships. Thus actual relationships that exist may be missed. Further complicating the picture are some spurious associations, which achieve significance solely by chance. These findings, of course, fail to replicate when some other researchers try to repeat the analysis, thereby creating a literature full of inconsistent findings. The heterogeneity of rape also complicates the search for relationships. It is entirely possible that various features would be significant predictors of trauma within one form of rape but not for others. For all these reasons it has proved impossible to develop a single profile of the person most likely to experience severe aftereffects of rape. In the following material, we discuss the few reliable associations and debunk others that are widely accepted but not supported by research.

Demographic Characteristics

Demographic variables appear to have little influence on victims' responses to rape (Kilpatrick & Veronen, 1984; Kilpatrick et al., 1985), nor are they predictive of subsequent recovery (Becker et al., 1982; Ruch & Leon, 1983). In contrast, preexisting mental health problems have regularly been associated with assault outcomes. For example, the severity of preexisting emotional problems was a significant predictor of the initial level of trauma (Ruch & Leon, 1983). Likewise, a history of psychotropic medication use, alcohol abuse, suicidal ideation, or suicide attempts was related to greater distress in the first month postassault (Frank, Turner, Stewart, Jacob, & West, 1981). A prior diagnosis of a psychiatric disorder also was identified as a predictor of both short-term response and recovery outcome (Frank & Anderson, 1987). Prior mental health problems predicted sexual assault trauma in a national sample of victimized college women (Gidycz & Koss, 1990).

Prior Victimization

Research is becoming more conclusive on the effect of prior victimization on the impact of and recovery from a sexual assault. Between 1 and 4 months postrape, Frank and colleagues found no significant differences between single-incident and multiple-incident victims on measures of depression, anxiety, or fear (Frank, Turner, & Stewart, 1980; Frank & Anderson, 1987). In a larger series of patients, however, trauma scores for women with prior victimization increased during the 2-week period following the crime while the scores for women without prior victimization decreased (Ruch & Leon, 1983). In addition, elevated risk for depression among multiply victimized women has been reported in two large community studies (Kilpatrick et al., 1987; Sorenson & Golding, 1990). For example, the percentage of women who had a lifetime diagnosis of depression was 46% among women who had been raped a single time and 80% among women who had been raped multiple times (Kilpatrick et al., 1987).

EVENT CHARACTERISTICS THAT AFFECT RAPE RESPONSE

There has been a common assumption in the public arena that some rapes are worse than others. Rapes by strangers and those that are more violent are assumed to be more traumatic for the victim. However, this may not be the case.

Victim-Offender Relationship

Comparisons between victims of stranger and nonstranger rape uncover no difference in reactions or recovery except that those who were attacked by acquaintances were more likely to have problems with self-esteem initially (Hassell, 1981). A comparison among victims of stranger, nonromantic acquaintance, date, and marital rapes found no differences in degree of psychological distress as measured by psychological tests of depression and anxiety (Koss, Dinero, Seibel, & Cox, 1988). Although rapes by acquaintances were less likely to be seen as rape or to be revealed to anyone, no significant differences in the levels of psychological symptoms were found among the victims. Acquaintanceship with the assailant may affect victims in other ways, however. For example, it was reported that women who delayed seeking treatment were more likely to have known their assailants and less likely to have physically defended themselves than immediate treatment seekers (Stewart et al., 1987).

Severity of the Assault

Brutality scores or indices have been developed in a number of studies to describe the overall severity of an assault and to examine the effect of severity upon the victim's reactions. Some investigators have found neither the presence nor extent of violence per se to be strongly associated with victim reactions (Sales, Baum, & Shore, 1984); others have reported consistent associations (Cohen & Roth, 1987; Gidycz & Koss, 1990). Dismantling the indices into examination of individual assault characteristics has yielded mixed results. Threats against the victim's life were found to predict symptomatology within the first three months but not at the six-month follow-up (Sales et al., 1984). Other assault variables that predicted symptoms were the number of assailants, physical threat, injury requiring medical care, and medical complications (Sales et al., 1984). Life threat, physical injury, and completed rape were found to contribute significantly to the prediction of severity of posttraumatic stress disorder (Kilpatrick et al., 1989).

The possibility that the actual violence of an attack is less crucial to victim reaction than the "felt threat" was first proposed by Sale and colleagues (1984). Subsequent studies that have measured the victim's perception of threat have found that it predicts the extent of later fear reactions (Girelli, Resick, Marhoefer-Dvorak, & Hutter, 1986) and the degree of posttraumatic symptoms experienced (Kilpatrick et al., 1987). Thus it seems that it is not the characteristics of the event alone that determine the reaction, but the event as perceived by the victim. More information about cognitive processes in the aftermath of assault is presented in subsequent sections.

POSTTRAUMATIC STRESS DISORDER IN RAPE VICTIMS

Victims of violence—regardless of whether they have been raped, mugged, taken hostage, or survived flood, fire, terrorism, or internment—often suffer both immediate and long-term psychological responses. These characteristic responses form a cluster of symptoms labeled posttraumatic stress disorder (American Psychiatric Association, 1987). Posttraumatic stress disorder (PTSD) is simply a hypothetical concept to describe a set of symptoms that are observed frequently to co-occur in the aftermath of trauma. Rape victims are thought to be the largest single group of PTSD sufferers (Foa, Olasov, & Steketee, 1987). We will first review the constellations of symptoms that comprise PTSD, then we will consider hypothesized models for the psychological processes that generate and sustain the symptoms.

According to the *Diagnostic and Statistical Manual of Mental Disorders III-R*, PTSD is a group of symptoms that may develop following a psychologically distressing event that is outside of the ordinary range of human experiences. Psychic numbing, which is defined as diminished responsiveness to the external world, usually develops in the immediate aftermath of the trauma. The hallmark of PTSD, however, is intrusive reexperiencing of the trauma, which may not occur until months or years following the trauma when recollections are triggered by some actual or symbolic reminder of the trauma. Recollections are in the form of intrusive daytime memories or nightmares and are accompanied by intense psychological distress. To reduce the distress of reexperiencing, trauma victims often go to great length to avoid reminders of the trauma. Trauma responses that diminish within one month are not considered to qualify as PTSD. The diagnosis of PTSD is considered only after a month of symptoms. When the onset is six months or more beyond the trauma, the term "delayed-onset PTSD" is used.

The formal diagnosis of PTSD involves the assessment of four criteria:

(1) *Unusual experience.* Experience of an event that is outside the range of usual human experience and would be distressing to almost anyone.

(2) *Persistent reexperiencing.* The trauma reoccurs through persistent intrusive memories, recurrent dreams, flashbacks (suddenly

feeling as though the traumatic event were recurring), or intense distress when exposed to events that symbolize or resemble the trauma. At least one form of reexperiencing must be present.

(3) *Avoidance.* Stimuli associated with the trauma are persistently avoided. At least three of the following must be present: (a) avoidance of thoughts or feelings associated with the trauma; (b) avoidance of activities or situations that trigger recollections; (c) loss of memory for important aspects of the trauma; (d) extremely diminished interest in significant interests; (e) feelings of detachment or estrangement from others; (f) inability to experience some affects such as loving feelings; or (g) a foreshortened future in which the victim does not expect to have a career, marriage, children, or long life.

(4) *Increased arousal.* At least two forms of increased arousal are observed that were not present before the trauma. Manifestations of increased arousal include: (a) difficulty falling or staying asleep; (b) irritability or anger outbursts; (c) difficulty concentrating; (d) hypervigilance (edginess); (e) exaggerated startle response (jumpiness); or (f) physiological reactivity such as sweating or fast heart beat when exposed to events that symbolize or resemble the trauma. (American Psychiatric Association, 1987, pp. 247-251)

PTSD Prevalence

The lifetime prevalence of PTSD in a large community sample of rape victims was 57% (Kilpatrick et al., 1987). Criteria for PTSD were currently met by 17% of the raped women who were, on average, 17 years postrape. In a prospective study of hospital-referred rape victims, 97% met PTSD criteria at initial assessment; 46% still met the criteria 2 months later (Rothbaum, Foa, & Hoge, 1988).

The DSM-III criteria for PTSD have been criticized by those who work with victims as biased toward reexperiencing symptoms. Because victims frequently cope with their victimization through denial, especially when it occurs at early ages, the extent of assault-related aftereffects would be understated by the

PTSD prevalence figures. Some have suggested the need for a category of PTSD that is characterized by denial and negative alterations in schemas. Many clinicians believe that victimization-induced changes in cognitive schema are rape's most disabling legacy.

A BEHAVIORAL/COGNITIVE CONCEPTUALIZATION OF RAPE AFTEREFFECTS

Thinking concerning the psychological processes that create and maintain rape aftereffects has changed rapidly. A comprehensive review and critique of several alternate conceptualizations is provided by Foa, Steketee, and Olasov (1989). They conclude that the primary difficulty with earlier thinking was the failure to adequately account for the changes in meaning that accompany trauma. To do so requires a semantic theory, and a classical conditioning model is insufficient. Foa and colleagues (Foa & Kozak, 1986; Foa et al., 1989) have developed a behavioral/cognitive conceptualization of rape aftereffects that rests on Lang's (1977, 1979) discussion of fear structures. Fear structures are viewed as schema that have numerous connections with other schema in the memory network. A fear structure contains three kinds of information: (a) information about the characteristics of the feared situation, (b) information about verbal, physiological, and overt behavioral responses that occur when the structure is activated, and (c) interpretative information about the meaning of the elements in the fear structure, including the stimuli—or features that characterized the feared situation—and responses—or behaviors that occurred in the feared situation. The strength of this conceptualization is the inclusion of both cognitive and affective elements into one model.

Fear structures that develop following rape differ from those that might be seen in someone with ordinary fears. The differences include greater intensity of the verbal and physiologic responses that occur when the structure is activated, larger size of the structure that results from a wide range of stimuli capable of activating the structure, and a lower threshold for activation. Because many stimuli activate the structure, frequent upsurges are experienced in emotional arousal as well as intrusive re-experiencing of the trauma through memories and nightmares. These upsurges trigger attempts to avoid or escape the discomfort, resulting in numbness, behavioral avoidance, and dissociative behavior. The fear structures of victims who experience chronic symptoms actually may differ from those who experience symptoms for a short while and then recover spontaneously (Foa et al., 1989). For example, the fear structures of those raped in previously safe places may include more stimuli than those of persons raped in dangerous places. Likewise, the fear structures of those who experienced imminent death may contain more intensive response elements than those who did not perceive their life to be in danger. Further, individuals who have a low tolerance for discomfort and anxiety will be more likely to avoid situations or images that lead to activation of the fear structure. This tactic is not adaptive because it prevents completion of emotional processing, which involves changes in the connections among the elements in the fear structure so that the stimuli no longer are connected with strong emotional responses and the adaptive reformulation of the meanings ascribed to the stimuli and responses.

Because the aftereffects of rape are persistent and long-lasting, one questions why victims fail to habituate when stimuli that signaled the rape repeatedly reoccur but the previous outcome—rape—fails to occur. Foa and colleagues (1989) suggest that the fear structures that follow rape are so large that no situations in daily life match enough of the elements to activate the entire structure. And even when a victim exposes herself to a feared situation, the extreme physiologic reactions that are experienced may interfere with information processing. Also, because of the proactive nature of cognitive schema, contradictory evidence may not even be perceived by the victim. For example, a schema consisting of beliefs about the basic bad nature of other people may fail to change because the individual does not notice or remember instances when others have been kind.

CLINICAL SCREENING FOR ASSAULT HISTORY

Consider the following clients:

- An 18-year-old woman begins her first session, "How old were you when you lost your virginity? How'd you feel if you were 9?"
- A 25-year-old working mother of two presenting depression and marital problems related that while she and her husband were making love, she suddenly began screaming, "Have I ever told you what happened when I was 17?"

These clients often represent the practicing clinician's encounter with rape victims. The incidents occurred some time ago, may or may not meet a legal definition of rape, may or may not be conceptualized as rape by the victims, and only rarely were reported to the police. Yet, as an emotional issue the rapes are traumatic and current. Anxiety, depression, withdrawal, and difficulties in relationships are among the most common complaints that bring people to psychotherapy. They are also the primary symptoms of the posttraumatic stress disorder from which victims of rape suffer. The long latency and wide range of symptoms of delayed posttraumatic stress disorder often make it difficult to establish a connection between the presenting symptoms and a past sexual assault. The difficulty is magnified if the history of assault emerges only after psychotherapy has progressed for some time. The scope of rape, however, suggests that the clinician more frequently considers sexual assault as an etiological factor for the client who presents the complaints of anxiety, depression, social withdrawal, or difficulties in sexual relationships.

Kilpatrick (1983) has wisely noted, "However eager clinical psychologists may be to apply their assessment and treatment skills, they cannot provide adequate services if victims cannot be located and their victim status detected. Thus, detection and case finding are of paramount importance" (p. 92). Therefore, we will now turn away from research tools for describing the prevalence of rape to a discussion of clinical rape case finding.

Features Encouraging Nondisclosure of Rape

Kilpatrick (1983) discusses five reasons why victims do not volunteer the fact that they have been raped.

(1) *Fear.* Fear may account for a victim's failure to disclose her experience to a clinician. She may fear retribution by the assailant, the stigma of being a rape victim, or being blamed for provoking the rape. These fears are similar to those that inhibit victims from reporting a rape to the police.

(2) *Negative expectations.* A victim may have encountered negative responses in earlier attempts to disclose or discuss her rape with family or friends. If earlier attempts were met with disbelief, silence, or victim blame, the victim may be reluctant to bring her assault up again.

(3) *Issue not raised.* The clinician may fail to ask the victim about her sexual assault history. Earlier discussion of the true scope of rape establishes the wisdom of including assault items in every historical interview of a female client.

(4) *Rape is unacknowledged.* A victim may not perceive herself as having been raped although she has had an experience defined as rape by the law. These victims can be detected via questions that spell out in concrete terms the behaviors that may have occurred and avoid the use of the word rape.

(5) *Symptoms not connected to rape.* Victims may fail to disclose a rape because they do not see a connection between it and their symptoms. An adult woman who seeks treatment for relationship difficulties during college may fail to relate these problems to a date rape that happened when she was 16.

When to Screen for Assault Histories

Because of the high prevalence of assault experiences we recommend *routine* inquiry into violence history. There are three situations, however, when screening for sexual assault is positively indicated:

(1) *Presenting problems could be induced by rape.* Compare the symptoms a client is presenting with the types of symptoms known to be rape induced. Whenever a client has the same types of symptoms as rape victims, one must consider the possibility that the clinical picture is rape induced.

(2) *Symptom severity has changed abruptly.* Attempt to develop a time line for the presenting symptoms. Symptoms that appeared suddenly or became dramatically worse in a short period of time suggest the possibility that they were triggered by a traumatic experience.

(3) *Vulnerability cues are present.* It is important to remember that rape is but one form of victimization of women. Lack of pay equity legislation, employment-linked retirement benefits, and health insurance are antiwomen federal policies that contribute to women's lower status relative to men. Clinical work with women who are economic victims in society often reveals a high rate of sexual victimization as well. A history of exposure to family violence, child abuse, and sexual abuse also elevate the probability of additional victimization having occurred (Koss & Dinero, 1989b).

How to Ask About Rape

Most people do not object to being asked about sexual assault experiences. Many are even relieved to know that there might be an explanation for how they are feeling. We have found the following suggestions very helpful in questioning about sexual assault (Kilpatrick, 1983):

(1) *Normalize the experience.* Assume that victims are reluctant to disclose assault. Give support and encouragement to do so. "Some things happen to many women that are not pleasant kinds of sex." Or, "It's now generally recognized that many women have had experiences where they were forced to engage

in unwanted sexual activity. Women often are reluctant to talk about these experiences, but it's important for me to know because they can sometimes produce long-lasting problems."

(2) *Phrase questions to detect unacknowledged victims.* Do not use the word "rape." Assume that many victims do not realize that their victimization was a rape, or even any kind of crime at all. "Has anyone had sex with you when you didn't want to by using threat or force?" "Have you ever had any unwanted sexual experiences?" Not, "Have you ever been raped?" Be aware that the person who has never revealed an assault to anyone may experience shock when first questioned about this area. We have found it preferable to ask several concrete questions about the various scenarios that qualify as rape in order to give plenty of time for some of the initial shock to dissipate and to allow the person to carefully search for relevant memories.

(3) *Avoid becoming judgmental.* Many people, including clinicians define rape narrowly,

A "real" rape involves someone of unquestionable virtue being suddenly attacked by a total stranger who uses considerable physical force. In contrast, if the assailant is not a stranger, the victim does not sustain serious physical injury, and/or the victim is not a Nun with respect to virtue, our culture tends to define the situation as "spurious" rape. (Veronen & Kilpatrick, 1983, p. 94)

Judgments are for courtrooms, not consulting rooms. When a clinician becomes judgmental, the victim is likely to discontinue service and become more reluctant to seek help in the future.

PSYCHOMETRIC ASSESSMENT OF RAPE AFTEREFFECTS

Several standardized psychological measures recently have become available for the assessment of the severity of rape-induced aftereffects. Most are brief and lend themselves nicely for use in measuring individual progress as well as evaluating program effectiveness.

Clinical Trauma Assessment (CTA)

This is a rating scale designed to be completed by clinicians to measure the severity of the trauma experienced by rape victims in the immediate aftermath of sexual assault (Ruch, Gartrell, Ramelli, & Coyne, 1990). After completing a structured interview with the victim that includes questions about the sexual assault and emotional trauma, each of the 16 specific trauma symptoms are rated by a clinician from 0 (no trauma) to 7 (extremely severe trauma). The symptoms included on the rating scale are depression, self-blame/guilt, shame/embarrassment, loss of trust in people, interpersonal sensitivity, concern about others' reactions, confusion-shock, blank mind, difficulty concentrating, disorientation, difficulty making decisions, fear/anxiety, anger, nervous activity, crying/sobbing, and tension/rigidity. A factor analysis of the items revealed three factors that accounted for 53% of the variance. The three factors were named as follows (the Chronbach alpha internal consistency reliability is indicated in parentheses): Controlled Emotional Trauma Style (.84); Cognitive Trauma (.85); and Expressed Emotional Trauma Style (.70). The specific trauma symptoms evaluated as most severe by crisis workers were fear, concern about other's reactions, and anger.

Impact of Event Scale

This is a 15-item, self-report test designed to measure post-traumatic symptoms of intrusion and avoidance (Horowitz, Wilner, & Alvarez, 1979). Respondents think of the last week and rate the items on a 1 (not at all) to 4 (often) scale according to how much trouble they have had. The two subscales are named Intrusion (alpha = .78) and Avoidance (alpha = .82). In previous use with rape victims, the IES has demonstrated the ability to detect changes in levels of distress following cognitive-behavioral treatment (Kilpatrick & Amick, 1985).

Rape Aftermath Symptom Test (RAST)

This instrument was developed by adopting the 30 items from the SCL-90-R (Derogatis, 1977), and 40 items from the Veronen-Kilpatrick Modified Fear Schedule that best discriminated victims from nonvictims of rape at three months postassault (Saunders, Mandoki, & Kilpatrick, 1990). Victims rate each item on a 5-point scale to indicate the degree of current disturbance associated with that item. A global distress score can be obtained from the RAST that ranges from 0 to 280. Good internal consistency (alpha = .93) and test-retest reliability over 2.5 months (r = .85) have been reported. The RAST has been found to discriminate between rape victims and nonvictims for up to three years postassault (Kilpatrick et al., 1985). Using a cutting score of >160 on the RAST alone or >100 on the RAST and >15 on the IES resulted in correct discrimination of 89% of rape victims who were and who were not diagnosed with PTSD.

Rape Trauma Syndrome Rating Scale (RTSRS)

Similar to the CTA is the Rape Trauma Syndrome Rating Scale (DiVasto, 1985). The scale is designed to assess the severity of eight symptoms of sexual assault trauma. Interviews ask open-ended questions about each target symptom (e.g., "Has your appetite changed in any way?") and then rate the answer on a 5-point Likert scale. Validity data demonstrated that victims scored higher than nonvictims on all indicators.

Sexual Assault Symptoms Scale (SASS)

This is a 32-item, self-report scale that is designed for the assessment of trauma in the immediate postrape period (Ruch et al., in press). The SASS consists of four factors, termed as follows: Disclosure Shame, Safety Fears, Depression, and Self-Blame. These factors accounted for 52% of the variance.

However, 23% of the women who entered the emergency room
in one study of the SASS were unable to complete the scale
because they were too exhausted, intoxicated, unable to speak
English, or had developmental or physical challenges (Ruch
et al., in press).

THREE

Rape as a Community Issue

In the spring of 1983, public attention was drawn to New Bedford, Massachusetts, where six men from the city's Portuguese community were arrested and charged with aggravated—"gang"—rape. Initial reports indicated that as they took turns sexually assaulting a young woman on a pool table in Big Dan's Tavern, not a single bystander came to her aid.

Accounts of the crime were read throughout the country, and, indeed, throughout the world. In New Bedford, outraged citizens formed the New Bedford Coalition Against Sexist Violence. A candlelight vigil decrying sexist violence attracted more than 2,500 persons: men and women from all segments of the local community and feminists from throughout the United States. Within a week, city officials agreed to provide start-up funds for a new community-based rape crisis center.

The trials began one year later. Court proceedings were broadcast daily to local audiences who debated their meaning on nightly radio talk shows. When the trials ended, four defendants stood convicted by a jury of their peers. Public attention was again drawn to New Bedford as 10,000-15,000 citizens now participated in a second demonstration, this one called to protest the convictions and express solidarity with the accused. For these marchers, the convictions stemmed not from evidence submitted in court, but from the anti-Portuguese sentiment of judge, jury, and dominant community. Their numbers included men, women, and children of Portuguese and non-Portuguese descent, many of whom argued that the woman was no victim but an active and culpable participant. Some maintained that she should have been tried and punished. A local priest declared: "She led those boys into sin."

When the trials ended, the victim left New Bedford in fear for her life, her attorney announcing that, in fact, five sentences had been rendered: prison terms for four rapists and "permanent exile" for one victim.[1]

The so-called "Big Dan's" rape incident became the basis for a film titled *The Accused* starring Jodie Foster in a highly acclaimed performance. It also served as a catalyst for legal reform. In Massachusetts today, the bystanders who encouraged these assailants and who themselves were never tried for criminal behavior could in fact be charged and tried.

Since 1984, a number of other highly publicized instances of rape have become the subject of widespread public attention and debate, providing new impetus for community action and legal reform. Recently, for example, an Iowa housewife decided to disclose her identity to the local press and to allow publication of a detailed, nonanonymous account of her rape experience. The article and this victim's decision created nationwide discussion of the rights and responsibilities of journalists and whether or not the press would harm the rape victim or destigmatize the crime of rape by routinely publishing victims' names. The victim herself recommended that victims retain the right to choose if, when, and how their names are made public. And, in New York City, the case of a 30-year-old jogger who was gang-raped in Central Park by a group of boys engaging in violent revelry that they called "wilding" caused city residents and citizens nationwide to confront the ordeal of a victim who, once nearly dead from the multiple and severe injuries she endured, now had to relate in open court her sexual relationships with men other than her assailants. The secondary trauma associated with this kind of courtroom experience was never more clear to the general public than when the victim left the courtroom facing spectator cries of "The boyfriend did it; the boyfriend did it."

These events and their sequelae give graphic illustration to the premise that rape is a community issue and demonstrate the profound effect the relationship between victim and community can have upon the rape victim's psychological experience and recovery process. The effect is no less profound when the rape is unpublicized and possibly unreported. Consider, for example, the phenomenon of unreported and unacknowledged or "hidden" rape.

Victimization researchers agree that rape is a significantly underreported crime. Knowledge and fear of ill-treatment by police officers, court officials, and medical and mental health providers contribute heavily to a victim's reluctance to report (Bart, 1979; Holmstrom & Burgess, 1975; Robin, 1977). Whatever the public pronouncements of local officials may be in the aftermath of rape, ill-treatment and inadequate treatment reveal the community's lack of awareness and concern and lend institutional legitimacy to "rape supportive belief systems" (Weis & Borges, 1973). Central to these belief systems are myths and misconceptions that foster ill-regard and rationalize poor treatment (e.g., "Every woman secretly wants to be raped." "You cannot be raped by someone you know.").

Rape victims, like other citizens, share community values and beliefs and interpret their experience in light of community values and traditions. Tragically, it is therefore probable that widespread and unanalyzed acceptance of rape-supportive beliefs further encourages underreporting by preventing victims from acknowledging their experiences as rape: from seeing acquaintance rape or "date rape" as rape, for example, and by encouraging them to disregard as irrelevant any so-called "compromising circumstances." The victim who acknowledges her experience as rape but anticipates poor treatment from an ill-informed community may not report and may or may not seek care. The victim who *shares* many or most of the beliefs that underlie ill-treatment may very well deny that her experience is rape. She will almost certainly manage the emotional aftermath of rape in troubled isolation.

In this chapter, we examine the interrelationships that exist among community attitudes, community services, and the psychological experience of the woman raped. Rape as a focal point of social action is considered, and the community as both setting for and target of social change is discussed.

DEFINING "COMMUNITY"

Kinds of Communities

The term "community" describes all kinds of human groupings. Anderson and Carter (1978), for example, distinguish between *place, nonplace,* and *kinship* communities, finding that they have in common not only structural properties but also purposive functions that mediate between community members and the larger society. A *place community* is defined in terms of geographic boundaries and might consist of a city, town, or neighborhood where community members live and nonmembers do not live. Residence defines community membership. In the examples given earlier the city of New Bedford, the metropolis of New York City, and a town in Iowa are all *place* communities.

Nonplace communities are innumerable. Membership is defined not by residence but by other attributes shared by community members. Membership may be established by virtue of commonly held interests or values, for example, or by shared professional pursuits. One can speak, therefore, of a "community of scholars," a "religious community," and "the feminist community." Some nonplace communities are national or even international in scope. Others exist within the geographic boundaries of place communities. New York and New Bedford, for example, are home to several ethnic communities, locally active feminist communities, and individuals who identify with professional or cultural communities having nationwide membership.

Kinship communities also transcend place. These are defined not by common purpose, but by common bloodlines and familial relationships. Clans, tribes, and large extended families constitute communities based on kinship relations.

In New Bedford, the existence of sizable and well-established Portuguese and Cape Verdian communities has acted as a magnet, attracting from these ethnic groups immigrant constellations comprising multiple generations of families and friends. These groups function very much as kinship communities.

Some communities blur the distinction between place, non-place, and kinship communities. An ethnic community (e.g., a black, Hispanic, or Irish-American community) has attributes of all three. A "campus community" is defined by place and by attributes that transcend place. Responding to these variations, Spergel (1974) distinguishes between *geographic* communities (presumably similar to place); *functional* communities, which define membership by shared purpose or activity; and *population aggregate* communities, which include kinship, ethnic, race, and age or gender communities.

Whatever typology is used to classify communities, the rape victim, like other individuals, will undoubtedly belong to a number of communities at once. Each will influence her psychological experience of rape, and each will facilitate or make difficult her recovery from that experience. Thus

- the 38-year-old, Irish-American, Roman Catholic mother who is raped in a parking lot when leaving a late night work shift in South Boston will find her response to rape and her feelings about herself influenced simultaneously by the services available to her in the city of Boston, the degree of empathy and support extended her by coworkers, and the reactions of church members, neighbors, family, and friends;
- a 21-year-old black coed who is "date-raped" will search for her new sense of self in the reactions of largely white service providers and in the compassion extended or withheld by her roommate, classmates, college officials, friends, and family; and
- in New Bedford, a 21-year-old mother of two raped in a neighborhood bar will find herself the recipient of services from medical and law enforcement agencies in her geographic community, the focal point of empathy and outrage among local citizens and feminists nationwide, and a target of scorn and anger among many in the ethnic community with which she is identified.

FUNCTIONS OF COMMUNITIES

The impact that communities have upon the psychological experience of individuals is best understood in terms of the functions that communities perform for community members. Most authors agree that communities *grant identity and a sense of belonging* to community members, serving as contexts for the development and expression of personal identity. If, in the aftermath of rape, a victim's membership in the community is affirmed, her recovery will be facilitated by awareness of the support and concern available to her. On the other hand, if rape marks her as deficient or causes her to be shunned and avoided, the community will have exacerbated her trauma.

Communities also *teach and foster traditionally valued behaviors* and provide members with a vehicle for expressing community values and traditions. In too many communities, the victim's behavior is called into question as much as, if indeed not more than, the assailant's. Victims find themselves explaining, for example, why they did not scream or fight back, why they went to such and such a party or, simply, why and how they ever found themselves in a situation of risk. The inquiry can heighten a victim's sense of responsibility and complicate her recovery by promoting an unfounded sense of shame.

Additionally, communities *socialize members to prescribed norms,* formally and informally defining their rights and their community responsibilities, and shaping individual identity within a context of social responsibility. Rape-supportive belief systems, when adopted by community settings, encourage victim isolation and blame. Communities that affirm as normative a woman's right to go where she chooses, dress how she chooses, and say "yes" or "no" as she chooses to sexual advances by men are prepared by these values to aid the rape victim's recovery and ameliorate her pain with evidence of community indignation at her experience.

Communities also *mediate between individuals and the larger society,* enabling community members to influence and adapt to a larger, more encompassing world. In performing this role, communities serve individual and society, providing two-way channels of communication and fostering mutual influence. For the rape victim, the community is an environment in which she experiences her own social value. Communities that encourage full participation by women and men alike and that amplify and respond to the voices and concerns of youthful, elderly, and minority community members are equipped to respond and give solace to the disempowered and disenfranchised and to reempower the rape victim through social support to her recovery.

Finally, *communities provide a set of intermediate institutions* through which members can pursue community aims and achieve community status. In geographic communities, these institutions include the schools in which community attitudes and values are expressed and reinforced and the law enforcement, medical, and social service agencies to which the rape victim must turn for assistance. Ethnic communities frequently offer church groups, neighborhood boards, and other formal and informal settings that exist to strengthen ethnic identity. Other kinds of communities will provide national policy boards, social clubs, or political action committees. Each of these institutions, too, has the potential for positively or negatively influencing a victim's recovery.

What do these community functions have to do with rape and the meaning of rape for the survivor? Simply put, in performing or failing to perform these functions on her behalf, each community of which the rape victim is member will help or hinder her physical and emotional recovery from rape. If the geographic community where she resides makes available to her a wide array of timely, accessible, and sensitively provided services, the woman raped will experience compassion, advocacy, and a continued sense of belonging. If such services do not exist or if sexist values and rape-supportive myths prevail in the communities from which she draws her identity, then the victim's needs will undoubtedly go unaddressed. Her sense of social identity will be threatened, and her continued membership in the community may itself be placed at risk.

Because she is a member of various communities at once and because each of these is transacting towards various ends on behalf of all its members, every rape victim will experience a difficult "potpourri" of community reactions. She will receive solace, support, and advocacy here, and skepticism or indifference there. She will experience unanticipated exclusion from a once-familiar world and equally unexpected acceptance in another. Some victims will find themselves closer to family members once seen as distant; others will feel abandoned by families and friends once seen as close. Some communities will intensify a victim's sense of identity and belonging; some will act in new advocacy of her; and some will actively or passively exclude her from continued membership. Together these reactions will define the victim's position relative to the larger society and will contribute to or detract from her sense of personal and social power. As these intersecting communities act or fail to act on her behalf, the woman raped literally will rebuild her sense of self.

THE COMMUNITY AS "ECOSYSTEM"

What determines a community's reaction to rape and how does the event of rape fit into the myriad of influences acting upon community dynamics? Many authors in the field of community psychology (Gottlieb & Todd, 1979; Harvey & Passy, 1978; Kelly, 1968; Trickett, Kelly, & Todd, 1972) find it helpful to view communities in much the same way that field biologists view natural environments (i.e., as dynamic and essentially conservative systems that evolve adaptively as the result of resource transactions taking place within the community environment and between that environment and the larger world). As discussed in Chapter 1, the ecological analogy offers insight into the etiology of varied reactions and varied recovery patterns among rape victims (Harvey, 1990). It also poses a view of community and community change processes that can aid understanding of the community's impact upon the recovery process.

A RESOURCE PERSPECTIVE

The ecological analogy maintains that communities, like other living environments, utilize, conserve, and *cycle resources* in transactions that shape and preserve community identity. By creating traditions, encouraging the expression of shared values, and cultivating the personal competencies of community members, the resource transactions of a community enhance the members' sense of belonging, foster stability, and enable or impede community change.

The resources available within the community ecosystem include the varied qualities of *persons, settings,* and *events. Persons* bring to the community varied interests, skills, and energies and encourage the community to cultivate these same qualities in others. Inherent to a resource perspective is the premise that *pluralism and diversity* characterize all communities and give to each a unique identity. However alike they may be in some respects, community members inevitably differ from one another as well. They will differ in age, gender, income, and ethnicity, for example, and in terms of their personal values, skills, and competencies. When these differences are expressed in an environment that devalues diversity and treats differences as troublesome, pluralism and diversity can heighten conflict among community members and impede healthy community development.

In both New Bedford and New York City, for example, a history of racial discrimination and ethnic divisiveness set the stage for new expressions of antipathy and caused some community members to turn against the victim and champion instead the causes of the accused. When valued and cultivated, these same differences broaden community identity, enrich the dynamic aspects of community, and provide for varied resource exchanges. In these same cities, juries composed of diversely representative community members found the accused guilty of aggravated rape and refused to allow race, ethnicity, or awareness of legitimate minority grievance to cloud their vision or

compromise their work. In both cities, multiracial and multiethnic groups of community members have initiated legal
reform efforts and helped to create new victim service programs. These efforts will continue to expand and enrich the
resources of these communities and, in them, change the relationship between rape victim and larger community. Thus the
ecological analogy views pluralism and diversity as assets for
ongoing community development and change. Healthy community ecosystems are able to take advantage of pluralism and
diversity.

Community settings are formal and informal institutions that
cultivate and respond to the qualities of persons within the
community. They bring organization to bear on these qualities
and provide opportunities for collective action by community
members, thus empowering factions within the community to
influence community identity. A community-based rape crisis
center, a women's consciousness-raising group, a self-defense
course for women at risk of crime victimization and sexual assault all are settings that speak to the validity of women's rights
and to the level of a community's advocacy on behalf of rape
victims.

Events also function as resources within the community. Cere-
monial and festive occasions invite members to celebrate and
affirm shared values and strengthen bonds among community
members. A neighborhood crime-watch meeting, for example,
and "Take Back the Night" marches are events that give expression to the community's rejection of sexual violence and offer
opportunities for community members to bond with one another in expressing a positive value for nonviolent behavior.
Catastrophic or threatening events may catalyze the community
into action and defense. A highly publicized rape will galvanize
community attention, for example, and a less highly publicized
event will test the adequacy of a community's response to rape.

An ecological view of community emphasizes the interdependence of community resources and their ongoing and
dynamic interaction with one another. Individual community
members will express and develop their unique competencies,
skills, and values, for example, in any number of community

settings. Each of these capabilities affect the individual's growth and development and each will undergo varying degrees of change even as it is utilized. Similarly, community events will provide opportunities for members and settings (e.g., schools, churches) to participate in community traditions and, on occasion, will unexpectedly prompt community members to create new settings and mobilize community change. In the aftermath of rape, for example, a victim may turn to local care settings only to discover the inadequacy of their services and a lack of preparedness on the part of agency staff. Her interchange with these settings certainly will add to her burden and complicate her recovery. It will also introduce into these settings new possibilities for change. In some instances, local settings will retrench and defend what they do; in others local service providers will begin to recognize the need for new services and skills and may initiate a needed relationship with the local rape crisis center. In the absence of such a setting, the event of rape and the victim's negative encounter with local care givers may prompt her friends and family to join local feminists in their efforts to establish a community-based rape crisis center. In the end, community member, community setting, and community event will have interacted to bring about varying degrees of change in the ecosystem of the local community.

Community Change

All communities undergo change over time. Because all of its members are simultaneously members of other communities, every community has as members individuals whose attitudes, values, skills, and emotional priorities are in flux. As individuals move naturally and informally from one community to another, they are subject to change and they introduce the possibility of change, first, to other members individually and, through them, to the community. Thus the community ecosystem serves as a *setting for change:* a context in which members share their experiences, set new priorities and goals, consider the promises and risks of collective action, and generate strate-

gies for accomplishing desired change. Unanticipated events
like rape may introduce the possibility of change into the community ecosystem, and new settings may emerge as community
members pursue their newly established aims.

Just as every community will undergo change, so each will
resist change and for some members become *target of change*
activities. Resistance to change is mobilized when community
identity is threatened—when new ideas call established beliefs
into question and when change-oriented actions and events
challenge the value and validity of community traditions.

CASE EXAMPLE:
DATE RAPE ON COLLEGE CAMPUSES

These aspects of communities and community change processes are evident in all community-based social change activities. Consider, for example, the process set in motion when a
group of college women—women who on campus are members
of diverse academic interests and social groups and who away
from campus are members of separate geographic and ethnic
communities—begin informally to discuss the impact that a rising incidence of date rape is having on their lives. Together,
these women may conclude that a range of protective services,
public education efforts, and rape crisis services are needed.
They may organize to achieve these ends and, as a new constitu-
ency of community members, they may seek

- changes in prevailing community attitudes, values, and priorities
  so that the concerns of women students and the problem of date
  rape are given new or more serious attention;
- institutional and community support in the search for resources
  with which to initiate on campus new educational programs, new
  safety measures, and new victim services; and/or
- a reallocation of existing college resources so that needed services
  and action plans can be implemented.

At this point, the campus community will have served as a
setting for change (or, more precisely, as a setting in which con-

cerns are shared, needs are identified, and social change goals are specified). Community members who find support for these new beliefs and priorities among other members will expect the larger community to adopt similar beliefs and priorities and to facilitate newfound purposes. And, indeed, many communities will do so.

Other communities will reject new ideas and resist change, however, and in the process will become *targets of change* activities. If, for example, the campus is one in which officials are reluctant to acknowledge the problem of date rape for fear that negative publicity will threaten enrollments or jeopardize alumni contributions, activists for change will have difficulty gathering support from at least some community leaders. Similarly, if the college is one in which sexist beliefs and values thrive and in which behaviors conforming to sex role stereotypes are valued as normative, then many in the community will be unready and unwilling to examine the problem of date rape more closely. They will be unwilling to recognize, for example, that date rape is rape, that date rape does meet the legal criteria for rape in all states and that responsibility for date rape lies with the offender and not with his victim. In these communities, *resistance to change* may be fierce. Advocates for community change will risk scorn, condemnation, and exclusion. Critical to their success will be their ability to manage the change process: to create a climate conducive to change and to introduce change possibilities in a manner that enhances rather than depletes community resources.

At some point, each woman involved in the process of bringing about change in the campus community will enter or reenter a separate geographic, ethnic, or occupational community. She may find that women in these communities also share a concern about rape and its rising incidence. As she brings her knowledge, energy, and skill into these environments and joins with new constituencies of women, these communities, too, may come to serve as *setting for change, targets of change,* and environments characterized by *resistance to change.* It is through this ecological process that the dynamic of community change finds influence upon society as a whole.

THE ADAPTIVE NATURE OF
COMMUNITY CHANGE

An ecological point of view defines change and resistance to change as indicative of the adaptive—and essentially conservative—nature of communities. Like natural environments, communities conserve resources. When change activities make positive use of community resources, they fulfill the positive potential of this adaptive quality and they enrich community identity, values, and traditions. Change activities that ignore community traditions, overwhelm community resources, and/ or strain the support capacities of community settings have maladaptive impact. They can drain change agents of their morale and stiffen community resistance.

In emphasizing the adaptive nature of communities, an ecological analogy defines lasting community change as a *proactive and successive* process. It is *proactive* in that it makes positive use of community resources—utilizing and thus affirming the competencies of particular community members, for example, or calling upon and thus validating the potential of particular community settings for positive contribution, and respecting the continued relevance of various community traditions. Proactive resource transactions provide for the strategic development of new resources—for the timely creation of new settings, the performance of new roles by community members, and the cultivation of new knowledge, beliefs, and values by the larger community.

Lasting community change also is *successive*. Rarely is sudden or dramatic change accomplished. Indeed, most attempts at sudden or radical change are resisted and misunderstood, viewed as potentially threatening, and seen as ill-planned or ill-timed. Lasting change is an incremental process by which the limited and discrete, but nonetheless real and adaptive, changes of today lay groundwork for ongoing community development and continued change.

Although the ecological analogy underlines the adaptive and conservative qualities of communities, it does not encourage change agents to limit their social vision or to abandon efforts

after substantial community change and far-reaching social reform. Instead, it alerts change agents to the nature of the process
they are entering upon—to the need for both short-term and
long-term planning, for example, and to the importance of con-
serving their own energy, morale, and purpose. Needed for success is deliberate and incremental social action planning, as well
as strategies for change that respond to the community's unique
character and history.

In his review of the social change literature, Glidewell (1976)
concluded that effective change agents and effective change
strategies are distinguished by their ability to (a) broaden and
enrich community knowledge, understandings, and beliefs; (b)
create for the community new linkages with the outside world
so that its prevailing beliefs are regularly challenged and re-
examined; and (c) help communities manage the tensions inherent in change. Tension management, in particular, requires
that change agents understand and attend to the delicate relationship between the community ecosystem and its environmental surround. Chapter 4 includes a discussion of exemplary
community-based rape crisis centers. These settings are distinguished by their effective initiation of community change and
by their ability to help local communities manage the tensions
inherent in change.

INITIATING CHANGE IN A COMMUNITY'S
RESPONSE TO RAPE

Citizens concerned about rape express their concerns in all
types of communities and employ in each a range of strategies
for accomplishing their aims. They may look to ethnic, occupational, or neighborhood communities to adopt new attitudes
and values, but they will invariably turn to the geographic community for more visible indices of change. Thus city, town, or
state becomes a focal point of social change activities seeking
improved services for victims, new offender treatment programs, or public policy reforms. In a geographic community,
the *objective* measures of prevailing beliefs and values are the

programs, policies, and actions to which it willingly commits its limited resources.

When a woman is raped, the geographic community that purports to include, serve, and support her is revealed anew. Its traditions, moral codes, and social values are subjected to new scrutiny. Community attitudes toward rape, rapist, and rape victim are measured not by the sympathetic and outraged pronouncements of public officials but by the services that are or are not available to victims, potential victims, and their families and friends. The quality, speed, and sensitivity of services provided by law enforcement, medical, mental health, and social service agencies measures the true regard, dignity, and safety that a community extends as a matter of course to members who become victims. The community's response to rape brings to light obvious shortcomings in public policy and clear gaps in available services. Typically, community change activities begin with a thorough assessment of local services.

ASSESSING LOCAL SERVICES

If concerned citizens are to effectively initiate change in local rape services, they must have a clear picture of community needs and a thorough knowledge of the kind and quality of services that already exist. In reviewing local services, five dimensions of assessment are important.

Availability. Whatever the issues of concern, one can turn to an array of agencies within the community and to a roster of services offered by them and ask, "Is a given victim service available or not available in this community?" Later in this chapter, we list and describe the desired components of a communitywide rape response system. The question of availability, when applied to this list, measures a community's overall response to rape and defines the resources that the community has thus far committed to the crime and trauma of rape. Together these services indicate a community's ability and willingness to respond to rape.

Accessibility. Having determined which, if any, rape services are available in the community, one can determine how accessible these services are to the citizens requiring them. If, for example, a community's roster of services for victims include a Rape Hotline that is operated 24 hours a day, seven days a week, this crisis service is *accessible* to a much greater number of prospective callers than one operated only during daytime or evening hours.

Similarly, if a community has several hospitals, each of which is experienced in the delivery of emergency medical services to rape victims, such services are likely to be accessible to a variety of victims: middle-class *and* poor, white *and* black, urban *and* suburban. All communities are plagued by service limitations. Important in examining the accessibility of rape services is a comparison of available services with incidence and prevalence data in various segments of the community. If services must be limited, their accessibility to groups at elevated risk must be maximized within these limits. If a majority of rape victims in a given city are minority women or women who work late hours, it is imperative that rape services within the community be particularly accessible to these groups. Cultural and linguistic considerations are important factors in examining service accessibility as well. If bilingual staff are not hired, then services will be less accessible to non-English-speaking women than they should be. In a multicultural or multiracial community, a service staff that reflects community demography will increase service accessibility. Proximity to public transportation, accommodations to address the needs of the physically handicapped—these qualities, too, contribute to or detract from service accessibility.

Quantity. Quantity is an important factor in conducting a community-needs assessment. The questions become, "Does this community have *sufficient* services to meet the needs of actual or potential victims?" and "Are there *enough* facilities and resources for arresting, incarcerating, and treating offenders?" The community with three hospitals offering rape victim services is better prepared to be helpful than the community with only one. A district attorney's office with one part-time advocate for sexual assault victims is more limited than the office that houses an entire sexual assault unit. Funding cuts and staff layoffs alter the quality of service available in the community and may portend serious shortages.

Quality. Among the most important dimensions against which to evaluate the rape services of a community is that of quality: "How *good* are the services that this community offers the rape victim?" No measure is more reflective of community attitudes and values than this one. If, for example, a city hospital provides emergency treatment for rape victims and is situated and staffed in a manner that makes its services accessible to persons at risk, these services still may be totally inadequate because of the way victims are treated upon entering the hospital. Similarly, police rape units may be quite responsive or notoriously insensitive to victims, particularly to victims who elect not to prosecute or whose cases seem, in the eyes of experienced police officials, too difficult to "make" in court. A thorough assessment of the *quality* of services available to rape victims requires that the evaluator(s) have a clear point of view about rape, its causes, and its consequences.

During the 1970s, the rape crisis center movement had a major impact on traditional thinking about rape in established medical, social service, and mental health agencies, which contributed to great improvements in the quality of services to victims (see Chapter 4).

Legitimacy. A final measure against which to evaluate a given community's response to rape lies in the degree to which rape services are viewed as necessary and legitimate by established service agencies, law-enforcement officials, policymakers, and general citizenry. Legitimacy is a quality not easily defined. When rape hot line numbers are publicized on city buses and in the corridors of private and public service agencies, legitimacy is apparent. When an established hospital requests staff training from a grass-roots, community-based rape crisis center, the legitimacy of the center, its services, and its philosophy is obvious. On the other hand, when such services are regarded with hostility and defensiveness by established agencies and local officials, when their availability is not recommended, the services may exist but their legitimacy is largely unrecognized. The legitimacy extended to rape services by established community representatives and institutions greatly influences a victim's hopes and expectations. These, in turn, help to determine the choices she makes with respect to reporting the crime, seeking adequate care, and understanding her experience. Because the legitimacy extended to rape services has a potentially profound impact on victims, it is a crucial dimension on which to evaluate local services.

Each of these five dimensions is important to a full assessment of local services. The next issue is determining to what set of services these measures should be applied.

COMPONENTS OF A COMMUNITYWIDE RESPONSE TO RAPE

Due primarily to the impact of rape victim advocacy and the rape crisis center movement (discussed in Chapter 4), new criteria exist for a satisfactory and communitywide response to rape. Listed in Table 3.1, and described in the paragraphs below, critical components of this response can be classified as victim services, offender treatment alternatives, and preventive and educative social change initiatives.

Victim Services

Crisis services. A community ready to respond to rape immediately, with the dual aims of care and empowerment, will offer the following:

- A 24-hour rape hot line, operated seven days per week and staffed by trained personnel (paid or volunteer) who are able to listen sensitively and respond with concrete information and appropriate referrals to additional avenues of care. In most communities,

the availability of bilingual hot line workers is critical to the overall accessibility and quality of hot line services.

- Crisis counseling provided not only on the hot line but in personal contact with trained staff. This contact may be made at the
  hospital or at another, less institutional setting but should probably not be at the site of the rape itself. Some volunteers have
  themselves been attacked by assailants who had not left the area!
  It is important that crisis workers reflect the demographic characteristics of the larger population and that settings offering crisis
  counseling familiarize themselves with the cultural values and
  beliefs that will influence the recovery process of women of varying ethnic and economic backgrounds.

- Hospital accompaniment—a crisis service of tremendous value to
  rape victims in hospital-based crisis counseling. Such services
  increase the probability that a rape victim will seek and utilize
  medical care. It ensures that victims are informed of standard
  hospital procedures, the rationale for such procedures, and the
  choices that victims may make for immediate and follow-up care.
  Increasingly, initial police interviews are conducted at the hospital. Accompaniment and hospital-based crisis counseling helps
  ensure that victims also are allowed to make fully informed
  choices about evidence collection, complaint filing, and
  prosecution.

Hospital care. Rape victims should be able to rely on local
hospitals and the medical personnel who staff them to provide
prompt and sensitive reception, escort to a private room within
the emergency ward or to an area reserved for sexual assault
victims, and full explanation of all medical examination and
evidence-collection procedures. These procedures should be undertaken only with the victim's consent. Nurses, physicians,
emergency room personnel, and other hospital staff should be
adequately trained to provide immediate and follow-up services to rape victims, and their training should be updated regularly so that they can answer changing victim concerns. In
recent years, for example, rape victims have expressed tremendous anxiety about the possibility of contracting AIDS from
their assailants and have questioned medical providers and rape
crisis personnel about the pros and cons of being tested for
AIDS.

Police services. A serious community response to rape requires that police departments operate specialized rape investigation units, staffed by trained officers—including female officers—who are able to take into account the victim's emotional *and* physical state during initial interviews. Appropriate police behavior toward victims will be nonjudgmental and informative and will respect the victim's right to choose whether or not to file a complaint and move toward prosecution. When a victim does opt to file a complaint and agrees to cooperate with law enforcement officials, police investigation should proceed in a manner that respects the victim's dignity and exercises proper concern for her privacy and safety.

The district attorney's office. Community services to rape victims are greatly enhanced by victim-witness advocacy bureaus that offer information, solace, and support to victims before, during, and after their involvement with the court and by special sexual assault investigation units that can ensure serious prosecution of the crime and provide the victim with complete knowledge and understanding of various lines of inquiry, testimony, and cross-examination, and of current law regarding admissible and inadmissible evidence. Either alone or in tandem with a local rape crisis center, the Sexual Assault Unit of the district attorney's office should ensure that victims who choose to prosecute have access to "court-watch," court accompaniment, and victim-witness advocacy services.

Mental health and social services. In the aftermath of rape, many victims will require only short-term service to facilitate their recovery from crisis-induced posttraumatic stress and to aid their families in adjusting to rape. Others will, for a variety of reasons, profit from long-term therapy with a therapist who is knowledgeable about rape and free of the mythology surrounding rape and responsibility for rape that can thrive in traditional mental health settings. Women who have been the victims of particularly savage violence, victims who have waited many years to talk about their rape, and children or adults who have suffered repeated incidents of childhood sexual assault or incest are among the individuals for whom relatively short-term crisis work will no doubt prove insufficient. Both long-term and short-term care should be available in the community, as well as an array of social services (e.g., clothing bank, housing assistance, help in planning new avenues of transportation to and from work at night). These services can aid recovery and help sexual assault victims reestablish a preferred way of living in the community. Chapter 2 considers in detail theory and research guiding a clinical response to rape. Chapter 5 reviews and examines the efficacy of a number of individual approaches to clinical work with rape victims, and Chapter 6 focuses on various models of group treatment.

Specialized victim services. Some rape victims have special service needs. In any community, therefore, some degree of specialized service is essential. Services to children, elderly citizens, minority victims, male victims, gay victims, and victims of severe and sadistic violence are among the special populations that individual communities should take into account when developing an overall pattern of rape victim services. Service providers need to anticipate that the experience of sexual trauma and the probability of prior rape experiences will be particularly high among women within refugee populations that have immigrated to the United States in flight from political violence and torture (Mollica & Son, 1989)—in Indochinese, Haitian, and/or Latin American refugee populations, for example. Service providers need to keep themselves apprised of the shifting demographies of their communities and become aware of other victim groups and special service needs that these shifts may entail.

Offender Treatment

A community's response to rape also is evident in the seriousness with which its law-enforcement agencies pursue arrest and prosecution, in the sentences that local judges render, and in the availability of offender treatment alternatives.

Arrest and prosecution. When a charge of rape is made against an adult or juvenile offender, local law enforcement officials must proceed with investigation, arrest, and case preparation in a thorough and fully informed manner. Historically, there has been great attrition of rape cases moving through the criminal justice system. Galvin and Polk (1983), for example, reviewed the disposition of rape cases in California during the mid-1970s and found that only 730 of an initial 22,400 instances of rape were taken by police and prosecutors through the justice system to a guilty verdict. Of these convictions, only 166 had been obtained without plea bargaining. These authors see this attrition as comparable to that of most felonies. Other authors, however, cite similar findings and view them as indicative of police and prosecutor indifference to the crime of rape (Feidman-Summers & Lindner, 1976; Robin, 1977).

Research indicates that legal reform can serve as a basis for improved law-enforcement practice and lowered attrition of rape cases. Marsh et al. (1980), for example, examined the impact of Michigan's 1975 reform Sexual Conduct law on report, arrest, and conviction rates in six counties. Although increases in reporting could not be attributed to the new law, increased arrest and conviction rates seemed the direct result of mandated changes in police and prosecutor practice. Interviews with police, prosecutors, and defense attorneys did not warrant the conclusion that these changes resulted from improved attitudes toward the victim. Instead, the lowered attrition and improved conviction rates were associated with: (a) the new law's clearer definition of criminal sexual conduct (and degrees thereof); (b) its rendering the victim's sexual history off limits; (c) its elimination of the requirement that prosecuting attorneys prove early and continued victim resistance; and, most importantly, (d) its reduction of discretionary behavior among police, prosecutors, and other law-enforcement officials. These findings suggest that a community's response to rape can be significantly improved through legal reform activities.

The courts. Local courts have been the target of considerable concern among rape victim advocates. "Court-watch" or court accompaniment services are critical to an adequate community response to rape. Often initiated by local rape crisis centers, these programs ensure social and emotional support to victims going through the rocky experience of a courtroom trial and the ordeal of facing the accused in court.

Once rape cases arrive in court, the attitudes with which local judges hear the evidence and the nature of their instructions to juries can have tremendous influence on the victim's experience and on the verdicts rendered. Historically, judges' instructions have made conviction difficult. In communities and courtrooms across the country, judges have routinely given "Hale's Dictum" to juries deciding the guilt or innocence of men accused of rape. A 17th-century British jurist, Hale had warned that rape was easily charged but difficult to defend or prove. His warning clearly encouraged a verdict favorable to the defense.

In reviewing a community's response to rape, it is essential to examine state law and local practice involving rape trials. Rules of evidence and permissible lines of inquiry as well as attitudes and practices of local judges are critical elements of the court-room component. Optimism generally is warranted by research on the impact of legal reform efforts (Largen, 1988; Marsh et al., 1980). These studies document improvements in the attrition rates of rape cases and in police and prosecutor behavior, and find that judges generally concur in the opinion that positive legal reform has not been achieved at the expense of defendant rights.

Alternative treatments. With offender convictions, judges must make sentencing determinations, selecting from a variety of incarceration and treatment alternatives. Influencing their decisions will be a number of factors: the adult or juvenile status of the defendant; his criminal record (particularly his history of violence and sexual assault); the relationship of defendant to victim; and any number of attributes of the rape itself. Such choices will be mightily influenced as well by the kinds of treatment alternatives available at the level of the local community and the degree of seriousness that judges, jurors, and community members assign to the crime of rape.

Treatment possibilities include maximum security prisons (with or without special programs for men convicted of sexual assault); specialized units for first offenders (where incarceration typically is combined with some form of mandated clinical treatment); local facilities for juvenile offenders (many of whom may themselves be victims of physical or sexual abuse); and community-based treatment programs in which incestuous fathers, pedophiles, and juvenile offenders voluntarily (or under court mandate) acknowledge and attempt to overcome the causes and consequences of their behavior. Some communities are beginning to experiment with victim-offender confrontation programs. Others are considering the pros and cons of medical intervention with Depo-Provera. This experimental drug is said by its enthusiasts to reduce the sexual drive and capability of prospective rapists. It is viewed by its critics as a questionable approach to treating offenders who may simply choose to victimize women in other than sexual ways (Ledray, 1986). Whatever treatment alternatives are available in the community, each should function as a research-demonstration effort, its efficacy measured not by an offender's expression of changed values but by reduced recidivism among program participants.

SOCIAL ACTION, COMMUNITY EDUCATION, AND PREVENTION

No aspect of a community's response to rape is as important as its capacity for social change and its resources for community education and rape prevention. Chapter 4 discusses in detail the social change and community education initiatives of local rape crisis centers. Chapter 7 examines prevention constructs and provides examples of exemplary preventive intervention programs. The following is a brief portrait of these essential activities.

Social action. Changes wrought in state law and in the practices of traditional law-enforcement, health, and mental health facilities have been achieved through the organized and concerted efforts of feminist activities. These efforts are crucial to ongoing improvement of a community's understanding of and reaction to rape. In the early 1970s, social change activities concentrated on improving victim services and securing legal reform. As these efforts met with success and as traditional practice began to embrace new standards, rape victim advocates turned their attention to the special needs of child, elderly, and minority victims and to the aims of social and cultural transformation. Today, victim advocates are concerned with increasing services for minority women victimized by sexual assault, proposing reforms in laws concerning marital rape, developing strategies to address a seeming epidemic of date rape on college campuses, and developing services and public policy initiatives to address the new phenomenon of "AIDS anxiety" among rape victims.

Community education. Community education programs educate citizens about rape. They demystify the crime, challenge rape-supportive belief systems, and promote safety through enhanced rape awareness and self-defense skill. Conducted in local churches, temples, schools, and workplace settings by rape crisis centers or citizen action groups, these programs build support for local reform efforts and inform citizens of available and needed services. Community education activities provide training to police, attorneys, hospital personnel, mental health care providers, and rape crisis volunteers. A community's capacity to respond to rape with a full array of needed services probably depends heavily on the adequacy and effectiveness of its community education programs. Virtually all community-based rape crisis centers sponsor community education programs (Burt, Gornick, & Pittman, 1984; Harvey, 1985).

Prevention. Prevention activities vary widely. They are generally classified into one of two categories. First, there are a large number of rape *avoidance* programs that seek to educate prospective victims about rape, the risks of rape, and strategies for avoiding, resisting, or lessening the brutality of rape. These programs often include self-defense and risk-awareness courses.

They may involve the development of car pools, escort services, or social gatherings designed to increase the latitude and safety of potential victims.

A second category of programs emphasizes *prevention* through knowledge development and attitude change. Such programs confront beliefs and values that support rape by condoning discriminatory treatment of and violence toward women. They challenge gender-specific role stereotypes and reach out to young audiences, in particular, by promoting new concepts of sex role and sexual responsibility. In any community, both avoidance and prevention programs should be made available to a variety of audiences, settings, and age groups.

A COMMUNITY NEEDS ASSESSMENT TOOL

Table 3.1 presents a chart that summarizes this discussion and may serve as a tool for assessing the quality and comprehensiveness of local services. Concrete goals for change activities in specific communities can emerge from this assessment.

CONCLUSION

Rape is a phenomenon that can promote both change and resistance to change in diverse communities. Although communities can be differentiated by a variety of typologies, all perform essential functions for community members and each can have tremendous impact upon the physical and emotional prognosis of rape victims. Because the victim is always a member of diverse communities, she will experience a wide range of reactions: compassion and hostility, advocacy and abandonment, service and skepticism. Every community can be seen as an "ecosystem" in which the community's reaction to rape is influenced by the nature and stability of its varied resources. Change agents are well advised to initiate reform activities with regard for the adaptive qualities of communities and for the proactive and successive nature of lasting change. A starting

Table 3.1 Assessing a Community's Response to Rape

Service Component	Avail- ability	Accessi- bility	Criteria Quantity	Quality	Legiti- macy
Victim Services					
Crisis					
1. Hot line	___	___	___	___	___
2. Counseling	___	___	___	___	___
3. Hospital accompaniment	___	___	___	___	___
Hospital care					
1. Emergency	___	___	___	___	___
2. Follow-up	___	___	___	___	___
Police services					
1. Rape unit	___	___	___	___	___
2. Investigatory procedures	___	___	___	___	___
District attorney's office/ court procedures					
1. Rape unit	___	___	___	___	___
2. Victim advocacy	___	___	___	___	___
3. Court accompaniment	___	___	___	___	___
Mental health/social service					
1. Short-term	___	___	___	___	___
2. Long-term	___	___	___	___	___
3. Special services	___	___	___	___	___
Offenders					
Police and district attorney					
1. Investigation	___	___	___	___	___
2. Arrest	___	___	___	___	___
3. Prosecution	___	___	___	___	___
Court systems					
1. Trial practice	___	___	___	___	___
2. Sentencing by judges	___	___	___	___	___
Alternative treatment					
1. Juvenile	___	___	___	___	___
2. Adult	___	___	___	___	___
Community Intervention					
Social action					
1. Victim advocacy	___	___	___	___	___
2. Law and policy reform	___	___	___	___	___
Community education					
1. Avoidance	___	___	___	___	___
2. Prevention	___	___	___	___	___

NOTE: For Availability: Y = Yes; N = No.
For other measures, use 1-5 rating scale (1 = Excellent; 5 = Poor) for individual services and categories of service.

point for change activities lies in the assessment of local services and the identification of unmet needs. In community after community, the development of a comprehensive community response to rape has relied on the efforts of local rape crisis centers.

NOTE

1. The victim died in a car accident in Florida two years later. According to reports by friends and family, she never recovered from her experience.

FOUR

The Rape Crisis Center

Until 1970, there existed in the United States no service agency or advocacy group giving needed attention to the phenomenon of rape and the adequacy of a community's response to rape. Except in relatively extreme cases of aggravated rape (i.e., a forced sexual assault involving extreme violence or threat of violence, a weapon, and/or multiple assailants), police and prosecuting attorneys were skeptical and disinterested. They viewed the charge of rape with great suspicion and dealt with victims of so-called "simple rape" (e.g., date or acquaintance rape, rape by a single unarmed offender) reluctantly, even begrudgingly (Estrich, 1987). The rape victim who could identify her assailant(s) and did wish to prosecute typically found herself subject to harsh interrogation by law-enforcement officers less concerned with her well-being than with their own chances of "making a case" and getting a conviction. The victim who chose not to prosecute fared no better. Noncooperation with the criminal justice process could call into question her status as unwilling victim and cast doubts about her right to needed care. In either case, her recovery from sexual assault would depend, first, on her own capacity to weather crisis and, only secondarily, upon the adequacy of local hospital procedures and the more or less informed advice of private physicians.

In many communities around the United States, this picture has changed dramatically. Today, for example:

- Rape victims in Philadelphia, Pennsylvania are escorted to a small but private suite of rooms in Philadelphia General's emergency ward. Here, clean clothes, hot coffee, crisis counseling, and victim advocacy are provided day and night by advocates from Women Organized Against Rape (WOAR). The service represents a degree of collaboration between hospital and grass-roots rape crisis center that was unheard of in 1970 and remains rare even today (Harvey, 1982a, 1982b).

- In Albuquerque, New Mexico, Hispanic victims are seen by bilingual advocates of the Albuquerque Rape Crisis Center where special services also exist for child victims, victims of extreme violence, and victims experiencing severe or prolonged distress (Harvey, 1982a, 1982b).

- In Cambridge, Massachusetts, volunteer advocates and staff of the Boston Area Rape Crisis Center work closely with clinicians from Cambridge Hospital's Victims of Violence Program to ensure a full range of mental health services to area victims. The two settings have cosponsored multidisciplinary training, minority outreach, and public policy reform programs (Hospital & Community Psychiatry, 1988).

In these and hundreds of other communities throughout the United States the 24-hour hot lines and trained advocates of grass-roots rape crisis centers provide rape victims in crisis with information, advocacy, and ongoing support (Harvey, 1985; National Center for the Prevention and Control of Rape [NCPCR], 1981).

During the 1970s, grass-roots rape crisis centers were established in communities throughout the United States, Canada, Europe, and Australia. By 1980, they had become influential settings for community action, legal advocacy, and service reform. Individually, rape crisis centers have enhanced rape awareness among local citizens and transformed the standard practices of local medical, mental health, and law-enforcement agencies. Collectively, they have advocated successfully for far-reaching social reform—challenging prevailing social values, confronting time-honored views of rape, initiating and securing needed public policy reforms. The emergence and proliferation of local rape crisis centers and their profound impact on virtually all aspects of the larger society's response to rape constitute major accomplishments of a unique social movement (Amir & Amir, 1975; Pittman, Burt, & Gornick, 1984).

In this chapter we consider the origins, scope, and impact of the rape crisis center movement. Attention is given to its feminist origins and to the unifying effect of feminist values on the aims, services, and organizational structure of the early and "prototypical" rape crisis center. Also considered are the social, political, and "ecological" forces that have created debate and fostered diversity among community-based centers. The chapter highlights, through case examples, the impact of the rape crisis center movement on the medical, legal, and mental health practices of traditional public service agencies. Rape crisis center research is reviewed, and the shared attributes of highly effective, exemplary rape crisis centers are discussed (Harvey, 1985).

THE RAPE CRISIS CENTER MOVEMENT

The first rape crisis centers were established in 1970 in six, possibly seven, cities across the United States. Originating independently, they nonetheless bore great resemblance to one another. All were initiated by feminist groups already active in their home communities, for example, and all shared an ardently feminist view of rape.

These early centers were followed rapidly by others and by antirape citizen action groups in increasingly diverse communities. In 1973, the National Organization for Women (NOW) turned its attention to the problem of sexual violence against women and began assisting local community groups with the initiation of antirape citizen task forces. By 1974, 61 community-based rape crisis centers had been established in 27 states, and NOW had helped to initiate 136 local antirape projects (either center or task force) in a total of 39 states (Brodyaga, Gates, Singer, Tucker, & White, 1975).

The rape crisis center movement continued its rapid growth throughout the 1970s. Local centers increased in number. State- and regionwide communication among them fostered multicenter action for social change. And national organizations were established. In 1976, federal legislation (Public Law #94-63) created the National Center for the Prevention and Control of Rape (NCPCR) to sponsor research, demonstration, and training programs that would shed light on the causes of sexual assault, its mental health impact on victims, and the efficacy of varied treatment and prevention strategies. NCPCR was located in the National Institute of Mental Health (NIMH) "in recognition that rape and sexual assault are serious crimes resulting in severe emotional trauma and other mental health consequences for victims, their families, and their communities" (NCPCR, 1982, p. 2).

Until 1982, NCPCR was a separate center within the NIMH. It had its own national advisory board and its own grant application review committee. Its research activities reflected the interests of feminist scholars and its training initiatives were closely linked with the concerns of grass-roots rape crisis workers.

In 1982, as the Reagan years were beginning and federal budget cutters were launching the "David Stockman juggernaut,"[1] NCPCR was reorganized as a unit of the newly formed Center for the Study of Mental Health Emergencies. Between 1982 and 1987, it lost its separate review committee and its national advisory board and was reorganized again and again. Today, NCPCR does not exist. NIMH-sponsored research on sexual assault was relocated to the Center for the Study of Anti-Social Violent Behavior, which did not fund treatment programs for rape victims and did not enjoy close working relationships with community-based rape crisis centers. In 1990 another NIMH reorganization resulted in the creation of the Center for Anti-Social Violence and Traumatic Stress Studies. Feminist researchers are hopeful that this reorganization will result in greater attention to the needs of rape victims and in renewed sponsorship of treatment research and demonstration efforts.

NCPCR exemplifies the movement's efforts to accomplish change through traditional political processes—and the vulnerability of these efforts to those same processes. Nontraditional, grass-roots political activism has realized the formation of more enduring and in many ways more influential organizations and coalitions. In 1979, for example, volunteers from more than 40 centers in 25 states met in Geneva, Wisconsin, to form the National Coalition Against Sexual Assault (NCASA). A nationwide network of antirape programs, NCASA's aims are to enhance communication and coordinate rape awareness and victim advocacy efforts among member programs. NCASA's membership is organized into six regional coalitions, each of which sponsors an annual or biannual meeting and a regionwide social action agenda. Membership fees and volunteer energy provide for NCASA's Annual Conference, its distribution of national and regional newsletters, and its nationwide legislative alert and lobbying efforts (NCASA, 1982). Eleven years after its formation, NCASA is the organization most responsible for transforming the grass-roots energy of rape crisis volunteers into the formal political accomplishments of new legislation, needed public policy, and substantive legal reform.

By 1979, an NCPCR survey (1981) indicated that community-based rape crisis centers could be found in at least one community of every state in the United States, in Puerto Rico, in the District of Columbia, and in every province of Canada. By 1983, a majority of these programs were NCASA members.

The number of rape crisis centers that exist today is difficult to ascertain. Many of those identified by NCPCR in 1979 had closed their doors by 1989, unable to sustain themselves through a prolonged period of fiscal conservatism and fierce competition for shrinking public resources. Others have drastically reduced their services. Despite these losses, the movement continues to reach out to new communities and to inspire new citizen action groups. Its continuing impact is best measured by the fact that when local citizens seek to refashion their community's response to rape, they invariably begin by establishing a local rape crisis center.

FEMINIST ORIGINS OF THE RAPE CRISIS CENTER MOVEMENT

The rape crisis center movement was born of and nourished by feminist theory, ideology, and debate (Brodyaga et al., 1975). Feminist thought was critical in at least four respects. First, feminist authors identified sexual violence against women as the embodiment of patriarchy, and sexual assault as a threat to all women. In doing so, they provided a societal analysis of rape that galvanized the energies and imaginations of women seeking concrete avenues to social change. Prominent among feminist strategies for change were collective action and legal reform.

Second, feminists articulated the physical and emotional trauma of rape and the extent to which that trauma was ignored and exacerbated by medical, mental health, and criminal justice institutions. A feminist analysis of rape called for new services on behalf of victims, drastic reformation of existing services, and an application of the movement's social action strategies to the clinical aim of ameliorating rape trauma. In the formative years of the rape crisis center movement, feminist activists viewed victim service and social change as equally necessary and generally compatible responses to rape.

A third contribution of feminists thinkers was their sharp critique of the hierarchical structure and authoritarian decision-making practices of traditional (i.e., patriarchal) public service agencies. This critique fostered the search for less hierarchical, more humane and egalitarian organizational forms. The goal was to create feminist institutions in which women could work collectively to help one another, sharing power even as they secured it. The goal was realized most clearly in the example of the collectively organized, feminist rape crisis center.

Finally, feminist activists encouraged already established feminist organizations to address the problem of sexual violence against women and to help in the development of uniquely feminist settings. This encouragement led NOW to follow its own national-level antirape task force with widespread sponsorship of community-based antirape citizen action groups. Many rape crisis centers trace their beginnings to these groups.

The rape crisis center movement also has been shaped and directed by ideological influences other than feminism (Amir & Amir, 1975). Other formative influences include, for example, the civil rights movement with its emphasis upon oppression and the need for political struggle against oppression, the student movement of the 1960s with its antibureaucratic stance and its initiation of street corner services for runaway youth, and a community mental health movement that affirmed the validity of alternative service workers and alternative service settings. These influences—combined with two decades of pragmatic decision making in idiosyncratic communities—have fostered intense ideological debate among local centers and witnessed in some a dilution of feminist fervor. Today, the field is characterized by tremendous diversity (Burt et al., 1984; Harvey, 1985). Nevertheless, the formative and continuing contribution of feminist thought and action to the course and accomplishments of the rape crisis center movement cannot be overstated.

A FEMINIST ANALYSIS OF RAPE

A feminist analysis of rape begins with the assertion that ours is a patriarchal society, comfortable with and reliant upon men's maintenance of political, economic, and physical control of women (Brownmiller, 1975; Griffin, 1971). Discrimination against and hostility toward women are not atypical realities. Instead, antipathy toward women and the neglect of women's rights are social norms. Violence against women and the sexual subjugation of women inside and outside their homes are not unusual events. In such a society, rape must be viewed not as a socially deviant expression of male power, nor as the insane act of deranged individuals, but rather as a terribly predictable consequence of prevailing social values.

In a patriarchal society, the feminist analysis continues, women are socialized to be passive, good-willed, and compliant, and to assume the status of property. Men, on the other hand, are socialized to be aggressors, predators, and "owners." Feminist authors note, for example, that early rape laws did not view sexual assault as a crime against the woman raped but rather as a property crime against her father, husband, or—if she were a slave—her master. In support of this analysis, Chappell and colleagues (National Legal Data Center, 1975) report that rape was first defined a crime in the 10th century by the English court of King Alfred. Never mentioning the woman raped, the law applied only to the rape of slaves and required that slave owners be compensated for damage done to their property. Free men who raped were obligated to pay fines to both owner and king; slaves who raped slaves were sentenced to castration.

Although contemporary American law differs substantially from this beginning, many feminists maintain that the "spirit" of the law has changed very little and that women continue to be treated as property, not as persons. Feminist researchers note, for example, that the crime of marital rape did not exist in the United States until well into the 1970s. In 1990, 26 states still treat as noncriminal at least some forms of wife rape and 8 states have not criminalized wife rape at all (Russell, 1990).

A feminist analysis also asserts that within a patriarchal society, it is women—not their assailants—who are held responsible for rape. Unless a woman can prove initial refusal and ongoing resistance, she may well be seen as culpable. The legal definitions of rape that prevailed until the advent of the antirape movement and the dehumanizing yet routine trial procedures to which rape victims were subject substantiate this point of view. As recently as 1975, rape legislation in the United States generally encouraged jurors to reject the victim's and accept the defendant's version of events surrounding an alleged rape. At that time, prevailing law (a) allowed the victim's sexual activity with men other than the defendant to be presented as evidence for the defense; (b) required that the occurrence of rape, resistance on the part of the victim, and/or the identity of the accused be established not by belief in the victim's testimony but by independent, corroborating evidence (e.g., the testimony of an eyewitness observer!); and (c) provided for judges to instruct juries of the difficulties faced by defendants seeking to disprove a charge of rape (National Legal Data Center, 1975). State by state, and case by case, feminist activists have secured legal reforms and instituted statutory protections for victims. The situation facing victims who choose to prosecute is decidedly better today than it once was—at least in instances of aggravated rape. It is also true, however, that the practices of police and prosecuting attorneys—who represent, after all, the law as victims and defendants experience the law—and the decisions made by appellate courts (which have the right to reverse trial findings) make successful prosecution of "simple rape" extremely difficult even today (Estrich, 1987). The victim who knows and may have dated her assailant, the victim who was too frightened to struggle or say, "No," the victim of a single unarmed rapist will have, at best, a very rough day in court and possibly no day at all.

A feminist analysis also emphasizes that both the fact of rape and the fear of rape function to reinforce male power and help to ensure the social control of women (LeGrand, 1977; Riger & Gordon, 1981). Lest they be raped, women are encouraged to lead restricted life-styles, limit their ventures into the outside world, seek male protection, and suppress inclinations toward autonomy and independence. Because patriarchal interpretations of rape encourage this restriction, a feminist response must do just the opposite: encourage choice, affirm independence, and aid women's cultivation of personal and social power.

A feminist analysis of rape concludes that social institutions (e.g., hospitals, police precincts, district attorneys' offices, and courts) have dismissed the seriousness of a rape victim's experience and have denied her the right to interpret that experience herself and to chart her own course of recovery. Social institutions have thus exacerbated the trauma of rape.

Feminists continue to examine the phenomenon of rape and the social context in which rape seems to flourish. Today a variety of feminist perspectives exist, each of which exerts its influence on the actions of antirape programs throughout the country. Still, the shared premises of a feminist analysis continue to give definition and direction to the social change strategies, victim service initiatives, and organizational forms of community-based rape crisis centers nationwide.

SOCIAL CHANGE INITIATIVES

Feminist rape crisis centers have pursued three avenues of social change: rape prevention, service reform, and legal advocacy.

Rape prevention. Eliminating rape is the overriding aim of the rape crisis center movement. Local centers have generally adopted one or both of two clearly feminist approaches. The first of these involves community education to challenge prevailing values, confront rape-supportive myths, and develop new understanding of rape and rape victims. The theory is that rape will decline only as the larger society disavows patriarchal values and rejects the validity of forced sexual assault. The aim, then, is to prevent rape by changing the knowledge base and belief system of society as a whole. Community education strategies that embody these themes are aimed at local citizens and at those social institutions (e.g., schools, courts, churches) that express and influence prevailing attitudes, values, and beliefs.

A second feminist approach to rape prevention addresses prospective victims directly and teaches rape avoidance through risk awareness and self-defense preparedness. Not all rape-avoidance programs are feminist in nature. Indeed, some have been condemned by feminists for perpetuating unrealistic fears and discouraging women's embrace of independence and autonomy (Bart & O'Brien, 1985). Rape-avoidance activities that offer accurate information, foster self-assertion, and help to develop women's mastery of psychological and physical self-defense skills are more directly attributable to feminist themes.

Feminist (and other) rape prevention strategies are discussed in greater detail in Chapter 7.

Service reform. Throughout the 1970s and 1980s, feminist activists advocated successfully for fundamental change in the long-standing practices of medical, mental health, and law-enforcement agencies. Change seems to have been most arduously accomplished in the medical field. Despite the fact that hospitals throughout the country have significantly revised their emergency room rape protocols, too many hospitals in too many communities continue to tend to the medical needs of rape victims in a perfunctory and insensitive manner, in settings that offer no privacy and in circumstances that offer no dignity. Twenty years after the birth of the rape crisis center movement, medical procedures are still implemented rapidly, without explanation, and without respect for the victim's right to make knowledgeable choices concerning her own treatment. Bart (1979) attributes the tenacity of insensitive medical practice to an internalization of patriarchal values by male and female physicians alike, and particularly by obstetrics-gynecology physicians of either gender. It is also true that the structure of the medical profession is fundamentally hierarchical—with patients first and then personnel at all levels deferring successively to one another and, finally, to the physician. A field so organized is at best an unlikely context for egalitarian and empowering reform.

Despite these barriers, many rape crisis centers have brought about change in the reception and treatment of rape victims by medical facilities and personnel. The facilities provided to Women Organized Against Rape by Philadelphia General Hospital, for example, and the continuing trend toward hospital accompaniment programs are indices of genuine change. Exceptions also are found in the innovative hospital-based rape crisis services of Harvard-affiliated Beth Israel Hospital in Boston and in the physician-directed Rape Treatment Center of Miami General Hospital. The Beth Israel program provides emergency room and follow-up crisis response services to rape victims throughout the greater Boston area and extends emergency room training and supervision to all medical interns and residents. Now in its 15th year of existence, the program has trained hundreds of physicians. In Florida, the Miami Rape Treatment Center, located at Miami General Hospital and affiliated with the University of Miami Medical School, has mobilized statewide training of medical, mental health, social service, and law-enforcement personnel. The center has dramatically changed the medical care of rape victims in the local community and is a heartening sign of change accomplished from within the medical profession (Harvey, 1985).

Mental health services have also been a focal point of feminist reform. Feminists have generally rejected (a) the validity of psychiatric inquiry into victim culpability; (b) the supposition that a victim's emotional response to rape is psychopathological; and (c) any assumption that an assailant's behavior can be accounted for by the psychological attributes of his victim(s) or the diagnostic classifications of traditional psychiatry (Bart, 1979). Though critical of traditional psychiatry, this position has met with positive response among researchers interested in psychological trauma and clinicians who see the "rape trauma syndrome" as an understandable response to extreme crisis (Burgess & Holmstrom, 1974a; Kilpatrick, Veronen, & Best, 1984; Russell, 1984). The concerns of feminist rape crisis centers also have met with positive response among community psychologists and community mental health practitioners, who have consistently emphasized the validity of alternative community-based services, the relevance of self-help and social support initiatives, the importance of citizen involvement in the design of alternative services, and the competence of nontraditional service providers (Alley, Blanton, Feldman, Hunter, & Rolfson, 1979; Bloom, 1984; Gartner & Riessman, 1977; Harvey & Passy, 1978; Heller & Monahan, 1977). Many of the activities of grassroots rape crisis centers can be viewed as actualizations of community mental health premises on behalf of women (Gonzales, Hays, Bond, & Kelly, 1983).

Cambridge Hospital's Victims of Violence Program illustrates the contribution of feminist activism and the rape crisis center movement to the development of community-oriented mental health services for victims. Located in a hospital-based, Harvard-affiliated department of psychiatry that is known particularly for its pioneering development of community-based mental health services, the Victims of Violence Program is an explicitly feminist trauma clinic providing comprehensive psychiatric services to victims of recent and prior physical and sexual violence. The program is collaboratively administered by a senior staff (psychologist, psychiatrist, and social worker) whose multidisciplinary training and professional credentials are augmented by close and continuing ties to the women's movement and to grass-roots feminist settings. These ties are reflected in the program's clinical training activities and comprehensive array of victim services, in its coordination of program services with those of the Boston Area Rape Crisis Center and other grass-roots community agencies and groups, in its political understanding of victimization, and in its commitment to demystifying and depathologizing the psychological sequelae of traumatic events such as rape and incest. Established in 1984, the program was awarded the American Psychiatric Association's Gold Award for innovative hospital and community service in 1988. It is the first time in that organization's history that a victim service program has received such recognition (Hospital & Community Psychiatry, 1988).

Legal advocacy and criminal justice reform. Police practices have been the targets of social change activities since the outset of the rape crisis center movement (Feldman-Summers & Lindner, 1976; Holmstrom & Burgess, 1975; Robin, 1977). In 1975, the Center for Women's Policy Studies together with the Law Enforcement Assistance Administration of the United States Department of Justice published a "prescriptive package" to guide the organization of rape investigation units in local law-enforcement agencies. Recommendations urged police and other law-enforcement officials to put aside their antipathy toward feminist rape crisis centers and to recognize them as allies in the criminal justice process (Brodyaga et al., 1975). These reform efforts yielded rapid and significant success. Bart (1979), for example, reports that by 1975, her interviews with rape victims contained remarkably few police "horror stories."

The rape crisis center movement also has sought to bring about change in the policies and practices of local district attorneys' offices and in the courtroom experience of rape victims who pursue prosecution. Historically, legal definitions have treated rape not as a violent crime but as an illicit sexual act, criminal only if the victim was underaged (as in statutory rape) or could prove early and ongoing resistance (Largen, 1988). In court, jurors were instructed to be on guard against false accusations and the standards of proof imposed on charges of rape encouraged a callous disregard of rape victims by police and prosecuting attorneys (Estrich, 1987; Feldman-Summers & Lindner, 1976; Largen, 1988; Robin, 1977).

State by state feminist legal reforms such as those initiated in Michigan, California, and Massachusetts have sought with some success to (a) secure legal definitions that focus on the assaultive nature of rape and on the use of force by an offender; (b) eliminate a burdensome and victim-blaming standard of proof (i.e., of nonconsent and ongoing resistance); (c) change the treatment of rape victims by law-enforcement officials; and (d) improve the arrest, prosecution, and conviction statistics of reported rape cases.

The most far-reaching revisions in rape law were realized in the State of Michigan's 1974 Criminal Sexual Conduct Law, which defines as criminal various kinds of sexual conduct under circumstances that presume criminal intent and nonconsent. Lack of consent is assumed in this definition, and the victim need not provide corroborating evidence of resistance in order to prosecute a charge of rape (Largen, 1988). Researchers generally agree that these reforms have witnessed genuine benefit for victims and needed change in the conduct of police and prosecuting attorneys. They attribute these gains to two features of the 1974 law: (a) it offered a clearer definition of sexual assault (and degrees thereof) than had previously existed, and (b) it greatly reduced the discretionary powers of police and prosecuting attorneys. *How* to proceed was made clear; that one *must* proceed was made even clearer (Largen, 1988; Marsh et al., 1980).

Feminist legal reform efforts have realized in many states a more humane response to victims by jurors, judges, and law-enforcement officials and have enabled convictions where convictions might not have been possible before. Consider, for example, the outcomes of two aggravated rape trials in the Commonwealth of Massachusetts, 1984:

In the first, the victim was a young army private who had willingly joined members of the Grand Slamm rock group on a bus she thought was headed to a party. Hours later, she was dumped from the bus and left in a roadside ditch, the victim of repeated sexual assaults. Some years ago, her case would not have found its way to court: the victim's behavior would be seen as naive and blameworthy, and the case would have been judged too hard to prove. By 1984, however, legal reform efforts in Massachusetts had established that neither unwise nor naive behavior is an invitation to rape. In March of that year, a Massachusetts jury found three members of the Grand Slamm rock group guilty of aggravated rape. On March 20, 1984, Judge Barton of Middlesex Superior Court in Cambridge, Massachusetts, interpreted the jury's verdict:

> No longer will society accept the fact that a woman, even if she may initially act in a seductive or compromising manner, has waived her right to say "No" at any further time. "No" means "nothing further" and whatever past excuses may have been accepted on sexual arousal in males that could not be terminated are no longer tolerated by this society and by jurors who are a cross section of this Commonwealth. Women are equal partners with men. They are not sexual objects. (*Commonwealth v. Crowe*, 1984)

The second trial was completed only five days later, one year after the gang rape at Big Dan's Tavern in New Bedford, Massachusetts. Here, too, a jury found four men guilty of aggravated rape. Judge William Young rejected defense arguments that compromising behavior on the part of the victim merited light sentencing of her assailants. He sentenced three of the four convicted men to terms of 9 to 12 years in a maximum security prison, the fourth to 6 to 8 years. Citing Judge Barton's earlier ruling, Judge Young added:

> To suggest that any course of conduct, however flirtatious or seductive, may reduce the sentence imposed for a subsequent act of aggravated rape is to impair the degrees of freedom we ought to guard zealously for all our people. These individuals stand convicted of most serious crimes— crimes of extreme violence that brutalized a defenseless young woman and sought to degrade her human, individual dignity. To lessen the sentence for aggravated, ongoing rape would virtually outlaw an entire gender for the style of their dress, the length of their skirts, or their choice to enter a place of public refreshment. (*Commonwealth v. Vierra*, 1984)

These judicial findings are eloquent examples of the impact that feminist activism and the rape crisis center movement have had on courtroom practice. Ultimately, both trials were governed by the laws of the Commonwealth of Massachusetts— laws that were the product of legal reform and victim advocacy efforts among community-based rape crisis centers nationwide.

EMPOWERING SERVICES

Feminists have viewed victim *empowerment* through the restoration of choice as a primary antidote to rape trauma. The emphasis on empowerment poses a challenge to traditional medical, mental health, and legal practices that too often exacerbate the trauma of rape by denying to victims the healing experience of informed choice. When practitioners "march on" with their work, implementing standard procedure without concern for the rape victim's right to know and choose among alternative procedures, they reinforce her status as victim, ignore her capacity for survival, and undermine her recovery. Consider the following examples:

- Susan G. is an articulate 27-year-old, white, middle-class victim who knows and can identify her assailant. The circumstances of her rape are such that the district attorney's chances of successful prosecution are good. The evidence gathered by medical and police personnel is judged by the police to be "solid," and they are anxious to proceed with arrest and prosecution. Mental health counselors see Susan as shaken, but essentially strong—articulate and intelligent, possessed of inner strength, good judgment, and clear familial support. They believe she could weather a courtroom trial better than most victims. Indeed, Susan is an "ideal victim." She will make a good witness; her case is strong and her assailant known. The problem is that this assailant told Susan that if she tried to prosecute, he would be back. She believes him. She is frightened. She is reluctant to prosecute.

- Jan E. is a 17-year-old college freshman who attended a party given by some friends and ran into a man she'd been wanting to get to know. She flirted with him, had a little too much to drink, was flattered when he offered to drive her home, excited when he came into her apartment with her, and horrified when he made it clear that she would have sex with him whether she liked it or not. He hit her, threatened her, and raped her. Now Jan feels wounded, frightened, and ashamed. She also feels angry and is intent on prosecuting. The district attorney and police agree that hers will be a difficult case to prosecute successfully. Jan invited her assailant into her apartment. Her behavior before the rape can and will be treated as compromising by the defense. Moreover, the mental health and medical people are not convinced that Jan will want to go ahead with prosecution two or three months down the road as she discovers what it will demand of her. Also, they are of the opinion that she might take a loss in court badly.

These cases are not atypical. They illustrate a main difference between traditional professional practice and a feminist view of victim care. In cases like Susan's, law-enforcement officials have wanted very much to proceed with prosecution. Historically, they have been less concerned with a victim's right to choose what happens to her than with her responsibility to help the state get a conviction. In situations like Jan's, these same officials have been reluctant to proceed. In both cases, the evidence on hand and prevailing professional opinion oppose victim preference.

A feminist position maintains that, above all else, *a woman has the right to choose what happens to her.* In Susan's case, feminist counselors might also hope that she would prosecute, but they would genuinely respect and take seriously the legitimacy of her fears. From a feminist perspective, the primary curative step for Susan is that of choice—of resuming personal authority over her own life. Rape crisis advocates might explore with her the extent to which her immediate choice is based on strong but possibly passing fear, and they would present to Susan the option of allowing evidence collection to proceed should she later change her mind and wish to prosecute. Peer support would encourage Susan to explore her feelings fully and would assure her that others would understand and support her final decision, whatever that might be.

In Jan's case, feminist rape crisis workers would know well the difficulties inherent in her desire to prosecute. Her case will be picked up and followed without enthusiasm by the prosecutor's office. Once in court, she is sure to find herself the target of harsh questioning and intense cross-examination. Nevertheless, feminist rape crisis workers would encourage Jan, too, to choose the course she feels best for her, knowing in advance the difficulties her choice will entail. They would advise Jan to insist on timely evidence collection and would give her detailed information about the procedures involved. Later, they might offer court-watch or court accompaniment services to provide her with visible evidence of continuing emotional support. Whatever the services offered, it is in their emphasis upon empowerment through resumed control and informed choice that feminist services have differed most clearly from traditional approaches to care.

FEMINIST ORGANIZATIONS

Feminists have been highly critical of the organizational structure of traditional institutions, seeing them as hierarchical and nondemocratic embodiments of patriarchal values and as settings that perpetuate the status quo and reinforce the political, social, and economic subjugation of women. A feminist response to rape has thus required the creation of uniquely feminist settings, settings that reveal the shortcomings of traditional organizations and provide alternatives to them.

In the early 1970s, feminist rape crisis volunteers were as concerned with the organizational structure and internal decision-making processes of rape crisis centers as they were with the social change and victim service activities of these settings. The first, and subsequently the most influential, centers were organized as feminist collectives. Few, if any, employed paid staff and all valued the "feminist credentials" of empathy, compassion, and commitment to social change over professional credentials and traditional training. All of these centers relied extensively, if not entirely, on volunteers who were members of the collective and who comprised an egalitarian decision-making board. As they had equal responsibility for the work, so they had equal right to participate in program development, direction, and debate.

Today, the all-volunteer feminist collective has largely disappeared (Gornick et al., 1983). In its place are a wide range of settings that differ in size and budget, staffing patterns, services, philosophical premises, and organizational structure (Burt et al., 1984; Harvey, 1985). Sources of this diversity include (a) *ideological debate* within the rape crisis center movement; (b) state and federal *funding opportunities* that have influenced local center structure, staffing, and affiliation; and (c) the *ecological processes* operating on individual rape crisis centers in their home communities.

Ideological debate. Despite their continued sharing of many feminist precepts (i.e., an emphasis on empowerment, a commitment to social change, and a desire for independence from established organizations), feminist rape crisis centers also have chosen different paths and have done so on the basis of ideological debate and division. In the late 1970s and early 1980s, for example, some centers began to examine the possibility that an emphasis on victim service could prove incompatible with the social change objectives of the rape crisis center movement. The ensuing debate created conflict and division among local centers (Burt et al., 1984; Harvey, 1985). Advocates who assigned priority to a social change agenda saw victim service work as requiring too much interaction and cooperation with established service agencies. They feared center cooptation and argued for autonomous settings concerned primarily with public education, legal reform, and social activism. Proponents of a victim services perspective seemed to shy away from community activism, arguing that victim needs could best be met in an environment of cooperation. During the most heated period of debate, some centers turned almost entirely to social activism and others sought to become more established and more "respectable" service entities. Ultimately, most programs arrived again at some acceptable blend of victim service and social action emphases. But, in the process of debating and arriving at independent resolutions of the issues, community-based rape crisis centers individuated and diversified.

Another debate within the field concerned the matter of volunteer staffing. In order to survive, most of the early rape crisis centers began to feel the need for at least some paid staff. Initially, these staff were part-time administrators who raised funds for center activities, developed center ties with local service agencies, and organized center communication with other rape crisis programs. As center activities met with success, however, and particularly as center-based victim services were elaborated upon and expanded, many rape crisis centers felt the need to employ direct service staff with professional training and credentials. Typically, these centers hired feminist lawyers, feminist therapists, and feminist administrators. But as they did so, they left behind the formative model of the all-volunteer feminist collective.

Funding opportunities. Ideological debate and program diversification were further encouraged by the appearance of state and federal funds for victim service programs. In the early 1970s, virtually all feminist rape crisis centers operated with minimal budgets drawn from membership fees and community donations. By the mid-1970s, rape crisis centers were eligible to apply for newly available federal funds from such sources as the Law Enforcement Assistance Administration (LEAA) and the Department of Labor's Comprehensive Employment and Training Act (CETA). These funding initiatives required, however, that centers demonstrate organizational stability and community support and that they document a capacity for program continuation beyond an initial period of start-up or demonstration funding. Few of the early rape crisis centers could meet these requirements. Raised for their consideration and discussion were such possibilities as (a) center affiliation with a more established agency; (b) the inclusion of agency representatives and influential citizens as members of a previously all-volunteer board; and (c) center expansion into a more elaborate and agency-like structure.

With these organizational choices before them, many in the field feared that funding would prove the ideological death knell of the rape crisis center movement. They speculated, for example, that individual centers would be overwhelmed or coopted by the funding process, or would develop into more traditional service agencies and forego social change, victim advocacy, and legal reform. In fact, these fears have not been substantiated over time. In their survey of representative rape crisis centers, Martha Burt and her colleagues at the Urban Institute (Burt et al., 1984; Gornick et al., 1983; Pittman et al., 1984) found that highly effective and decidedly feminist social change activities had been launched by large and small, by both primarily volunteer and professionally staffed, rape crisis centers of relatively simple and of more elaborate, agency-like structure. Harvey (1985) came to similar conclusions about rape crisis centers designated highly effective by others in the field. Among these programs, center decisions with respect to agency affiliation and structural form had less to do with program accomplishments than did such qualities as consistency between program services and program ideology and center knowledge of change activities appropriate to the local community.

The ecology of community change. As the rape crisis center movement spread, antirape programs were initiated by women of varied interests and backgrounds. Some brought with them organizational and political skills cultivated in "new left" and counterculture activism; others brought to the field the lessons of more mainstream political involvements. When federal and state support became available in the mid-1970s, and as some representatives of medical, mental health, and law-enforcement agencies expressed new understanding of rape and new commitment to improved treatment, already existing and newly emerging centers drew upon the skills and resources of professional women and women experienced in organizational administration. Women from diverse professional backgrounds thus joined the rape crisis center movement. As they did so, their personal qualities and expertise interacted with the attributes of already established community settings and the resources and traditions of local communities to generate rape crisis centers uniquely suited to the ecologies of their host environments.

RAPE CRISIS CENTER RESEARCH

Rape crisis centers have been the focal point of nationwide survey research and exemplary project/case-study investigation.

Survey Research

The survey researcher typically selects a representative sample of rape crisis centers from a nationwide population of programs and queries these with respect to any number of attributes. Some surveys have yielded descriptive portraits of the field and chronicled its development over time (Brodyaga et al., 1975; O'Sullivan, 1976); others have sought to identify factors contributing to program diversity and effectiveness (Burt et al., 1984; Harvey, 1985).

Rape crisis center services. O'Sullivan's (1976) nationwide survey of 90 representative programs identified the service and advocacy initiatives that in five short years had come to typify grass-roots rape crisis centers in communities throughout the country. All of these programs operated a community speakers bureau, and almost all offered hospital and police accompaniment services to victims (89 and 90 percent, respectively). Court accompaniment programs were offered by 80% of those surveyed, and 78% had initiated volunteer rape hot lines. Brodyaga et al. (1975) reports similar findings. Crisis, advocacy, and support services for victims combined with community education and social change activism described the rape crisis center of the early 1970s. In addition to these services, individual rape crisis centers were offering short-term and long-term counseling (60%); rap groups, group counseling, and peer support sessions (38%); training to police, court, medical, and mental health professionals (56%, 13%, 59%, and 49%, respectively); court-watch programs (25%), and self-defense training (29%) (O'Sullivan, 1976).

In their survey of 50 representative rape crisis centers, Martha Burt and colleagues (Burt et al., 1984; Gornick et al., 1984; Pittman et al., 1984) found that the majority of centers continued to offer some combination of direct service and community education well into the 1980s. Direct care services included a wide range of emergency assistance, crisis intervention, hospital and court accompaniment, advocacy, and follow-up counseling programs. Continuing education initiatives included public education forums, professional training activities, and lobbying and political action at local, state, and national levels.

Among the programs they surveyed, Gornick et al. (1983) identified four organizationally distinct types of rape crisis programs: (a) small, primarily volunteer, clearly autonomous, politically active centers that resemble the prototypical feminist collective and are marked by a flexible pattern of services and a loose organizational structure; (b) larger, more substantially funded, agency-like centers that make use of paid and volunteer staff, provide a variety of victim services, and differ from one another primarily in terms of their clearly feminist or essentially apolitical orientations; (c) centers embedded in the structure of more established agencies (typically community mental health centers) that provide substantial administrative and financial support; and (d) hospital-based, emergency room programs that concentrate on delivering services to victims and training to emergency room personnel. These programs engage in little or no political activism and enjoy limited visibility in the community.

These researchers found considerable ideological diversity among these centers and, in some, a disturbing inability of newer center staff to articulate the once-organizing feminist precepts of their programs. Neither had a feminist perspective been replaced by other, equally organizing constructs. The authors speculated that diversity per se was not a drawback to the rape crisis center movement, but that over time this kind of "philosophical drift" could obscure program direction and undermine program effectiveness.

Exemplary Project/Case-Study Investigation

The issue of program effectiveness underlies exemplary project/case-study investigation. Here, interest is directed not to a large and representative sample of rape crisis centers, but to a small and decidedly unrepresentative group of highly effective programs. The aim is to determine what, if anything, these programs have in common and which, if any, of their shared attributes might underlie center effectiveness. Harvey (1982a, 1982b) site-visited three highly effective, though organizationally varied and philosophically diverse programs (Women Organized Against Rape in Philadelphia, the Albuquerque Rape Crisis Center in New Mexico, and Community Action Against Rape in Las Vegas, Nevada). Dissimilar to one another in terms of their educational backgrounds, professional credentials, feminist values, and preferred approaches to internal decision making, the directors of these three centers shared personal backgrounds rich in political and community activism. All emphasized the importance of social change, and all had spearheaded success-ful legislative reform campaigns. The programs they directed shared ideological clarity, a planning process that ensured con-sistency between program actions and values, and strong, mutually supportive ties with other community agencies and groups. This investigation served as a pilot study for a more extensive NCPCR-sponsored investigation that combined na-tionwide survey research with the case-study investigation of nine "exemplary" rape crisis centers (Harvey, 1985).

A STUDY OF NINE EXEMPLARY
RAPE CRISIS CENTERS

The project was conducted in two stages. Stage one involved a telephone survey of 50 sexual assault treatment and prevention programs deemed highly effective by regional representatives of the NCASA network of community-based rape crisis programs according to criteria set forth by an NCPCR/NCASA Advisory Panel (see Table 4.1). From these programs, nine were selected for site visitation and in-depth case study. Selection criteria at stage one emphasized program effectiveness; those at stage two ensured geographic, demographic, and programmatic variation among the case-studied settings. Whenever consistent with these aims, the advisory panel included programs known to have had a particularly formative influence upon the field.

The Stage One Programs

The stage one programs included independent, publicly and privately affiliated settings that could be classified as *collectives*, *modified collectives*, or *agency-like hierarchies*. This organizational typology is clarified in Table 4.2.

Table 4.1 Selection Criteria: Stage One Sample

  1. Program longevity and survival
  2. Clearly defined organizational structure
  3. Clearly defined planning process
  4. Initial and ongoing staff training
  5. Volunteer utilization and training
  6. Attentiveness to client choice and feedback
  7. Sensitivity to special populations
  8. Recognition within local community
  9. Positive impact upon local community services
 10. Utilization of community resources
 11. Regional/national impact upon sexual assault programming
 12. Record keeping and data analysis
 13. Willingness to participate in study

A summary portrait of the stage one programs is presented in Table 4.3. As a group, they reflect the diversity that today characterizes the sexual assault field. They are like one another, and different from less effective programs in two important respects, however. First, all of them give coequal attention to social change and victim service objectives. Second, in all but the publicly affiliated programs, the empowerment of women and victims is a unifying theme and organizing premise.

The Stage Two Programs

The nine programs selected for case-study investigation also included programs of each organizational type and affiliation. They are listed and briefly described in Table 4.4.

Origins. All of these settings were initiated early in the rape crisis center movement. Despite rocky starts and turbulent times, all have maintained a continuing and expanding presence in their home communities. These communities range from Sweetwater County, Wyoming, with its small and economically

Table 4.2 An Organizational Typology for Stage One Programs

Type	Program Characteristics	N
I. *The collective* *(N = 13, 26%)*	1. Volunteer, volunteer/staff or mixed volunteer/community board 2. Nonhierarchical, egalitarian structure 3. Primarily volunteer staffing 4. Participatory decision making 5. Little or no divisional structure	Independent *(N = 11, 85%)* Public *(N = 0)* Private *(N = 2, 15%)*
II. *The modified* *collective* *(N = 22, 44%)*	1. Community or mixed board 2. Squat hierarchy (2 to 3 tiers) 3. Primarily volunteer or mixed staffing 4. Participatory decision making 5. Minimal to considerable divisional structure	Independent *(N = 15, 68%)* Public *(N = 1)* Private *(N = 6, 27%)*

III.
The hierarchical
program
(N = 15, 30%)
	1. Community board
	2. Hierarchy (4 or more tiers)
	3. Mixed or predominantly professional
	    staffing
	4. Clear chain of authority for program
	    and policy development
	5. Three or more divisions
		Independent
		(N = 5, 33%)
		
		Public
		(N = 8, 53%)
		
		Private
		(N = 2, 13%)

stressed mining towns to metropolitan Pittsburgh in the East, and the bilingual, agricultural milieu of California's San Joaquin Valley in the West. With few exceptions, these programs began as groups of women drawn together by a sometimes alarming rise in the incidence of rape and by knowledge that similar groups in other communities had begun to develop antirape programs. Seven of the programs were started by NOW-affiliated or local governmental task forces that provided an initial

Table 4.3 A Summary Portrait: Fifty Effective
Sexual Assault Programs

Funding sources:	Primary dependency on local dollars, public or private, or both
	Funding sources vary with program affiliation and program type
Affiliations:	Varied
	Independent private nonprofit (62%)
	Publicly affiliated (18%)
	Privately affiliated (20%)
Structural types:	Varied
	Collectives (25%)
	Modified collectives (44%)
	Hierarchical (30%)
Philosophical themes:	Empowerment of women and victims (90%) unifies all but publicly affiliated.
	Additional themes vary with program type and program affiliation.
Program goals:	Rape awareness and elimination (98%)
	Victim advocacy (92%)
	Additional goals vary with program type and program affiliation.
Services:	Community Education (100%)
	Hot line/crisis counseling/medical and police advocacy (90%)
	Additional services vary with program type and affiliation.
Volunteer utilization:	Level of use, board involvement, and roles performed vary with program and type of affiliation.

forum for debating program philosophy, direction, and form. Few of these programs had the luxury of extensive planning, however. Only the Miami Rape Treatment Center program opened its doors after two full years of collaboration and planning by hospital personnel and local task force members. More typical beginnings were those in which task force immediately

Table 4.4 Nine Exemplary Programs

The Multiservice Programs

Lexington Rape Crisis Center: Established 1972 as Women's Center Task Force, today an *independent collective* run by volunteer board/director. Comprehensive victim services, community education, professional training, and prevention.

Sexual Assault Center of San Joaquin County: Begun 1976 as independent volunteer program, today a *modified collective, privately affiliated* with San Joaquin County Women's Center. Serves bilingual, multicultural, rural/urban population.

Sweetwater County Task Force on Sexual Assault: Established 1976, *independent staff collective* providing victim services, community education, professional training, school-based prevention, and sponsoring sexual harassment and child pornography initiatives.

The Direct Care Programs

Austin Rape Crisis Center: Established 1974, *independent modified collective* utilizing the services of more than 150 volunteers. Integrates feminist values with holistic healing; uses male advocates; includes client evaluation of services and grievance procedure.

Miami Rape Treatment Center: Physician-directed, hospital-based *publicly affiliated and hierarchical* program of emergency and follow-up care to rape victims. Utilizes "floating medical team"; provides statewide professional training.

Pittsburgh Action Against Rape: Established 1971; among earliest programs in country, today an "agency-like hierarchy" that integrates feminist values, participatory milieu, and increasingly specialized professional care.

The Prevention Programs

Alternatives to Fear: Begun in 1971 as a university-based karate course, AFT is today an *independent modified collective* specializing in self-defense, risk-awareness/rape-avcidance education for women and others at risk.

Illusion Theater: A working theatrical company providing childhood sexual assault prevention education for schools and community. Established 1975. *Privately affiliated, hierarchical.*

Syracuse Rape Crisis Center: Established 1974 as volunteer collective, now an *independent hierarchy* providing model services, and community education/rape prevention programs.

---

yielded program, and program survival relied on moment-to-moment innovation and ongoing experimentation.

Ongoing experimentation and internal change. Conscious experimentation with program form, identity, and affiliation distinguishes these from other, less effective rape crisis centers. Pittsburgh Action Against Rape, for example, began as an all-volunteer feminist collective, later made a near-fatal move out of Pittsburgh in search of LEAA funds, and ultimately returned home to construct a professionally staffed feminist program that is among the largest and most elaborately organized in the country. Lexington moved from affiliated to independent status while San Joaquin did the reverse. The Sweetwater task force began as a hierarchical program with a director, paid staff, and volunteers. Today it operates as a staff collective. Although these programs differ from one another in their initial as well as their contemporary affiliations and forms, they have in common this capacity for thoughtful experimentation and the ability to continually refine program identity in service to program effectiveness.

Program philosophy. Like the stage one programs from which they were drawn, these centers tended as a group to emphasize the *empowerment of women and victims* and to stress both *victim advocacy* and *societal responsibility for rape*. None viewed social activism as incompatible with a victim-service orientation, and most saw both as critical. Three of the programs were remarkable in their ability to mobilize public support in essentially conservative communities despite avowedly feminist platforms and program histories filled with social activism and legal reform.

The Sweetwater County Task Force on Sexual Assault, for example, serves a handful of small mining communities in which self-reliance, privacy, and rugged individualism are highly valued. In the mid-1970s, the area experienced a temporary economic and cultural traumatization when the energy crisis created new interest in mining and brought to the area large

numbers of transient workers. The incidence of rape and attempted rape rose dramatically. In 1976, a local women's group
organized a task force and initiated the first of its many community education campaigns. Since its inception, the Sweetwater
County program has introduced an incredible range of service
and social change initiatives, including school-based prevention
and child sexual abuse detection programs, state legislation protecting the confidentiality of rape crisis center records, a statewide antipornography campaign, and a campaign to combat
sexual harassment in the workplace. The program operates as a
feminist staff collective and enjoys unprecedented community
support.

Findings

Together, the stage one and stage two findings suggest that
highly effective rape crisis programs share (a) philosophical precepts that emphasize empowerment and stress the coequal
validity of social change and victim advocacy; (b) a "philosophical centeredness" that guides program development and ensures consistency between program action and values; (c) a
capacity for internal change based on ongoing program self-
study; and (d) the ability to instigate and successfully manage
social and community change. It is likely that these qualities
constitute the organizational underpinnings of program effectiveness among community-based rape crisis centers and antirape programs of diverse organizational form, affiliation, and
program.

Internal consistency and philosophical centeredness. Common
across these settings is a high degree of consistency between
expressed program values and actual program services, training, and social action strategies. Among these programs there
was no evidence of "philosophical drift" (Burt et al., 1984). Instead, all gave the impression of settings in which program
philosophy served as a platform for program development.

This impression is strengthened by the case material gathered at stage two. A feminist analysis of rape and the implications of that analysis for both community education and victim service roles are made explicit in Lexington's volunteer-screening process, for example, and in the volunteer training curriculum of the Syracuse Rape Crisis Center. Similarly, the value placed on professional involvement and on professional outreach to the larger community is clearly evident in the training and consultation initiatives of the Miami Rape Treatment Center. In Seattle, Washington, the self-defense classes developed for varied citizen groups by Seattle's Alternatives to Fear Program (see Chapter 7) express that program's emphasis on rape avoidance through the development of individually appropriate psychological and physical self-defense competencies. Whatever their differences in philosophy or form, each of these programs is self-consciously determined and vigilant with respect to program purpose, behavior, and identity.

This conclusion is compatible with those drawn by Alley et al. (1979) in their investigation of 12 community mental health centers, each distinguished by innovative and effective utilization of paraprofessional workers. The centers studied shared many qualities, the most important of which was a strong and unifying philosophical stance: a "mission" that united staff in common purpose and imparted direction and identity to the organization.

Program self-study. Another characteristic of these exemplary community mental health programs was an approach to program development and planning, which the authors labeled "program self-study" to stress its reliance upon ongoing internal evaluation (Alley et al., 1979). Self-study also typified these rape crisis programs. Indeed, the data are replete with examples of nondefensive, self-critical program review and reorientation. Pittsburgh Action Against Rape's return to its urban origins in order to reestablish program mission and identity after an ill-formed quest for available federal dollars illustrates "program self-study" and the accomplishments it fosters. Back in Pittsburgh, with its feminist identity reaffirmed and its ability to survive as an independent organization established, the center has expanded its services, elaborated its structure, and added credentialed professionals to its staff. One of the earliest, most influential, and respected programs in the rape crisis center movement, Pittsburgh Action Against Rape has continued to exhibit this capacity for internal change and the ability to undertake such change only as it is adjudged to be consistent with both community need and program values.

Other examples could be given as well. However idiosyncratic in other respects, all of these programs compile and make programmatic use of evaluative materials (e.g., client evaluations, follow-up interviews, aggregate reports). In each, the process of program development reveals staff attentiveness to program mission and to the compatibility of program aim and action. The process maintains within the organization an enduring capacity for program improvement through self-assessment and internal debate.

Social change and community intervention. The need for widespread social change is a premise of the sexual assault field— a premise guiding public awareness campaigns, efforts aimed at legal reform, and attempts to substantially revise prevailing concepts of care. Among community-based rape crisis programs, the most direct expressions of social reform are found in the changed attitudes of local citizens and in the more responsive services of local medical, mental health, and law-enforcement agencies.

Heller and Monahan (1977) propose that although social action projects rely for initial success upon the energy of highly committed constituents, their impact over time depends upon their ability to enlist cooperation and support from more established institutions. The case materials compiled at stage two echo this theme, revealing each program's extensive interaction with and remarkable impact upon local institutions. The Sexual Assault Center of San Joaquin, for example, has built strong ties with all key agencies in the area. Local police and sheriff's deputies routinely notify the center's staff of new rape cases and invite center advocates to be nearby during official interviews with victims. The local hospital uses a rape investigation kit developed by the center, and the center trains hospital staff in its use. The district attorney's office relies on the center for legal advocacy, case management, and coordination of rape cases proceeding through the courts.

San Joaquin is not alone among these highly effective programs either in its extensive community ties or in its skillful management of community change processes. Illusion Theater, for example, is adept at bringing its Minneapolis-based productions into schools and communities around the country. Advance planning with local sponsors and preliminary contact with local school officials characterize its entry into new communities. In one instance, when a planned performance met with unexpected opposition from local religious leaders, the theater opted not to encourage the battle brewing between warring factions in the community but to invite parents, teachers, ministers, and school officials to an adults-only preview of the production. Today, the play *Touch* is regularly performed in that community's elementary schools—by local groups trained and franchised by Illusion Theater. The prevention initiatives of Illusion Theater are further detailed in Chapter 7.

In short, whatever qualities may distinguish these programs from one another, none is "separatist" in its orientation to social and community change. Instead, each is a leader and a participant in community affairs, able to catalyze change in other settings. The most prominent talent these programs seem to share is that of bringing to bear upon their host communities the values and reforms of a nationwide antirape movement, thus prompting social change at the local, grass-roots level.

According to Glidewell's (1976) theory of induced social change (see Chapter 3), successful change agentry involves three "arts." They are (a) the ability to introduce into the host community new knowledge and new possibilities for change; (b) the ability to create system linkages between that host community and the larger world, linkages that will encourage and support the accomplishment of desired change; and (c) the ability to help a community manage the tensions that arise as it experiences and begins to undergo change.

Skillful implementation of these arts typify these highly successful programs. All of them, for example, emphasize community education as a catalyst for change and each has successfully introduced into its home community educational initiatives for diverse segments of the local population. Within its home community, each has created new linkages among existing community settings and, in doing so, has accomplished a significant enrichment and realignment of local resources. Each also has ensured community contact with a nationwide antirape movement and cultivated community support for social change and legal reform. Finally, each has provided clear leadership to the collaborative process of community change, serving as a lightning rod for community debate when necessary and acting, when possible, to ease tensions posing barriers to community reform. In performing these "arts," none of the settings studied has camouflaged or compromised its ideological stance. Instead, each has used that stance as a firm platform for effective leadership.

A final quality worth noting in these and in previously studied highly effective rape crisis centers (Harvey, 1982a, 1982b) is the kind of attention they give to the process and timing of community change and the awareness they exhibit of local possibilities for change. Illustrations of this quality are diverse. In the earlier example, Illusion Theater patiently and creatively diluted community resistance to child sexual abuse prevention activities by working with local parent and teacher groups. In Philadelphia, when a 9-year-old girl was raped on her way to school, Women Organized Against Rape immediately developed citywide school assembly programs, establishing its ability to respond immediately to local needs and to garner widespread regard among once "standoffish" agencies.

Finally, there is the resourcefulness of Community Action to Stop Rape in Las Vegas. Minimally funded and particularly reliant on volunteer services, this center has carefully recruited a cadre of volunteer specialists from throughout the local community: a teacher who works well with adolescent victims, a family willing to house victims sexually assaulted while visiting Las

Vegas as tourists, a nurse who is particularly helpful with victims of brutal or sadistic assault, and a host of others able to address special needs.

From his review of successful community interventions, Kelly (1979) concludes that "'taint what you do, it's the way that you do it." He suggests that the success or failure of community change initiatives depends ultimately on the sensitivity, resourcefulness, and sense of timing evident in these examples.

CONCLUSION

The community-based rape crisis center has become the primary setting for improving a community's response to rape. Initiated in the early 1970s as a result of feminist activism and debate, rape crisis centers are today found in hundreds of communities throughout the United States and in nations throughout the world. With increasing numbers has come program variation and diversity, particularly in the organizational forms, program affiliations, and ideological orientations of individual centers. Sources of this diversity include ideological debate within the rape crisis movement, federal and state funding programs that encouraged program conformity to new organizational requirements, and ecological factors operating at the level of the local community. Despite this diversity, the core activities of rape crisis centers remain largely the same as they were in the early 1970s: community education to change prevailing attitudes and beliefs about rape and rape victims; social activism for legal and institutional reform; and crisis response and victim advocacy services. Case-study investigations of highly effective rape crisis programs suggest that what may distinguish them from other centers is neither organizational form nor program affiliation, but a clear sense of program mission, an enduring emphasis upon victim empowerment and social change, an internal process of program self-study that ensures compatibility of program philosophy and action, and skillful management of community change processes.

NOTE

1. David Stockman was appointed by President Reagan to direct the Office of Management and Budget. During his first months in this position, federal agencies endured high financial cutbacks.

FIVE

The Clinical Treatment of Rape Victims

The professional clinician comes into contact with rape victims through one of the following avenues: clients who are referred by rape crisis centers, hospitals, physicians, or prosecuting attorneys' offices; clients who enter therapy for another stated purpose but subsequently reveal a history of rape; self-referred clients; or clients who are raped during ongoing therapy. Studies of rape victims have suggested that relatively few seek professional help immediately after a rape. For example, a survey of college student rape victims revealed that 4% had utilized rape crisis centers (Koss, 1988). Likewise, fewer than half of victims three months postrape who were judged to need treatment agreed to participate (Veronen & Kilpatrick, 1983). Further, only one quarter of the victims who entered immediate postrape treatment completed a 14-hour treatment program (Frank, 1979). These observations suggest that many women attempt to cope on their own in the immediate postrape period. However, as many as 48% of one sample of nonrecent victims stated that they eventually sought help for rape-related concerns (Ellis et al., 1981). Among the reasons victims gave for finally seeking aid were impending trial, persistent symptoms that did not diminish with time, first sexual encounter after the assault, breakup or argument with significant other, and withdrawal of support by family or friends (Stewart et al., 1987).

These data imply that the professional clinician is far more likely to be called upon to treat nonrecent cases. They further reveal that the number of rape victims who do not seek treatment is larger than the number who do. To address the implications of these findings, we will provide four different approaches to intervention. The first section describes a single-session trauma debriefing procedure for recent rape victims. The second section describes an individual integrative treatment for nonrecent victims who seek therapy months or years after their assault. We begin this section with suggested criteria for recovery from sexual assault. We conceptualize these criteria as the hallmarks of the survivor of rape and as a road map for the goals that psychotherapy is intended to achieve. The third approach to intervention is group treatment, the subject of Chapter 6. The final intervention, public education designed to reach that large group of victims who do not seek any formal services, is addressed in Chapter 7.

CHALLENGES OF WORKING WITH RAPE VICTIMS

Rape creates strong feelings in the therapist as well as in the victim.

Feelings of Vulnerability

It is a basic need of all individuals to find an explanation for violent and brutal crimes (Symonds, 1976). Exposure to a victim of brutal crime makes one feel vulnerable unless one can believe that the other person did something, or neglected something, that plausibly contributed to their victimization. Feelings of vulnerability can lead to a self-protective adoption of a blaming attitude toward the victim. These feelings may pose barriers toward establishment of a supportive relationship. For example, among the common mistakes made by emergency room attending personnel when treating rape victims are several behaviors that appear to reflect uneasiness about dealing with rape, such as appearing extremely busy (i.e., running in and out of the room without communicating verbally with the victim); leaving the victim completely alone; relating to the victim on an unemotional level avoiding any possibility for touching, holding, or caring; making premature evaluations and judgments; placing blame; and talking down to the victim (Warner, 1978).

Burnout

Rape victims often are challenging to work with, require a high level of commitment, are emotionally intense, and may cause clinicians to feel rejected. Immediately after a rape, as a natural protective maneuver, victims may need to avoid dealing directly with their experience. Therefore they may be guarded in responding to overtures to enter a therapeutic relationship. They cannot be expected to make a firm commitment for return visits or contacts. Later, victims' anger at the rape and the rapist, denied any other channel of expression, may be directed toward the clinician or agency. Then, rape-induced moves and changed telephone numbers may make it difficult for the clinician to follow up victims and obtain any sense of closure with them. Finally, victims become survivors at their own pace. Therapists who treat victims must have patience, an enormous amount of energy to nurture, and healthy ways to reduce their own stress and recharge themselves.

Special Problems for Male Clinicians

Although many rape victims express a preference for a female clinician, not all do. Some rape specialists have strong negative feelings about men working with rape victims, but what little is known about their performance suggests that men with interest and training can be effective (Resick et al., 1989). We believe that it is preferable if those who contact the rape victim immediately after the crime are gender-matched. The immediate aftermath of the crime does not offer the luxury of time to create a relationship with the victim so that she or he may judge the clinician as an individual rather than as a representative of a particular gender. Outside the crisis period, male clinicians may be effective with those victims without a preference for a female therapist.

The inexperienced male practitioner often is especially anxious about working with rape victims (Silverman, 1977). He may wish to please female supervisors or peers and may feel pressured to prove to them and to the victim that he is liberal and liberated. As a result, his behavior may appear overly gratuitous and patronizing. Even experienced male clinicians may experience a wish to make up for the pain inflicted by a male offender, to make the intervention a compensatory and corrective experience, and to prove that some men can be gentle, empathic, and trustworthy. This is a heavy burden for one person to try to shoulder.

Observations of male clinicians treating rape victims have revealed modifications in their use of space, physical contact, and tone of voice (Silverman, 1977). Most spoke more softly than usual. While some increased their normal physical distance from the client, others sat closer. Some clinicians held the woman's hand or patted her shoulder while others felt that any such gestures would be inappropriate. Male clinicians in particular, must study videotapes of their therapy so that they can be aware of any undesired seductive or distancing messages their nonverbal behavior might communicate. It can be expected that eroticized feelings experienced in the course of treatment of a rape victim (on the part of the therapist or the client) will prove more disquieting and anxiety provoking than they normally would be.

A firmly established gender difference in attitudes toward rape (Burt, 1980; Feild, 1978) is the tendency for men to see rape more as a sexual crime and for women to view it more as an act of violence. Thus from the female victim's viewpoint the male clinician may seem to focus too much on the sexual aspects as opposed to the violent aspects of her experience. To her then, he seems to lack empathy. Men also have a harder time identifying with the victim. Women clinicians have often had to confront feelings of vulnerability, powerlessness, and helplessness in their own personal lives much more directly than men do. Consequently, they may have an easier time accepting such feelings in themselves, conveying empathy to the victim, and assisting her in experiencing, containing, and tolerating her feelings.

SINGLE-SESSION DEBRIEFING FOR THE VICTIM OF RAPE

The material that follows describes procedures for the debriefing of the recently raped woman. The goal of debriefing is to present an accessible, nonstigmatizing, one-session response to the victimized person that will have a stabilizing influence on long-term response. The term debriefing is used to connote that rape victims are experiencing normal reactions to an abnormal experience and to avoid the automatic assumption that psychotherapy or counseling is necessary in the aftermath of trauma. Training and material on debriefing is available from the National Organization for Victim Assistance [NOVA], (1987).

In most hospitals and crisis centers these immediate interventions are provided by trained paraprofessionals. The initial response to rape among most victims is homogeneous and predictable. Thus the paraprofessional can be trained to apply a standard approach and to identify those instances where atypical responses to rape (particularly toward reactions among victims with a history of diagnosed mental illness) require the attendance of a trained clinician. In recognition of the contributions of paraprofessionals to rape crisis work, we have used the term "service provider" rather than the word "therapist" in this first section.

The most practical approach to the recent rape victim is to assume only a single session of intervention. Many victims enter a denial phase soon after the rape during which they are unable to think about, talk about, or deal directly with their experience. Thus many will fail to follow through on commitments for further intervention made during the first session. Additionally, victims may perceive premature insistence on acceptance of treatment as a second assault. Although response to a trauma like rape is relatively the same in everyone, providers must be aware of intersections between ethnicity, response to rape, and the recovery environment (see Parson, 1985; Williams & Holmes, 1981).

Materials on responding to the rape victim in crisis are available that reflect the psychodynamic (Burgess & Holmstrom, 1979), behavioral (Kilpatrick & Veronen, 1982), and crisis theory perspectives (NOVA, 1987). We have benefitted greatly from these writings in formulating our thinking about the components of postassault debriefing. The following intervention goals are suggested: establish a supportive relationship; handle immediate needs; involve the social network; allow for ventilation and validation; make practical arrangements; anticipate the future; and set up telephone follow up. If follow-up telephone contacts reveal a desire for additional sessions, appropriate referrals for advocacy and individual or group interventions can be made.

Establish a Supportive Relationship

Without a therapeutic relationship no therapeutic contact can be effective (Goldfried, 1980). The primary ingredients of a good relationship with a traumatized person are acceptance, empathy, and support.

Behaviors that help to convey *acceptance* include attentiveness to the everything the client says; a calm and accepting facial expression; frequent encouragers (verbal reinforcement, head nodding); restating what has been said; a lack of expressed or implied condemnation or reproach; respect for the client's style of coping; and communicating on the level of the client's current capacity to understand. In particular reference to the rape, the quality of the relationship is enhanced by the provider who can listen attentively to the victim—even when her need to ventilate dictates repeated recollections of her experiences—and can understand and accept her hesitancy to make commitments.

A second ingredient in building a relationship is the communication of *empathy*. All people have a craving to be liked (Wolberg, 1967). Because of their problems, many clients feel unloved or incapable of evoking sympathy. This observation is especially true among rape victims, who often feel that they have been soiled or damaged by their experience. Among the ways the provider can communicate empathy and caring are (a) verbalizing for the client how upset they must feel, (b) seeing things from the client's point of view, and (c) demonstrating empathy even when the client displays hostility.

Some persons with mental health training have been taught to minimize the use of *support and reassurance* out of fear of creating dependency in clients. This concern stems from long-term psychotherapy. It is groundless in the treatment of rape victims due to the extremely short duration of the contact. Furthermore, withholding of support from the traumatized person is very likely to neutralize the provider's effectiveness. Support is one of the primary factors that augments the coping capacity of the rape victim and allows equilibrium to be reestablished. Expressions of support that are helpful to the rape victim include stating that the victim was not at fault, acknowledging that the victim did all she could to resist, reassuring her that rape often is not avoidable but is survivable, and recognizing that the victim has not lost worth by the experience.

The following case of a 17-year-old rape victim treated by a rape crisis center victim advocate illustrates the positive impact of support:

Diane went out on a date with someone she had met in a restaurant. He had telephoned her at her home and arranged the date. When he picked her up, he suggested that they go to his aunt's home and watch television. She agreed, although with some trepidation. They drove to the "aunt's" house and there were no lights on. Her instincts told her not to go in, but she told herself she was just being foolish and nothing bad was going to happen.

She was raped in the house and then driven about two miles from the house and dropped off. At this point she realized that she did not know the man's last name nor where he lived. She was very scared as to her parents' reaction and also very upset that she had not followed her own instincts.

She called the rape crisis center from a phone booth, and they urged her to go to the hospital. She did so and as they had agreed, an advocate met her there. The advocate concentrated on supporting Diane throughout the examinations and police procedures. She counseled Diane that although she had done a stupid thing, that was no reason for being raped and that all people do stupid things at times. She attempted to convey to Diane that it was not her fault.

She also spoke to Diane about how her family might respond and did a bit of role playing with her. The therapist played the role of mother and father as Diane tried to find a way to share the incident with her parents. Diane responded very positively, and it was expected that she would indeed tell her parents. She was also encouraged to seek further counseling at a local children's services center but she responded tentatively to this suggestion.

Kilpatrick (1983) observes that sometimes clinicians feel they must determine in their own minds whether a "real" rape has occurred before they can offer support. This inclination represents a confusion of roles because it is the courts, not clinicians, that decide whether a rape has occurred. To the extent that rape can be predicted, it is most related to a history of past victimizations, something that is beyond the control of the victim. Other risk factors for rape are economic characteristics (e.g., being poor, living in high crime areas, lacking a car) that also are not in the victim's control and are not within the realm of therapy to remedy. Finally, no research has suggested surefire ways to avoid rape or to identify rapists. For all these reasons, rape victims deserve to be supported wholeheartedly, to have their sense of violation validated, and to be reassured that their responses were all that was possible under the degree of fear that rape induces. It is through support that the trauma specialist helps to dispel erroneous, guilt-inducing beliefs that many rape victims, like everyone else in our society, may harbor. The rape victim needs the reassurance of someone's presence throughout the immediate postrape phase, someone who can express to her verbally and nonverbally that she is still a worthy person.

The following case illustrates the outcome in a case where the victim was viewed by the clinician as at least partially responsible for her rape:

Doreen relates her experience as follows: "I'd been friendly with him for a long time when the trouble started. I was pretty clear in my mind that we were just buddies. He had been over to my apartment many times—we hung out there talking. This time he started saying that he was tired of games and that he knew what I wanted, to screw him. I was amazed as I didn't want to. I said so, but he said that I was just playing the game. Again I said no, I didn't want anything but to be his friend.

"At that point he picked me up, brought me into the bedroom, and threw me down on my bed. I didn't do anything else. I just lay there as he took my clothes off and had sex with me.

"I continued to see him occasionally as friends and tried to clarify what I saw as our relationship—friends, just friends. Eventually I became acquainted with another of his buddies. A little while later the same thing happened with him. I have always had a circle of male friends who I have only seen as just that. Now I keep them all a bit further away. I got into therapy a while after this after telling a friend about it."

The therapist notes on this victim state, "Doreen entered therapy upon a friend's suggestion. Although she had intercourse with two men against her will, she did not identify herself as a rape victim. The initial therapy dealt with her sense of being a perpetual victim to others' actions. I conceptualize her as an hysteric. I attempted to help her connect her behaviors to the events that happen to her. Doreen came for eight sessions before prematurely ending therapy."

Rape victims' immediate response to rape may be expressed or controlled. The more controlled victim often can relate her experiences with little interference. The victim who is manifestly upset, however, frequently requires more structure and activity on the part of the interviewer. Subsequent to the establishment of supportive contact, the provider can turn attention to handling the victim's immediate needs.

Handle Immediate Needs

Over 85% of the requests of rape victims who were seen immediately after their assault in a hospital emergency room were for psychological support, medical intervention, or police attention (Burgess & Holmstrom, 1979). We will consider each of these needs briefly.

Social Support

Among the earliest concerns of the rape victim is notifying significant others including parents, friends, husbands, and boyfriends. Many victims simply require the physical means to carry out the notification while some may want the provider to do it for them. Although in longer term therapy it is often desirable for clients to master tasks themselves, here there is no time to set the stages for mastery. Therefore it is appropriate to assist the victim in notifying significant others. Quite frequently a victim experiences disclosure fears about how significant others will react. Or she may be unsure that she wants to notify anyone. In both instances the provider will want to explore the victim's thoughts about the potential reactions of her significant others. Victims with children may desire a professional opinion concerning the means and advisability of telling their children about the rape. Counseling of family members, discussed in more detail later, may be helpful in assuring that their reactions to the victim are supportive.

Medical Assistance

Medical treatment is recommended for victims of rape for several reasons. First, in cases of violent rape, serious injuries may require immediate medical care. Second, even in cases where no obvious injuries exist, preventive treatment is indicated for sexually transmitted diseases, including AIDS, and for pregnancy. Also, reassurance regarding the absence of internal injuries may also be helpful. Third, many victims may desire explanation of the psychological shock-related physical symptoms they are experiencing. Additionally, medical personnel collect forensic evidence for potential use in prosecution.

Unfortunately, medical personnel appear to concentrate on evidence collection and to minimize attention to psychological concerns. Because of the potential for medical procedures to exacerbate a victim's sense of powerlessness and their superficial resemblance to acts of sexual assault, a victim advocate, a specially trained emergency nurse, or a female police officer should be present continually during any examinations. To prepare the provider to be present at a rape exam, the following information is included about medical and nonmedical aspects of the procedures. The material was prepared on the basis of two sources (Burgess & Holmstrom, 1988; Hicks, 1988).

Emergency room considerations for rape victims. Medical personnel should have special training regarding the collection of evidence subsequent to rape and, if possible, should use a prepackaged standard rape evidence kit so that the correct specimens are collected and the samples are labeled and analyzed appropriately. Most victims will be exhausted and withdrawn, which can lead medical personnel to underestimate the extent of trauma. Rape is a medical emergency and should be so treated from the moment the victim is brought in; however, the word "rape" should not be used in referring to the victim. The primary reason is that this may cause distress to the victim, but secondarily it is a legal term, not a medical term. A friend or relative should be allowed to accompany the victim if desired. When they cannot be with the victim, they should be taken to a quiet area separate from the public waiting room. Rape victims should not be left alone in an exam room. The sex of people caring for the rape victim is less important than individuals' attitudes toward rape. Only those who feel that they can be accepting of the victim and her situation should work with her. One who harbors any feelings that a rape victim in some way brought the experience on herself or secretly enjoyed it should not come into contact with these patients.

Psychological aspects of the rape examination. There are several helpful expressions that should be memorized for use with the victim of rape. They are (a) "I am so sorry this happened to you"; (b) "You're safe now"; (c) "No matter what you did, you did not deserve to be a victim of a crime"; and (d) "I know you handled the situation right because you're alive." It is essential that all aspects of the examination and treatment must be subject to the patient's decision in order for her to begin attempts to regain control over her life. Ensure that procedures are carried out gently, slowly, with full explanation of what is being done and why, and with responsiveness to the victim's wishes. Ask permission to begin the examination, especially the pelvic exam, in order to provide the victim with control in a situation that is most reminiscent of the rape. If patients refuse any aspect of the physical examination, note that in the medical record and abide by their wishes.

The conduct and documentation of the rape examination. Obtain the history of the assault in as factual a manner as possible. To decrease the stress for the patient, prepare her for the questions that will be asked and then ask her permission to begin the questioning. Explain that the questions you will ask are necessary to allow you to give her the best possible examination (and in the event she decides to prosecute, the best possible collection of evidence). Do not rush through the examination. Alternate the questions about humiliating acts that were done to her with questions that relate to her feelings about the violence. Examples of nonhumiliating questions include "Were you threatened?" and "Do you feel safe now?"

The findings from the physical examination, along with the victim's brief description of the rape, must be recorded and should include the following information: (a) length of time elapsed between the incident and the examination; (b) presence of abdominal, anal, pelvic, or skeletal muscle pain, dysuria (painful urination), or tenesmus (painful spasms of the anal or vesical sphincter with an urgent desire to evacuate the bowel or bladder); (c) type of sexual penetrations (oral, anal, vaginal); (d) culture of the throat and anus, if these areas were penetrated, (e) evidence of stains on clothing that fluoresce under an ultraviolet lamp; (f) the victim's activities following the assault, such as bathing, douching, urinating, or changing clothes; (g) precise location and description of the injuries including perineal lacerations, bruises, erythema, anal tears or cuts, as well as injuries to other body areas (take photographs or make sketches and place these in appropriate files, according to the institution's procedures); (h) results of the pelvic examination, done with a warm, water-moistened speculum. After the exam is completed, discuss protection against pregnancy and venereal disease. Be prepared to respond if the victim initiates a discussion about possible testing for exposure to the AIDS virus (see Jenny et al., 1990). Follow-up should be scheduled for six weeks, or sooner if there are any complaints.

Legal Assistance

Many states have statutes governing mandatory reporting of sexual assault with which the provider should be familiar.

Rapes may be reported with the intention of pressing charges against the offender, or they may be reported anonymously. Law-enforcement authorities strongly encourage victims to file, at minimum, an anonymous report. Such reports build a more accurate statistical picture of rape and make it harder to maintain the illusion that it is an infrequent crime. However, the decision to report and/or to prosecute is absolutely a personal one. Many police departments and prosecutors' offices maintain a rape response team consisting of specially trained female personnel. A properly trained police officer can be quite effective at the hospital emergency room in ensuring that evidence is collected correctly. Although currently most police officers have received at least some instruction regarding the proper questioning of rape victims, it is recommended that a victim advocate be present whenever a rape victim is questioned by law-enforcement authorities. Even months after rape, police questioning is highly disturbing to victims because it requires that they relive their assault. The presence of an advocate provides support to the victim and offers some degree of protection against harassing questioning.

Encourage Ventilation

An important step along the road to resolution of a traumatic experience is to desensitize it. Repetitive nightmares and "compulsive" retelling of an experience are natural psychological mechanisms through which a traumatic experience is gradually robbed of its impact on the victim. The provider can assist the process by encouraging the victim to talk about her experience. The emotional arousal that accompanies psychological trauma often creates an intense pressure to talk. Therefore most victims need no prodding to communicate the events that took place and the emotions they experienced before, during, and after their assault. Should it be necessary to assist the victim to verbalize her experiences, however, several avenues are available to heighten ventilation. First, the provider may use prompts that could include the following: Where were you when it happened? What did you see? What did you hear? What did you feel? How did you react? And what happened after he did that? (NOVA, 1987). Validate the key emotional reactions. For example, to the statement "I feel so ruined," the provider might respond, "It's understandable that you feel that way. It's a common reaction to what you've been through."

Involve Significant Others

Rape is both a personal crisis and a family crisis. Unfortunately, friends and family, like anyone in our culture, may hold false stereotyped views of rape. Because of these views, significant others can desert or further isolate the rape victim. Additionally, lack of understanding of the trauma of rape and the length of the recovery process may lead family members to fail to adequately support the victim.

The dynamics of the male partner's reaction to rape have been described by Rodkin, Hunt, and Cowan (1982). During the course of a support group for the male relatives of rape victims, they observed the men's reactions. Like the victims, many of the men experienced fear when they first learned of their partner's rape. Like victims, they experienced anxiety symptoms and disturbances in eating and sleeping. However, their symptoms subsided sooner than the victims' symptoms, often as soon as it was determined that the victim was safe and her injuries were not serious. Then a protective stage ensued during which the men felt very guilty for not having been protective enough and fearful that rape could happen again. During this period, they spent more time than usual with the victim. Finally, the male partners began to lose patience with the length of time recovery took and began to resent the victims' dependency. Often, they channeled this anger into increased work commitments that made them appear less understanding and supportive. The victims then became resentful because they perceived their partners as unresponsive to their needs. A book designed especially for the husbands, fathers, and male friends of rape victims is available (McEvoy & Brookings, 1984).

These observations suggest that it is wise to prepare family members before they join the victim and debrief them more extensively afterwards. Several goals in debriefing the family members of rape victims are suggested: (a) to challenge rape myths by portraying rape as a crime of violence, not a victim-precipitated sexual act; (b) to facilitate constructive release of feelings especially guilt and threats to self-esteem and masculinity; (c) to present a realistic picture of the length and phases of the recovery process through which rape victims pass; and (d) to support the important contributions of family members to the recovery period.

Make Practical Arrangements

Due to the psychological disequilibrium induced by a trauma such as rape, victims may be impaired or unable to meet their everyday commitments such as parenting and work. For example, dealing with an assault experience often strips the mother of the psychological "cushioning" necessary to respond to the demands of her children. The rape victim may be able to bring herself into psychological equilibrium faster if the needs and demands placed on her are lightened. The provider can explore with a victim the possibilities for obtaining short-term assistance in caring for her children from friends or relatives so that she has more time to attend to her own needs and more energy to devote to recovery. Help with children is not always desired by victims, however. As the following case illustrates, the need to care for children sometimes serves as an immediate coping strategy:

> Chris, a 47-year-old mother of a teenage daughter, called the rape crisis center after being raped in her home while her daughter was forced by the rapist to watch.
> Chris called the hot line seeking help for her daughter in the form of counseling referrals. She said her daughter was very upset by having to watch the rape. Chris was concerned about the effect of the rape on her daughter's future sexual life and relationships with men.
> The counselor provided referral information for both the daughter and the mother. But she also tried to suggest that while the daughter's needs were important, it also was essential for Chris to focus on the personal consequences of

the rape. She pointed out that the daughter's ability to accept and deal with what had happened is tied to the mother's ability to respond adaptively to the rape. While Chris responded positively to these suggestions, she continued to focus on her daughter's needs during the remainder of the 30-minute contact.

While a long absence from work is inadvisable, a short respite is clearly justified and beneficial. The provider can support the need to take some time from work and can assist in making arrangements with the victim's supervisor.

The victim's physical safety is the final practical issue that the specialist should address. The victim needs some immediate ways to begin rebuilding her sense of security and control over her life. Although restoring the sense of security is a long-term goal that will require assimilation of the assault, concrete steps may begin the process. If the victim were raped away from home by a stranger, she may need to stay somewhere else for several days while awaiting apprehension of the rapist. It is dangerous for the victim to return immediately to her old routines and routes while her attacker is still at large because stranger rapists often stalk their victims and are aware of their habits. Changes that may increase the victim's sense of security include changing her route to work, changing to daytime work hours, making contact with someone else who follows her route and traveling together, arranging for an escort to the parking lot, alerting her employer to the need to set up more secure areas for employees to park or to meet public transportation. Participation in a self-defense class may provide a greater sense of security to the victim as well. The victim raped at home can be assisted to consider ways in which the security of her residence can be increased. These include installing additional locks and changing the name on the mailbox. Frequently, however, victims choose to move to a different residence in the safest neighborhood they can afford.

In cases in which the victim is raped by someone she knows, a different set of problems is posed. When the victim can avoid

the offender, she can choose to move to a different neighborhood, change schools, and obtain an unlisted phone number.
But often these situations prove more difficult as they frequently
involve an offender who cannot be avoided because he is a
relative or coworker. To increase the victim's future security in
these instances, it is extremely helpful if some authority figure
makes it clear to the offender that his actions were undesired by
the victim, were wrong, and will result in serious consequences
should he approach the victim again. At work, sexual harassment guidelines may be used to remove the offender from the
victim's environment or at a minimum can serve as the justifica-
tion for a stern warning and future monitoring of the offender's
behavior.

In the following description, a counselor focused efforts on
meeting the victim's immediate needs and handling practical
arrangements:

> Beth is a 27-year-old woman with myasthenia gravis who
> was raped in her apartment by a man who followed her
> home from work. She went immediately to the hospital.
> When asked if she wanted friends or family called she said
> no. She did not wish anyone in her family to know what
> happened to her out of fear that they would use it to argue
> that she was too ill to take care of herself.
>
> The hospital staff then suggested calling the rape crisis
> center and having a victim advocate come to the hospital.
> Beth agreed to this. The advocate who responded had a
> masters' degree in counseling and had been working for the
> crisis center for 18 months. She spent two hours with Beth
> discussing her fears about her friends' and family's likely
> reactions to the rape. She stressed the need to mobilize
> some support system for her. Beth expressed concern that
> just as she had begun to regain control of her life this had
> happened. She was distraught that she had gone through so
> much to gain some mastery over her disease, only to have
> this occur. She said that she knew it was not her fault but
> felt as though fate were dealing her a very rotten hand.
>
> The advocate supported her belief that this was a rotten
> thing to happen to her and her belief that it was not her

fault. Again and again she was encouraged to think of someone she would be comfortable telling or going to for support. Finally, she did agree to telephone a friend, and arrangements were made for her to stay at the friend's house for the next few days. A police report was made and a physical exam was conducted. Beth was encouraged to seek further counseling or to call the rape center again. However, she did not recontact the center and could not be reached when follow-up calls were made.

Anticipate the Future

Victims as well as significant others can benefit from some discussion of the usual symptomatic responses to rape, the psychological impact of rape, and the length of time required to feel recovered. Such information may prevent more serious problems from developing by altering the expectations of involved others and by lessening the tendency for victims to blame themselves for symptoms and to feel they are taking too long to recover. The information that could be shared with victims and their families might be similar to the comments included in the paragraphs that follow. We have written this material as a provider would actually speak. Of course, these general comments need to be adjusted to the capacities and specifics of each individual case.

Expectations Regarding Physical Problems

"Rape is a trauma just like a major disaster such as a tornado or a bad car accident. Because of the shock these events cause to your system, some physical problems usually develop afterwards. You may experience symptoms you usually associate with extreme fear, such as pounding heart, shortness of breath, or dizziness. You may find your appetite or sleeping is changed as it is when you're worried about a major traumatic event like a court appearance or are under a lot of pressure at work. You may notice problems with sex that you've rarely experienced before. Often this is a signal that you're not ready to resume your former activities so quickly. It's perfectly okay to substitute other forms of feeling close and to avoid intercourse until you feel ready. Even though these physical symptoms are typical, they will still upset you. Seek a doctor's care, but be sure to tell him or her of your recent rape so that they can properly understand the cause of your symptoms."

Expectations Regarding Psychological Distress

"Nearly everyone experiences some psychological problems after a rape. Particularly upsetting are nightmares or flashbacks of the experience and the feeling that you need to talk about your experience over and over again until everyone around you is fed up. These are normal psychological processes that operate after a major trauma. Their purpose is to gradually wear down the frightening impact of an experience. They will eventually help you put the experience behind you. Even if you don't have any problems now, it's not unusual for some to crop up six months or a year from now. The problems that are most common are fears that you never had before or were not as severe, feeling bad about yourself and about life in general, conflicts in your intimate relationships, and problems getting back to your former enjoyment of sex. You may find that the rape has affected your whole family. Don't be surprised if you develop negative feelings about someone that are stronger or different from those you've had before. Try to talk your feelings over and be specific about what the other person can do to help you feel better. Family members may feel pretty impatient that it is taking you so long to get on top of things."

The Availability of Services

"You may find that although your enjoyment of life is less, you can live with your symptoms and cope. But, there may come a time when you feel that the toll is too great and you need relief. A number of people are available to help you at this point. I'm going to give you a sheet listing some of them so that you'll know who to call. Besides talking to someone privately, it is possible to become a member of a group made up of women who have experienced sexual assault. If it's okay with you, I'd like to call you at home in a few days and see how you're doing. Then, or at a later time, I'd be glad to see you again or help you make an appointment."

Expectations Regarding the Course of Recovery

"It usually takes over a year to feel fully recovered from sexual assault, to be able to think of it without losing control, and to feel the same level of health you enjoyed previously. Going through a court process, or anything else that reminds you of the assault, may make you feel temporarily worse after you thought you were finally getting on top of things. It's not unusual for there to be ups and downs on the way to recovery."

Arrange Follow-Up

Rather than relying on the victim to keep future appointments, we recommend asking permission to keep in contact by telephone. If this is acceptable, then the provider can telephone within a few days to talk with the victim and consider how she is coping. From her responses, it can be gauged whether there is interest in arranging further face-to-face appointments. If at any point the victim expresses the desire to forget her experience, obviously the provider would discontinue follow-up and close with the invitation to the victim to call at any time in the future that help is needed. If the victim does not want future appointments but is amenable to brief telephone contact, the specialist can place follow-up calls for several months at gradually lengthening intervals.

The follow-up of rape victims, however, is often difficult. Binder (1980) reported the results of attempted follow-up of 25 women who received rape-related emergency services. At three months postrape, clinicians were unable to contact 68% of them. Among explanations of the high attrition were the observation that victims moved or changed their phone numbers, displaced their anger about the assault onto the provider and refused to talk, and did not want to be reminded of their assault. At the same time, some of these individuals possessed characteristics that rendered them more vulnerable to assault and less accessible to follow-up such as transience, intravenous drug use, severe mental retardation, and serious mental illness.

There is widespread agreement that a considerable amount of improvement occurs in the first three months following a sexual assault. To date, empirical data have failed to demonstrate that immediate interventions hasten recovery or lessen long-term problems. For example, brief behavioral therapy was designed as prophylactic treatment to prevent the development of phobic reactions and was offered immediately after rape (Kilpatrick, Veronen, & Resick, 1979b). Unfortunately, repeated assessment only proved more successful than administration of the treatment in reducing rape-induced aftereffects. Studies of alternate interventions must continue to ensure that those techniques that are widely used are also effective.

CRITERIA OF RECOVERY

We think of recovery as the victim-to-survivor process. It is the process by which a victim not only survives a sexual assault but "survives standing up," as one of our colleagues has termed it. The abilities that we would like to see in a person who is recovered from sexual assault are described below (Harvey, 1990).

Memory. The individual has control over the remembering process and not the reverse. The individual can elect to recall or not recall events that previously intruded unbidden into awareness, taking the form of frightening dreams, troubling flashbacks, and distressing associations.

Integration of memory and feeling. Memory and affect are joined. Things are remembered with affect that is appropriate in intensity to the thing remembered. Sad memories elicit sadness once again.

Affect tolerance. Affect is no longer overwhelming: feelings can be felt and named and endured without overwhelming arousal, without dissociation, and without numbing.

Symptom mastery. Symptoms of anxiety, depression, and sexual dysfunction have receded and are more tolerable and predictable.

Attachment. The individual is reconnected with others; the pull to isolation and detachment is replaced with a new or restored capacity for affinity, trust, and attachment.

Meaning. The individual has assigned some tolerable meaning to the trauma and to the self as trauma survivor. Some victims will discard the sense of being damaged by their experience and embrace instead the belief that personal strength and compassion have been enhanced. Losses have been named and mourned and given a meaning that allows the victim to move forward through life. Feelings of self-blame have largely been replaced by new or restored self-esteem. Critical, obsessive review of the past has been replaced by more realistic assessment of it.

Consistent with the model presented in Chapter 2, these criteria of recovery are not conceptualized as achievable only through formal intervention. The criteria do serve well as goals to strive for in psychotherapeutic treatment, however. Individual psychotherapy with rape victims is the subject of the remainder of this chapter.

INTEGRATIVE TREATMENT OF NONRECENT RAPE

The material that follows describes an integrative approach to the treatment of the nonrecent victim. The conceptual foundation of the approach is cognitive/behavioral in that the aftereffects of rape are seen as conditioned fear reactions, avoidance responses to the situations that trigger the fear, and associated alterations in central beliefs about safety, esteem, trust, intimacy, and control. The following material builds on the pioneering innovations that characterized Stress Inoculation Therapy (SIT) as developed by Veronen and Kilpatrick (1983) and modified by Foa, Rothbaum, Riggs, and Murdock (1990). Because this presentation is intended as a guide to clinical practice, greater flexibility existed than was possible in earlier efforts to create treatment manuals for research. The main modifications in the present approach as contrasted with SIT include the focus on the development of a therapeutic relationship, which is necessary if one is to work with clients whose assets do not include the ready ability to form trusting relationships; an expanded discussion of methods for achieving cognitive reappraisal and restoring mastery; and the absence of a suggested duration and sequence of techniques. Because of the variability of victims' responses to the various phases of treatment, the length of therapy may range from brief (<25 sessions) to long term. The components of the integrative approach to treatment of rape aftereffects include (a) assessing rape resolution and the rape-relatedness of presenting symptoms; (b) developing a relationship; (c) processing painful memories of the trauma; (d) reformulating shattered beliefs; (e) restoring mastery; and (f) treatment of specific symptomatic aftereffects, including anxiety (fears, avoidance reactions, intrusion), depression, sexual dysfunction, and relationship difficulties.

Clinical experience of many in the field is that group treatment alone or as an adjunct to individual therapy is the treatment program of first choice for victims of sexual violence; yet, there are several situations under which treatment directed at emotional processing of rape trauma is not appropriate. Poor candidates include: (a) persons who do not have an organized day and something else to do besides therapy; (b) persons suffering from borderline personality disorder who have addressed psychological trauma by cutting or slashing themselves in order to feel alive, or drinking or taking drugs in order to numb themselves; and (c) persons who are still suicidal, still drinking heavily, still drugging themselves heavily, living with their perpetrator, or still having contact with the perpetrator. The first order of business with any patient involves safety, self-care, and stabilization of life routines. This may mean treating alcoholism and drug abuse before you treat trauma. It may mean employing a considerable number of behavioral self-help techniques and self-care journals. Some people who seek help in outpatient and inpatient treatment facilities have experienced repeated victimizations at various periods across their lifespan beginning with incest in early childhood. We have not addressed treatment of incest survivors because other excellent sources are available (Briere, 1988; Courtois, 1988).

It must be stated at the outset that there is little evidence of effectiveness of any therapeutic approach designed for rape victims. Research in this area is very difficult and few have met the challenges. Most of the studies that do exist have examined group interventions (Becker & Skinner, 1983; Cryer & Beutler, 1980; Resick et al., 1989). The bulk of the literature on individual psychotherapy consists of evaluations of behavioral interventions. Included in this group are studies that examined the effectiveness of systematic desensitization (Becker & Abel, 1981; Frank & Stewart, 1983, 1984; Turner, 1979; Wolff, 1977); cognitive therapy for depression and anxiety (Frank & Stewart, 1984); emotional flooding involving prolonged imaginal exposure to disturbing fear cues (Haynes & Mooney, 1975); and packaged therapy that combines multiple interventions (Kilpatrick & Amick, 1985; Pearson, Poquette, & Wasden, 1983). In general, the results of these studies suggest positive outcomes for women who are three or more months beyond rape at the start of therapy. There have been very few comparative studies of alternate therapies for rape, and those that have been published tend to find no significant differences in effectiveness. Accumulated clinical wisdom suggests, however, that it is a *major* mistake to attempt to look for linkages between a person's childhood development and a recent rape. Such a tack belittles the importance of the trauma and reinforces the myth that the victim somehow was responsible for what happened to her (Spiegel, 1987). Several reviews of this literature are available (Ellis, 1983; Foa, Olasov & Steketee, 1987; Holmes & St. Lawrence, 1983).

Even a cursory review of the treatment evaluations reveals some critical deficiencies in the literature including the absence of control or compassion groups from whom can be gauged the simple effects of the passage of time on rape recovery. In addition, therapy durations in many studies were very brief (4 to 10 sessions). Such brief therapy durations may be realistic only in uncomplicated cases of single, relatively recent victimizations among previously well-functioning women. Treatment studies also have not adequately reflected clinical reality. Caseloads consist primarily of women who have delayed seeking treatment for years and manifest the effects of violence compounded with their individual psychology, the negative reactions of their social network, the consequences of avoidance behaviors, and the deleterious impact of intervening life events. Most treatment studies have been focused on cases in which there has been a relatively short delay between assault and treatment initiation. Work with rape victims cannot wait for badly needed feedback on effectiveness. Informed refinements in our approaches are hampered by the absence of systematic evaluations, however.

Assess Rape Resolution

When pretherapy interviewing reveals an assault history, the possibility must be considered that the rape is resolved and is unrelated to the presenting symptoms. If so, the fact of an assault history would not influence normal treatment planning. When rape is unresolved and is a source of symptoms, however, the need for a treatment plan that addresses resolution of trauma is suggested. Unresolved sexual trauma occurs when a woman is raped, shares little or no information about the experience with others, and is unable to settle her reactions to the experience (Burgess & Holmstrom, 1979). Several criteria exist that the clinician can consider to determine whether intensive psychotherapeutic work needs to be directed toward a client's remote assault experience (Forman, 1980).

Ability to Discuss the Rape

The ability of the victim to discuss her assault and its aftermath openly but without undue emotions is an indication of resolution. "This is particularly so if the event is integrated into the past in a meaningful way, without either glibness or overreacting. . . . Incomplete or maladaptive resolution is seen in expressions of outrage, blame, and vindictive motives concerning various elements of the criminal justice system" (Forman, 1983, p. 518). Reluctance to discuss a sexual assault is a clear indication of nonresolution.

Postrape Responses

Few women experience no symptoms after a sexual assault. The victim who denies that she is experiencing or ever experienced any rape-related symptoms may be coping with her experience by encapsulating it. Postrape symptoms that were not evident or not as severe prerape clearly suggest a relationship to rape. Particularly suggestive of unresolved sexual trauma are persistent phobias, guilt feelings, lowered self-esteem, and avoidance of sexuality (Burgess & Holmstrom, 1979).

A comparison of the victim's preassault to postassault adjustment also may be revealing. Coping behaviors that are regressive compared to the victim's prerape behavior are suggestive of unresolved assault, as is the occurrence of an increased number of nonnormative crises and life changes (Forman, 1983).

Meaning Ascribed to the Rape

The meaning given to an assault by the victim and by her significant others is related to the likelihood of resolution. Resolution is less likely to occur when responsibility for the assault is ascribed to the victim, particularly if she is experiencing guilt and self-blame. Resolution is more likely to be associated with views of the rape as a turning point, or a terrible but growth- or insight-inducing experience.

Social Support

If the rape resulted in permanent deterioration in the victim's social support system, the likelihood of successful resolution is reduced. Total avoidance of social contact with men or clear-cut deterioration of relationships also suggest an unresolved sexual assault. Also indicative of unresolved sexual assault are instances where the victim has informed no one about her experience.

Evidence of Overreaction to a Minor Event

Occasionally the clinician will encounter a client who is experiencing obvious psychological disequilibrium and serious symptoms in the context of what appears to be a disagreeable but relatively minor sexual molestation. These instances suggest that a reactivation of an earlier unresolved sexual assault has occurred. The recent experience may have opened the floodgates to the feelings and reactions generated by the earlier assault. The assault that requires clinical attention, then, is not solely the recent one but the earlier, unresolved one.

Time Since Rape

The length of time since an assault occurred has been noted to be a poor predictor of residual impact or the likelihood of resolution (Forman, 1983). In fact, victims raped years ago may be less likely than recent victims to have resolved their assaults because of the less accepting social climate they faced and the unavailability of crisis services.

A short case summary follows of a woman whose experience is an extreme—but not uncommon—example of the emergence during the course of ongoing therapy of long unresolved sexual trauma:

Elizabeth entered therapy following numerous bouts with depression that were infringing more and more on her academic performance. She was referred to therapy by her mother's psychiatrist and was seen by a female clinician in private practice. For the first three years of therapy, Elizabeth revealed nothing about physical and sexual assault. When she did begin to focus on her experiences, her references were tentative and she was reticent to fully accept her experiences as fact. With support and reassurance, Elizabeth was able to share the following experience with her therapist:

"I was about five or six the first time. Mother was in the hospital for depression and housekeepers were taking care of us during the day until father got home from work. I really don't remember the first time, and I just remember some of the details. What I remember most clearly is the time Dad made me take his penis in my mouth. He warned me not to make any noises. Well I just couldn't help it. I was terrified, but who was there to hear me? My sister was asleep, and my mother was in the hospital. He also put his penis in my bottom. After he was finished he made me say my prayers. I remember how funny it felt to say, 'Now I lay me down to sleep, I pray the lord my soul to take,' because I did. I'd always been scared saying this prayer but then I prayed anything would stop it all.

"After Dad left I felt down there, and there was blood. I was really scared but I didn't tell anyone. The first person I've told in 25 years is you."

After a review of the considerations listed above, the clinician is in a position to gauge the extent to which a remote sexual assault has been adaptively resolved and to estimate the likelihood that the presenting symptoms are related to sexual trauma. If the past sexual assault appears to be incompletely resolved, therapeutic assistance in assimilation of the experiences is indicated. As always, treatment begins with the establishment of a therapeutic relationship with the client.

Build a Relationship

The case of Elizabeth illustrates dramatically that the ability to discuss the painful details of a long-hidden sexual assault requires the existence of a secure therapeutic relationship. The establishment of a strong relationship can take anywhere from one day to a year—or as in Elizabeth's case—over a year. Particularly in cases where sexual assault occurred at an early age, there may be considerable interference with the normal development of trust and the ability to relate to others. Therefore, establishment of a relationship with victims of nonrecent rape is a primary therapeutic goal. Techniques beyond those geared toward basic relationship building should be held in abeyance until the clinician observes in him- or herself and in the client signs of a working relationship.

Earlier, we discussed some of the positive steps to building a relationship. Along the road to a therapeutic relationship, however, the therapist may also encounter a number of resistances to recovery from rape. Resistances can include behaviors that are characteristic of the client's habitually disturbed attitudes toward people (Wolberg, 1967). Attitudes that can delay or interfere with the establishment of a therapeutic relationship include clinging dependency, fear of getting too close, hostility, submissiveness, perfectionism, distrust, and detachment. Dependency, for example, may require that the clinician recognize the client's needs but also explain that experience suggests that making all the decisions will inhibit self-growth. It is out of respect for self-growth that clinicians are not more active. Such an explanation may help avert some of the hostility at what the client may be perceiving as negligence or rejection. The client who fears getting too close may chart out a therapeutic course where a retreat follows every new revelation. Such clients often fear harm should they reveal too much. The clinician may have to undergo a number of tests to demonstrate that he or she is not malevolent or potentially destructive. Finally, hostility and guilt may identify a client who automatically expects the clinician to condemn or punish for past behavior. The client may feel contempt for the clinician who fails to act as a strong authority "should" respond and may desire a more competent (more punitive) clinician. As clients recognize that they can speak their mind, they may begin to reevaluate their concept of the clinician as an arbitrary authority and develop feelings of warmth.

The following clinician behaviors stand as evidence of a working relationship: a feeling or conviction that he or she likes the client, will be able to help the client, is making contact with the client, and that the client is responding well to the relationship (Wolberg, 1967). The following behaviors suggest the client's engagement in the relationship: evidences of liking, feeling relaxed with the clinician, and being confident of the clinician (Wolberg, 1967). On the basis of a secure foundation, more specific treatment goals such as assimilation of the experience may be pursued.

Foster Processing of Painful Memories

Talking about painful memories helps to strip them of their distressing potential and return a sense of control to the victim. Before beginning the processing of memories, it is necessary to provide a rationale for asking the client to do something that in the short run will make her feel worse. The following model was developed by Foa, Rothbaum, Riggs, and Murdock (1990):

> It is not easy to digest painful experiences. If you think about the rape or are reminded of it, you may experience extreme fear and other negative feelings associated with the assault. It is unpleasant to feel this way, so most people tend to push away fearful, painful memories or ignore them. We may tell ourselves things like, "Don't think about it, time cures all." Other people may even advise you to use such tactics believing that this is the best way to cope with traumas. Also, friends, relatives, or partners may feel uncomfortable hearing about the rape and may subtly influence you not to talk about it. Unfortunately, with highly traumatic events, ignoring your feelings and fears does not make them go away, and therefore these memories recur. (If trying to ignore the experience stopped it from affecting you, you would not be here.) Often the experience comes back to haunt you through nightmares, flashbacks, phobias, and other ways because it is "unfinished business." What we are going to do is the opposite of our tendency to avoid. We will help you to process the experience by having you remember what happened and stay with it long enough to

get more used to it. The goal is to be able to have these thoughts, talk about the rape, or see cues associated with the rape without experiencing the intense anxiety that is disrupting your life. We know from research that this treatment is effective: if you expose yourself to a memory, image, or feared situation long enough, your fear and anxiety will decrease. (pp. 5-6)

Elements to be recalled include any features about the situation surrounding the assault including sights, sounds, or smells, and anything that was said; feelings experienced just before, during, and after the event and now as the memory is recalled; responses that occurred including physiologic reactions as well as overt behaviors; and what the victim thinks about each of these elements. Foa et al. (1990) suggests the following instructions:

I'm going to ask you to recall the memories of the assault. I'll ask you to close your eyes so you won't be distracted. I will ask you to recall these painful memories as fully and as vividly as possible. I don't want you to tell a story in the third person, but to describe it in the present tense, as if it were happening now, right here. You will close your eyes and tell me in detail what you see and feel. We'll work together on this. If you start to feel too uncomfortable and want to run away or avoid it by leaving the image, I will help you stay with it. (p. 9)

Support and reassurance are important aids to bringing out painful memories (Burgess & Holmstrom, 1979). For example, where the offender was a friend or relative, the victim may be struggling to avoid thinking about and exposing the negative characteristics of those she loves. The clinician may offer support that people frequently hold conflicting feelings about close acquaintances. Recognizing these contradictory feelings, rather than ruining a relationship, can make it more open, realistic, and stronger. Some victims may believe that their feelings are so strong that should they open up "Pandora's box," they will lose control and stay angry forever. Reassurance may help the victim realize that it is failure to discuss these feelings rather than discussing them that is more likely to lead someone to feel angry forever. Furthermore, the clinician is there to assist the victim to proceed at a pace that she can handle. Multiple exposure to the memories in imagination usually are necessary to achieve habituation and control over the process of recalling. It is important to provide frequent encouraging feedback on the progress the client is making in desensitizing the memories.

Often, the constraints that have kept the memories suppressed for so long are still apparent to the clinician. The victim who has been unable previously to share her experience with anyone frequently requires assistance to facilitate remembering and verbalizing. Consider the following instance:

> Cindy is a 20-year-old, single, first-year college student. Her presenting problems included being overweight. Additionally, she stated, "I'm not exactly sure, but I don't think I care too much for men." She experiences anxiety attacks including revulsion, nausea, and tenseness whenever she believes a man is interested in her in a romantic sense. She relates these problems to her father's restrictiveness and to her weight problem. (She is approximately 60 pounds overweight.)
>
> Cindy states that she has had many boyfriends starting at an early age. She was first kissed at age 12 and reported enjoying it. She further stated that she had no problem with closeness or touching until she reached approximately 14 to 16 years of age. After that age, any contact of a "boyfriend-girlfriend" nature revolted her and precipitated only thoughts of escape. She had attempted to reciprocate and "go along with it" but could not bring herself to do it. She also denies feelings of attraction to women and states that if she ever did feel such interest she would "ostracize herself from society."
>
> In response to questions regarding her sexual assault history, Cindy reported that at age 13 she was cornered in a barn by a cousin who tried to force her to kiss him. She doesn't remember this as having been traumatic or particularly significant. But she does state that she has a long-

standing hatred of this cousin and can't recall any reason why.

In cases where the inability to verbalize freely is limited, techniques such as deep breathing or muscle relaxation may assist the victim to recall her experience. Use of these methods also are desirable because they promote counterconditioning wherein a new set of responses can become associated with the memories. The following instructions for teaching controlled breathing were developed by Foa et al. (1990):

> Most people realize that our breathing affects the way we feel. For example, when we are upset people may tell us to "take a deep breath and calm down." However, we don't need to take a *deep* breath, but rather a normal breath and exhale slowly. For example, when our ancestors, thousands of years ago, were walking through the forest and spotted a lion, they probably gasped and held their breath. When the lion walked away, they sighed in relief (exhaled). There- fore, it is *exhalation* that is associated with relaxation, not inhalation.
>
> While concentrating on the exhalation and dragging it out, we will also have you say the word CALM to yourself while you are exhaling, and I will say it aloud. [May also use RELAX if client prefers.] CALM is a good word to use because in our culture it is already associated with nice things. If we are upset and someone tells us to "calm down," usually it is associated with comfort and support. It also sounds nice and can be dragged out to match the long, slow exhalation: c-a-a-a-a-a-a-l-m.
>
> In addition to concentrating on slow exhalation while saying CALM to yourself, we want to slow your breathing down. Very often when people become frightened or upset, they feel like they need more air and may hyperventilate. However, usually just the opposite is true. Unless we are preparing for one of the three "Fs" (fight, freeze, flee) in the face of a real danger, we often don't need as much air as we are taking in. When we hyperventilate and take in more air, it signals our bodies to prepare for one of the three "fs" and to keep it fueled with oxygen, just like a runner before a

race takes deep breaths to fuel her body with oxygen and continues to breathe deeply and quickly throughout the race. Usually when we hyperventilate, though, we are tricking our bodies and what we really need to do is to slow down our breathing and take in *less* air. We do this by pausing between breaths to space them out more. After your slowed exhalation, literally hold your breath for a count of four [may be adjusted if necessary] before you inhale the next breath. (p. 3)

Where forgetting is as complete as that described in Cindy's case history, hypnosis may be helpful. Hypnosis produces a relationship with the clinician where the client accepts suggestions and experiences psychic and somatic effects. Hypnosis may modify or remove repression, which may be helpful in restoring lost memories. Wolberg presents a script for the clinician to follow in inducing hypnosis through muscle relaxation (Wolberg, 1980, pp. 223-234).

Promote Reformulation of Shattered Beliefs

Rape victims are no different from nonvictimized women in the extent to which they subscribe to myths about rape (Koss & Dinero, 1989b). Many misperceptions about rape may exist. It is helpful to learn what the victim thinks about the cause of her rape, the degree to which she feels responsible, and the changes in her identity and thoughts about others that she has experienced. Cognitive psychological theories teach us that the victim's thoughts on these topics are important correlates of the symptoms that she experiences.

Several styles of thinking about rape occur spontaneously and seem to be associated with recovery (Burgess & Holmstrom, 1979). They include suppression ("I don't think about it at night; I try to keep my mind off it"); minimalization ("Compared to what a young girl would experience after a rape, my experience wasn't that bad"); rationalization ("He was a sick man who needed help, and it was just a one-in-a-million chance that he broke into my house"); and dramatization (i.e., repeatedly expressing the anxiety and thereby dissipating it). Self-affirming ways exist whereby rape eventually can be assimilated as a positive event. These include considering the event as a consciousness-raising experience ("I wasn't much of a feminist before my rape but it kind of crystallized for me the way women are treated in our society."); as a life-appreciation lesson ("During the rape I said to myself, 'If I come out of this alive, there's a lot of things I'm going to change in my life and I'll be grateful for every minute of every day I live.' "); and as a challenge to overcome ("I've always been a strong person. I realize that now that I've been raped, I'm at a crossroads" [Kilpatrick & Veronen, 1982]). These examples illustrate the cognitions that occur spontaneously in the rape resolution process.

Therapeutic work on cognitive appraisal actually begins during the processing of painful memories when the clinician elicits a victim's thoughts about the cause of the assault, her reactions during and immediately afterward, and her views of herself and others now that this has happened. Particularly relevant are beliefs about safety, trust, power, esteem, and intimacy that are thought to be challenged or shattered by rape (McCann et al., 1988). Cognitions are maladaptive when they operate to maintain symptoms (e.g., thoughts such as, I know I'll never be the same after this; I'm damaged for life. No man would ever want to marry me; Sex will never have meaning for me again; That shows you how bad my judgment about men is; My mother told me was I asking for it because I dressed like a slut).

Therapeutic handling of maladaptive cognitions involves tactfully challenging them on the basis of their factual accuracy or the logic of their conclusions (e.g., "Yes it's true that your dress was extreme, but does every woman who dresses punk get raped?"). At the same time beliefs that are adaptive are supported and reinforced. The goal is to assist the victim to reformulate her appraisal of her experience into terms that will promote adaptive coping in the future and support a decision to get on with her life. Such reappraisals do not minimize rape but aim to guide the victim to positively assimilate it into her picture of who she is, how she got that way, where she is going from here, and what other people mean to her.

Integration of rape into one's beliefs hinges on sharing it with significant others. As long as an assault remains a dark secret, the victim must continually wonder if others have guessed or would respond differently if they knew. Thus a constant source of tension is introduced into human relationships. Telling others may not be easy when the secret has been hidden for months or years. It may be helpful to discuss in advance who to share the information with, how to present the experience to them, and what their reaction is likely to be.

Restoring Mastery

The feedback that comes from concrete life experiences undertaken outside of therapy may positively influence the reappraisal process. The clinician can be helpful by guiding the survivor toward involvements that satisfy important needs and support changes in thinking. A range of possibilities exist for therapeutic activities, and they must be tailored to the individual client's needs. The following examples are but a few of the possibilities. Those who feel damaged and soiled by the rape may greatly benefit from attending a support group. These groups often are led by rape survivors who provide positive, vibrant models of lives that are not ruined. Further, the supportive feedback of group members may counteract beliefs that one has been rendered unlovable. Sometimes participation in a self-defense course may help solidify changes in views about personal control and power. Also helpful can be turning attention to other ways of regaining control over life such as moving, reorganizing personal priorities, and making plans to achieve a new goal (which could include reaching a career objective or adopting a more healthy life-style).

The following case describes how a clinician consistently supported adaptive coping during a two-year course of therapy:

Joyce is a woman in her late forties who was raped during ongoing therapy focused on problems of general self-esteem. She was accosted by a stranger as she was entering her car. He forced her to drive to a remote area where he raped her and then shot her. During the interval she was with him, she made numerous attempts to make some connection with him. She did so hoping that she could thus influence him. Following the rape and shooting, the police found Joyce and brought her to the hospital. Once there, the emphasis was on life-supporting interventions. The rape took secondary importance to the physical assault.

She was in the hospital for a prolonged period during which time her therapist continued to see her. As a result of the shooting, Joyce was left disabled and needed several months of rehabilitative therapy. While she was recuperating, the police interviewed her many times. She found their continual questioning and probing to be analogous to another assault.

Generally Joyce's reaction was one of feeling violated. Her life had been violated, as well as her body, and then the police continued to violate her mind and memories. Initially she did not express anger. When she did begin to do so, it was directed toward the police, and then eventually toward the rapist. It was harder for her to rage at the rapist as she had purposefully tried to connect with him, and she continued to try to sort out his motives and needs. Eventually, she was able to let go of these attempts and to permit herself to be enraged at him for violating her.

The course of therapy was one of gently and solidly supporting Joyce. She determined how much of the incident she wanted to deal with and at what pace. Frequently the first 40 minutes of the hour-long sessions were devoted to tangential material, and the last 20 minutes were focused on Joyce's feelings. This pattern was supported by the therapist, who wanted to help her reestablish (a) a sense of control, and (b) a sense of potency. She did not want to further "violate" Joyce by pressing forward faster than Joyce was prepared to move.

At this time, about two years after the rape, Joyce is once again living on her own and is contemplating what type of work to return to doing. She has continued pain and a disability. An acceptance of the numerous changes she has had to make is gradually building. She no longer sees herself solely as the victim. She is aware of her strengths, which she has utilized in coping with this major trauma—and is connecting more with that awareness versus the sense of impotence and violation that flooded her initially. She relies more on friends and family than in the past and has found increased depth in these relationships than she knew previously.

Joyce was a strong and courageous woman before the rape, and she continues to be so now.

The next case summary illustrates the accomplishment of similar treatment goals; however, the absence of the complications associated with physical injuries allowed treatment to be completed in four months. The case is a good illustration of the resolution of rape-related problems through emotional processing and reappraisal.

Kathy also is in her late forties. She was raped by a stranger while jogging. Her experience was presented in more detail earlier.

Initially, Kathy was seen by a rape crisis center advocate who helped her through the medical exams and police investigation. Treatment was clearly crisis-oriented. The advocate referred Kathy to a woman's therapy collective. The development of rape-related fears led Kathy to seek therapy approximately one month after her rape.

Therapy focused on affirming Kathy's strengths and encouraging her to become involved in projects that would put her in a position of controlling her environment. She became active in a "green light" project in her neighborhood as a result of this suggestion. The therapy also centered on learning some assertive, self-defense maneuvers. An attempt was made to validate Kathy's fears and at the same time to help her put them into perspective. She continued therapy for four months.

Where clinical judgment reveals that a victim's symptoms are so severe that they interfere with the process of therapy, or when symptoms are failing to resolve as a result of the methods suggested above, specific procedures to treat target symptoms are needed.

Treat Target Symptoms

When the rape-related symptoms of anxiety, depression, sexual dysfunction, and relationship difficulties remain disturbing and intense, they must be targeted for specific attention. It is not possible to provide comprehensive information on the treatment of each of these symptoms, to which whole books are devoted. Instead, we have attempted to highlight useful techniques that have demonstrated effectiveness for victims of rape.

Anxiety

Anxiety, fears, and intrusive thoughts are among the most long-lasting symptoms induced by rape. Among the treatment approaches to fear and anxiety in rape victims are the visual-kinesthetic dissociation treatment derived from neurolinguistic programming (Koziey & McLeod, 1987) and cognitive/behavioral treatment (Veronen & Kilpatrick, 1983; Foa et al., 1990). The cognitive/behavioral approach consists of procedures to lessen the distress created by traumatic memories and to develop coping skills for use in distressing situations. The components of the cognitive/behavioral approach are summarized below.

(1) *Preparation for treatment.* Clients need a realistic appraisal of what a therapist expects can be accomplished by the proposed treatment. For example, "The goal of treatment is not to eliminate anxiety. Anxiety is a fact of life. The goal is to learn to manage your anxiety" (Veronen & Kilpatrick, 1983). Also important is a rationale for how the symptoms developed and an explanation of the therapeutic techniques that are proposed to lessen symptoms. Foa et al. (1990) suggests the following model:

> Rape is experienced by most women as a sudden traumatic event in which the woman fears she will be killed. She may

be overpowered, incapacitated, held down, restricted, or in some way, made to feel powerless. Sex is then forced upon her. Fear, anxiety, anger, depression . . . following a rape are normal responses. The development of rape-related fear can be understood through a process called classical conditioning. Forced sex is an intrinsically unpleasant and aversive experience which brings about automatic responses of pain or fear of being harmed or killed. Persons, situations, or events which are present at the time of the assault become associated with the rape experience and may also bring about negative emotional responses. Rape-related fears may also generalize; that is, persons, situations, or events which appear to be similar to those present at the time of the assault may also bring about fear and anxiety and other responses. (p. 5)

Next, information about assault-related fear stimuli and the avoidance reactions they trigger are collected. Areas in which information is needed include the following: (a) external cues such as objects or situations that are sources of discomfort; (b) internal cues such as thoughts, images, or impulses that provoke anxiety, shame, or disgust; (c) feared consequences of the cues; and (d) avoided situations or objects (Foa et al., 1990). This information is used to develop a list of feared situations that can be imagined in the therapy room as well as faced in the real world. Examples of typical fears that are the target of treatment among rape victims are being alone, going places alone, men who look like the assailant, strange men, going out, seeing violence, and darkness. To indicate how strong a level of discomfort is caused by a particular thought or scene, a scale is used where 100 stands for extreme upset and 0 stands for no discomfort whatsoever. Ratings of discomfort on this scale can be used to monitor the progress in anxiety reduction within and across sessions.

(2) *Exposure to imagery.* The goal of exposure is to obtain habituation when the stimuli associated with a rape are remembered and the associated physiologic and cognitive responses are experienced, but the feared outcome no longer occurs. Exposure may occur in imagination as the client vividly remembers,

or exposure can occur in vivo when the client remains in feared situations until the anxiety decreases. Foa et al. (1990) recommend that imaginal exposure takes place in therapy and in-vivo exposure be carried out as homework.

Taking situations from the data gathered in preparation for treatment, the client is asked to vividly imagine themselves in the situation. Objects such as a photo of the assailant or clothing worn during the assault may be brought to therapy if it enhances the imagery the client is able to experience. Details of the situations are varied systematically to accomplish exposure to the variety of stimuli to which anxiety has become generalized. Tape recordings may be made of the session for the client to play at home to increase the exposure to each scene. In the therapy session and on homework forms the client indicates the level of discomfort experienced on each exposure. Thus progress can be followed and the therapist has a guide for giving supportive feedback. For example, after decreasing anxiety Foa et al. (1990) suggest a comment such as, "You see, your anxiety decreases if you just continue to stay long enough in the situation you were afraid of," or, "I want you to notice that you are much less anxious than you were in the beginning of the session" (p. 10). Reinforcing comments such as, "You've done very well. It took some courage to stick it out even though you were quite afraid," should be made throughout exposure (p. 10).

(3) *Provision of coping skills.* To teach a coping skill a specific sequence is followed: define the new skill, tell what it can do, and how it is used; practice the skill on a problem unrelated to the assault; and then apply the skill to a rape-related problem.

Muscle relaxation and breathing control. These coping skills give the client a strategy for managing the physiologic components of fear. Procedures for teaching breathing control were reviewed previously. Muscle relaxation can be taught using the Jacobsonian (Jacobson, 1938) tension-relaxation contrast training. This procedure includes relaxation of all major muscle groups with the addition of controlled breathing at the end. A script therapists can use to make a relaxation tape is found in Wolberg

(1980, pp. 223-231). Clients take this tape home and practice using it twice daily.

Thought stopping. This skill is used to counter ruminative thinking. It is taught by asking the client to think the bothersome thought for 35 to 45 seconds. Then the therapist says in a loud voice, "STOP" (Foa et al., 1990; Veronen & Kilpatrick, 1983). This procedure is repeated several times and then the client is encouraged to silently verbalize the word "STOP."

Rational thinking. This skill is used to illustrate the impact of interpretations on the reactions one experiences and is the traditional ABC paradigm (*A* = antecedent event, *B* = belief about event, *C* = consequences [Beck, Ruch, Shaw, & Emery, 1979; Ellis & Harper, 1961]). This model demonstrates that the same event can lead to two different consequences in individuals whose beliefs differ. For example, the emotional consequences will vary greatly if a tapping noise is believed to be a branch blowing against the house as opposed to an intruder in the process of gaining entry.

There are five steps to rational thinking. To begin, the client generates an experience unrelated to the assault where she became upset, such as being overruled by her boss during a meeting. The first step of rational thinking requires the client to provide the *A* and *C* for the experience (*A* = being overruled; *C* = feeling anxious, upset, worthless). Next, the *B* or automatic assumption that links *A* to *C* is generated (*B* = My boss does not think I'm smart; he's rejecting me). Third, the reality or rationality of the assumption is tested by weighing the evidence for and against it. If the evidence is insufficient, the client can decide to throw out the assumption or try to get more information. Finally, when the evidence is insufficient, the assumption needs to be reformulated ("It would be preferable if the boss liked my ideas but it doesn't say anything about my worth as a person").

Guided self-dialogue. This skill teaches the survivor to focus on her internal dialogue and is modeled on Michenbaum's (1977) stress-inoculation procedures to prepare for a feared event such as surgery. Basically, stress inoculation is a lot like coaching. Irrational, faulty, or negative dialogue is identified, and rational, facilitative, task-enhancing, dialogue is substituted. Inner dialogue is created for four categories: preparing for the stressor; confronting and handling the stressor; coping with feelings of being overwhelmed; and reinforcing self-statements. Examples of self-statements are found in Veronen and Kilpatrick (1983). For example, to *prepare for the stressor* the client is asked to rehearse inner dialogue such as, "Don't think about how bad I feel; think about what I can do about it, " or, "I have the support and encouragement of people who are experienced in helping people deal with problems," and "I have already come a long way toward handling this problem, I can go the rest of the way easily." To *confront and handle the feared situation* the client may say, "One step at a time, I can handle the situation; there's no need to doubt myself, I have the skills needed to get through," or, "Focus on the plan. Relax . . . take a deep breath, I am ready to go." To *cope with feelings of being overwhelmed* the client may say, "I can expect my fear to rise, but I can keep it manageable"; "My fear is expected and it has enabled me to survive and avoid being killed, but I must manage its intensity and not let fear incapacitate me"; "This will be over soon"; "This fear may slow me down but it won't stop me"; or "I may feel nauseated and want to avoid the situation, but I can deal with it." *Reinforcing self-statements* at the completion of the stressful task include "I did it—I got through it, each time it will be easier"; "I am avoiding less and less, I am making progress"; and "When I manage the thoughts in my head, I manage my whole body." Self-statements can be written on index cards for the client to practice with at home.

Covert modeling and role playing. Role playing is the acting out of behaviors by rehearsing lines and actions. It helps the client substitute new behaviors and words for old ways of doing things. The client and the therapist take turns acting out scenes in which a feared situation is confronted, including what will be said and the actions that will be taken. The repeated practice of a behavior reduces anxiety and makes it more likely that the new behavior will be used when it is called for. Covert modeling is similar to role playing except that it is done in the imagination. With covert modeling one can have the client visualize in imagination the steps to complete a task and the feelings upon successful completion. Many experts consider it necessary to have a cognitive map of the possible outcome in order to achieve that outcome in actuality.

Depression

The cognitive approach is considered effective for use with victims of rape (Frank & Stewart, 1983). The relevance of cognitive techniques to rape-induced depression has been summarized by Frank and Stewart (1983):

> Beck (1972) theorizes that the individual's negative and distorted thinking is the basic psychological problem in depression. According to Beck, negative thoughts, even of brief duration, stimulate abnormal physiological reactions that are experienced as sadness, anxiety, anger, guilt or a variety of other negative emotions. . . .
>
> Beck further believes that depressive cognitive content is often related to thoughts of loss or perceived loss from one's personal domain. The personal domain includes the individual and his or her circle of significant others, together with things of value (objects, attributes, ideals, principles, and important goals). Rape victims frequently experience a number of losses in their personal domain. Often a rape may mean a significant reduction in the victim's friendship circle, either because individuals are frightened off by the rape event itself, or because of antagonistic social interactions which develop between the victim and those who make it clear to her that she ought to have handled the situation differently.
>
> Furthermore, rape often produces physical dislocation, in that rape victims frequently move from their place of residence, which can be another actual loss. The social disruption which follows a rape, as well as the enormous time commitment required to pursue a prosecution, often means

a victim loses her job or is forced to drop out of school either permanently or temporarily.

Not infrequently, the victim sees these temporary setbacks as not at all temporary, but rather magnifies them out of all proportion, viewing them as indicative of her abilities and her prospects for the future. Such over-generalized negative interpretation of events drives the recent victim into increased dysphoria, dejection and discouragement. Once the victim is reduced to a moderately depressed state, her perceptions, interpretations, and evaluations no longer require outside confirmation. . . . This negative view of the self and of the future also prevents the depressed victim from realistic testing of ideas, active problem solving, and use of appropriate help and advice from others. (p. 97)

Distortions in thought patterns result in selective attention to outside reality and inaccurate anticipation of consequences. Among thinking distortions are arbitrary inference (i.e., drawing a conclusion where evidence is lacking or supports a contrary conclusion); magnification (i.e., exaggeration of the meaning of an event); cognitive deficiency (i.e., disregarding important aspects of a life situation); dichotomous reasoning (i.e., overly simplified perception of events such as good versus bad or right versus wrong); and overgeneralization (i.e., generating a fallacious rule from a single incident). Cognitive treatment of depression is directed toward identifying these stylistic qualities of a client's thinking and developing an understanding of the connection between the thinking processes, affective experience, and maladaptive behavior.

Treatment consists of the following four procedures: the daily activity schedule; the mastery and pleasure method; the daily record of dysfunctional thoughts; and problem-solving techniques. The first two methods may be unnecessary in cases of mild depression. The Beck Depression Inventory (Beck, Ward, Mendelson, Mock, & Erbaugh, 1961) can be used initially to gauge the severity of depression and periodically to follow progress.

(1) *Daily activity schedule.* Activities are scheduled for every hour of the day. A list is made of the tasks to be done each day moving from the easiest to accomplish to the more difficult. Activities are checked off as they are accomplished. This procedure is particularly helpful with severe depression.

(2) *Mastery and pleasure record.* More good things may be happening than the client realizes. On the daily schedule, write "M" next to those activities that involved some mastery of a difficult situation and "P" next to those activities that brought some enjoyment.

(3) *Daily record of dysfunctional thoughts.* The daily record is based on the ABC method discussed previously. Whenever clients feels sad, they are instructed to stop and review their thoughts: "Try to remember what has been passing through your mind. You will probably find that these thoughts were very negative and that you believed them." During each session, the client's negative thoughts that were recorded during the previous week are considered and their accuracy evaluated. The clinician guides the client to reformulate more logical and correct alternative statements to their automatic negative thoughts. After this task has been accomplished, clients are instructed to correct their thinking on their own and to keep a record of their reformulations.

(4) *Problem-solving techniques.* Clients are taught procedures to follow when burdensome problems arise. The first step is to break problems down into steps; if at a loss for what to do, seek advice. Second, write down all the steps that have to be taken to solve the problem. Take one step at a time.

Sexual Dysfunction

A treatment package structured on the P-LI-SS-IT model (Annon, 1974) has been developed to treat rape-related sexual dysfunction (Becker & Skinner, 1983). The treatment is designed for the dysfunctional woman alone and does not require a sexual partner. Thus it can be used regardless of a woman's sexual orientation and partner status. The treatment is designed to involve 10 one-hour sessions weekly in either a group or individual format.

Becker's treatment approach involves moving a client through increasing levels of therapeutic intervention, starting and stopping according to her individual needs. The levels of intervention include giving permission (P); providing limited information (LI); making specific suggestions (SS); and providing intensive therapy (IT). The 10-session time estimate for treatment does not include sessions necessary for intensive treatment. The techniques that comprise this treatment approach are drawn from several sources including sensate focus exercises (Masters & Johnson, 1970); Kegel exercises (Deutsch, 1968; Kegel, 1952); masturbatory training (Kaplan, 1974); masturbatory conditioning (Marquis, 1970); the use of dilators (Annon, 1976); thought stopping (Geisinger, 1969); behavioral rehearsal (Lazarus, 1966); and systematic desensitization (Lazarus & Rachman, 1960; Wolpe & Lazarus, 1966).

Relationship Difficulties

Relationship difficulties can take the form of withdrawal from social participation as well as deterioration of established intimate relationships. Although both problems fall under the heading of "relationship difficulties," each necessitates its own therapeutic interventions.

The persistence of serious problems in a rape victim's established intimate relationships usually dictates the need for conjoint sessions with her partner to occur after initial work on rape resolution has been undertaken. To date, no clinical literature addresses the special impact of rape on a relationship. Forman (1983) suggests, however, that rape is more likely to have devastating effects on a newly formed relationship that lacks established communication patterns than on an existing relationship.

Conjoint therapy with couples who have been victimized by rape has not been studied systematically so we can only speculate about treatment approaches. Some of the statements made previously regarding work with significant others during the crisis period also may be relevant here. That is, attention may have to be devoted to clarifying misperceptions regarding rape and its impact, the length of the recovery process from rape, and the important role of involved others. Communication training (Lazarus, 1981), which focuses on development of sending skills and receiving skills, may be valuable:

When expressing ideas or conveying feelings, many people send messages that are vague, ambiguous, contradictory, and difficult to follow. To improve sending skills, the client learns about the importance of eye-contact, voice projection, body posture, the use of simple, concrete terms, the avoidance of blaming and pejorative remarks, forthright rather than manipulative intent and statements of empathy. Good receiving skills call for active listening, verification and acknowledgement, and rewarding the sender for communicating. Role playing and behavior-rehearsal are especially suited for promoting the development of communication skills. (Lazarus, 1981, p. 232)

Work with the rape victim whose level of social interaction is very low begins with consideration of the causes of the withdrawal. Withdrawal in a victim with a past history of good social participation and usable social skills often is an indication of depression. Interpersonal psychotherapy techniques (Klerman, Weissman, Rounsaville, & Chevron, 1984) may be helpful here because they are predicated on the ability of failed expectations in interpersonal relationships to generate depression and social withdrawal.

Social withdrawal that selectively involves heterosexual relationships suggests sexual anxiety that might best be approached through components of Becker's treatment package. Generalized social withdrawal in a rape victim with deficits in social skills may benefit from friendship training and social skills training (Lazarus, 1981). As Lazarus observes,

It may seem trite if not absurd to stress that friendship is predicated on sharing, caring, empathy, concern, self-disclosure, give-and-take, positive reinforcement, and complementarity, whereas power plays, one-upmanship, competitive striving, and self-aggrandizement are apt to undermine friendship and truncate the development of intimacy. Yet, when observing the behavior of many people, one wonders why these self-evident truths are so frequently ignored, and why people who neglect them are perplexed by their social isolation. In friendship training, one identifies and discusses the prosocial interactions that constitute affectionate interactions, and the client is urged to put them into practice. (1981, p. 234)

The components of social skills training that address the ability to express positive and negative feelings, and the ability to initiate, continue, and terminate conversations also can be employed.

SIX

Group Treatment for Survivors

In the course of their recovery, many rape victims will turn to rape crisis centers, women's advocacy centers, self-help organizations, and a variety of mental health facilities for support and assistance. Increasingly, the kind of support available in these settings is group support. Many, if indeed not most, community-based rape crisis centers offer drop-in discussion groups for women at any and all stages of recovery and rape survivor support groups for women six months or more postrape (Harvey, 1985). These groups provide rape victims with an opportunity to meet with other survivors in a safe, supportive, and egalitarian setting, and to both give and receive a degree of validation, solace, and understanding that may have eluded them in their daily lives. Generally, these groups are designed to perform an educative and empowering function as well as a therapeutic one and to normalize for survivors of sexual assault the psychological distress they may be feeling months or even years later. The emphasis is on "survivorship" not victimization, and the aim is to help women to understand and take charge of their own recovery (Sprei & Goodwin, 1983; Yassen & Glass, 1984).

Within the mental health field, too, and particularly among clinicians interested in the treatment of psychological trauma (Coons, Bowman, Pellow, & Schneider, 1989; Flannery, 1987;

Goodwin & Talwar, 1989; Herman & Schatzow, 1984; Janoff-Bulman, 1985b; Scurfield, 1985; van der Kolk, 1987b), group psychotherapy increasingly is viewed as a treatment of choice for individuals who have experienced life-threatening events, including sexual assault. The groups offered to rape victims by mental health settings are varied. They differ from one another in terms of treatment goals, duration, structure, selection criteria, format, and process. They include inpatient as well as outpatient groups, short-term behavioral groups to facilitate understanding and management of posttraumatic symptoms, short- and long-term supportive psychotherapy groups to address various aspects of rape trauma and assist with specific recovery tasks, and ongoing psychodynamic psychotherapy groups that encourage participants to work through traumatic memories and feelings in the relational context that group treatment offers.

In this chapter we review a wide range of treatment models and we consider the probable usefulness of various models for rape victims whose psychological attributes, needs, and circumstances may vary widely. The indices of recovery and resolution presented in Chapter 5 are again considered, first, in relationship to those attributes that most group treatment approaches share, and, when applicable, in terms of the means by which specific group models might address specific recovery issues. Various types of groups are described and briefly discussed, and three approaches are presented in some detail. These approaches reflect a feminist view of rape trauma and an approach to treatment influenced by an ecological view of psychological trauma and recovery. They are currently being implemented by clinical staff and clinical trainees at Cambridge (Massachusetts) City Hospital's Victims of Violence Program. These approaches—and other clinical interventions on behalf of victims—were developed in collaboration with community colleagues, including staff of the Boston Area Rape Crisis Center and the Women's Mental Health Collective.

RESEARCH ON GROUP TREATMENT

Despite the wide range of group treatment approaches that have been developed on behalf of rape victims and victims of other psychologically traumatizing events, little research has been conducted to assess the efficacy of group treatment per se and/or to examine the comparative efficacy of various group treatment models with respect to specific treatment goals and particular survivor populations. In her review of the literature on violence against women, Koss (1990) points out the lack of group treatment research in the sexual assault field and the need for evaluation studies of community-based treatment groups such as those developed by rape crisis centers and other feminist settings.

This gap in the literature is an important one. In one of the few studies available, Cryer and Beutler (1980) report that while the group approach they evaluated did appear to reduce isolation among rape victim participants, group participation also was associated with increased depression. Herman and Schatzow (1984) examined the self-report data of incest survivors participating in their short-term, task-oriented, survivor groups six months postgroup to find reported improvements in self-esteem and a lasting sense of reduced isolation, shame, and stigma. As a group, however, these participants did not report great improvements in other aspects of their lives: in their work situations, for example, or in the quality of their sexual relationships with partners. More recently, Resick et al. (1989) examined symptom and self-esteem data pregroup, immediately postgroup, and at 3- and 6-month follow-ups among 37 rape victims assigned randomly to one of three short-term behavioral groups or to a waiting list control group. The findings indicated improvement among all subjects studied, regardless of group assignment, and indicated no differences whatsoever due to group treatment approach. The groups that they studied included a stress inoculation group, a behavioral group, and a supportive psychotherapy group, each led by both a male and female therapist and consisting of six sessions plus a pregroup and postgroup interview. How different these groups actually were for the participants and what the effect of male-female coleadership may have been upon all groups is not clear. Certainly, sexual assault survivor groups with male-female coleadership are not normative in the field.

In general, the studies to date raise at least as many questions as they attempt to answer. Together their collective findings suggest that the workings of group psychotherapy are far more complex than is currently known. Which kind of group might be most effective for which victim at what stage of recovery and/or towards which recovery goals—and why—are questions that require empirical exploration.

THE RATIONALE FOR GROUP TREATMENT

With or without hard data, a number of authors have offered convincing rationales concerning the probable benefits of group treatment for rape victims (Sprei & Goodwin, 1983; Yassen & Glass, 1984); for victims of other types of sexual assault and abuse (Coons et al., 1989; Goodwin & Talwar, 1989; Herman & Schatzow, 1984); and for victims of traumatic and life-threatening events (Flannery, 1987; Janoff-Bulman, 1985b; Scurfield, 1985; van der Kolk, 1987b). Among these and other authors, at least nine benefits of group treatment have been identified and discussed. These are identified and briefly summarized in the paragraphs below:

• *Reduced isolation.* Because sexual assault involves the willingness of one person to violate and humiliate another in deeply personal ways, rape can lead to a heightened fear and mistrust of others and to a pervasive sense of shame and separateness. In the face of these feelings, rape victims can withdraw from the company of others and suffer alone. The group offers these victims an opportunity to meet with others who have shared their experience and know what it is like. The group can thus reduce isolation and counter self-isolating behaviors that may be complicating the traumatic experience of rape.

• *Clear and unambiguous support.* In the aftermath of rape, well-meaning friends and family often pose questions and offer assistance to rape victims in an unhelpful and essentially victim-blaming manner. Additionally, support figures can recommend and model coping mechanisms that are frankly maladaptive (e.g., "What you need is a stiff drink," or "Look, you simply cannot go out alone at night anymore") or offer protection in a way that is overbearing and disempowering ("Call me before you do anything!"). The group is specifically designed to offer clear and unambiguous support to rape victims and to promote recovery by informing members about and encouraging them to make use of coping strategies that are adaptive and empowering (e.g., "Let's start naming some things that you believe you can do to mobilize yourself when you feel depressed or to create safety when you start feeling afraid," or "What do you need to remember about who you are when you start feeling ashamed? What group feedback can you take with you and hold on to?").

• *Validation of feelings.* Whether it is feelings of guilt and shame that follow upon the experience of rape or feelings of anger, fear, and rage, other group members know these feelings and can reassure rape victims that they are normal, familiar reactions—reactions that are known and understood in a very immediate way by others in the group. The discovery that one is not alone in these reactions and that they do not brand the victim as crazy or "over the edge" is an important piece of recovery that awaits the rape victim in group. When feelings are normalized and understood, the victim can begin monitoring her emotions and finally recognize signs of recovery in her changing emotional state.

• *Confirmation of experience.* Just as feelings are validated and confirmed by participation in group, so too are experiences and behaviors. While others in the victim's natural support network may question, for example, whether or not date rape is or is not "really rape," the rape survivors' group is clear: "Yes, this experience was rape; yes, what you experienced was real." In groups, rape victims have the opportunity to learn not only that other victims have felt what they feel, but also that other victims, too, had to do certain things and behave in certain ways in order to survive. They learn that others, too, are coping daily with flashbacks and nightly with dreams in which the terror of rape is reenacted over and over again. As they share the experience, they also can share strategies for managing these experiences.

• *Counteracts self-blame, promotes self-esteem.* Many rape victims blame themselves in the aftermath of rape, asking themselves, for example, "Why did I open the door?" or "Why did I go to that party?" or telling themselves, "I should have known better." Yet when they hear the stories of other victims—victims who behaved similarly and who also blame themselves—they experience these stories differently. They may begin to think, "These others are not to blame. Perhaps, therefore, I'm not to blame." As the victim examines and is able to reject self-blame, she emerges from the group experience with greater self-awareness and self-esteem. She is more aware of her own capacity to extend help to others and is able to take help from the group as well.

• *Egalitarian mode of care.* Individual therapy, whatever its other pluses and minuses may be, is not an egalitarian mode of care. Invariably, the dialogue is a one-way dialogue and hierarchy is present in the relationship. The therapist can be idealized in both negative and positive ways; she or he can be seen as too powerful and too much in control of the process, or depended upon to excess and seen as one's sole source of salvation and strength. Because rape is an act of violence that involves the abuse of power, it is important for victims to regain personal power and resume control over their own lives. Because the group is a more egalitarian mode of care, it is potentially less threatening than a more hierarchical form of care and better able than individual psychotherapy to dilute dependency needs and promote reempowerment.

• *Opportunities for safe attachment.* Traumatic experiences involve ruptures in human attachments and can render the prospect of intimacy and attachment frightening. Because the group is bounded by time limits, structure, and rules of conduct for members and leaders alike, it offers a safe context in which to meet, share feelings with, and again experience closeness to others. Bonding with others in the group can be for many victims a first and major step towards recovery.

• *Shared grief.* Rape and trauma involve loss: a lost sense of self, a lost innocence, a lost sense of safety in the world, and a lost trust in the essential goodwill of others. Whatever the losses and however they are framed, they must be grieved. When grief is shared, as occurs in the context of group, the past is mourned and located in the past, leaving the victim free to live in the here and now and to look forward again to the future.

• *Allows assignment of meaning.* Ultimately recovery from rape requires that the individual victim assign to her experience some kind of meaning that is self-affirming and life-affirming. In group, victims can join with one another and give collective meaning to their experience: acknowledging the changes it has wrought in their lives, for example, and committing themselves to ongoing recovery. For some victims, meaning-making will take the form of collective social action against rape; for others it will take a more private form. In any case, the group process will encourage each member to make her own peace with her experience and will support her as she does so.

Case example. Georgia L. is a 27-year-old, married woman. She and her husband Rick have been married 8 years and have 2 children, ages 6 and 4. A year ago—and against her husband's wishes—Georgia took an evening job in a supermarket not far from her home. Five months later she was accosted in the supermarket parking lot by a stranger who held her at knifepoint and ordered her to drive to a deserted spot. Once there, he raped her. Georgia did all of the "right" things. She contacted the police, called the rape crisis center, and went to the hospital where a rape crisis advocate met her and explained to her various medical and legal procedures. The advocate also helped her decide what she would say to her husband—and how. She filed a police report and is currently cooperating with the assistant district attorney assigned to her case. Her husband has been understanding and supportive and also very protective of her. She quit her job the day after the rape. She has not gone back to work. She tells herself that she should be "over" the rape, and that she should not feel so guilty, that she should be "grateful" for her husband's understanding and caring response. Instead, she feels angry, guilty, ashamed—and alone. She even feels angry at her husband for being understanding and for being so protective. She can't imagine talking with him about how she feels. Indeed, she doesn't feel like talking with anyone in her family. She does think about the rape crisis worker who met her at the hospital, and occasionally she thinks about calling her again.

Georgia is an ideal candidate for a rape survivors' group. She is not in crisis now and the initial trauma is behind her. Yet she is still feeling the psychological effects of rape and she is facing her feelings silently and alone. The literature on group treatment for victims of sexual assault suggests that sharing her story and her feelings with others who have had a common experience can reduce Georgia's sense of isolation, validate her experience, and repair her damaged self-esteem. The means by which groups are presumed to accomplish these ends are empowerment, social support, and safe attachment.

Empowerment. Feminists associated with grass-roots rape crisis centers and community-based sexual assault treatment programs have emphasized the humiliating and disempowering
nature of rape, the sense of powerlessness that rape trauma
entails and the *empowering potential* of rape survivor groups
(Harvey, 1985; Yassen & Glass, 1984). Sprei and Goodwin (1983)
emphasize the need for group treatment models which, by virtue of their egalitarian structure and respectful, supportive process, counter a disempowering socialization of women. The
rape survivor groups that these researchers initiated at the Sexual Assault Center of Prince Georges General Hospital in Mary-
land have three goals: (a) to educate women about rape and
rape trauma; (b) to counter victim-blaming self-perceptions by
addressing common myths and misconceptions about rape; and
(c) to promote recovery by reducing isolation, on the one hand,
and modeling effective coping, on the other.

In a feminist-inspired support group, Georgia is likely to meet
other survivors who blame themselves in ways that do not
really make sense and who also feel things they cannot explain
to themselves or to those who love them. She will learn that her
reactions are common, not unusual, and that distress at one's
own anger is a familiar experience to victims of violence and
abuse. Her feelings and her experiences thus will receive confirmation and validation. She will no longer be alone with them. In
group, Georgia also will extend understanding and support to
others. Together, she and other group members will recall the
disempowering nature of rape and begin to discover the recovery that lies in making efforts to resume control. Georgia might
be helped to understand that some of the anger she feels towards her husband has to do with the powerlessness she continues to feel in the face of his protectiveness. With group
encouragement and support, she may take upon herself the task
of freeing herself from his protection or of talking to him about
how she feels and setting some limits on his protectiveness.
Depending upon the setting in which her group is located, her
husband might himself be invited to attend a partner's group
designed to help male partners better understand the nature
and trauma of sexual violence. Finally, Georgia will be encour-

aged to grieve her experience and to place it in the past, to free herself for a future of heightened awareness and control, and to recognize in herself her skills and her status as survivor.

In emphasizing the empowering role of groups, van der Kolk (1987b) compares the benefits of group participation to those of individual psychotherapy, noting that the group can mobilize the helping capacities of the victim/survivor and enable victims to reexperience themselves as capable, help-giving individuals. Through its empowering influence, the group thus offers an alternative route for development and recovery, and counters unrealistic and ultimately disempowering dependency upon an individual therapist.

Social support. Among researchers and clinicians interested in the psychological trauma of victimization, Janoff-Bulman (1985b) has discussed the shattered assumptive world of victims and the sense of self-blame and stigma that can follow from it. She proposes that social support is critical to recovery: first, in countering a victim's self-perceptions of deviance; second, in helping her rebuild positive self-assumptions, and third, in countering a sense of the world as a dangerous and malevolent place. She suggests that peer-support groups comprised of individuals who have experienced a similar life crisis can provide needed support, particularly when it is not forthcoming from family, friends, and others. In his discussion of posttraumatic reactions and symptoms, Scurfield (1985) also stresses the importance of social support and proposes that group treatment can (a) counter a victim's sense of isolation with a sense of community; (b) help to reduce the stigma of victimization and aid the development of self-esteem; (c) make positive use of confrontation by peers; (d) help individuals process unfinished business; and (e) help group members identify, acknowledge, and express difficult emotions. The vehicle by which group treatment is supposed to accomplish these ends is social support.

When rape victims like Georgia turn to family, friends, and other support figures in the aftermath of sexual assault, they may do so in a state of extreme vulnerability: uncertain of themselves and needing clear indices of concern and unambiguous signs of support. For many victims, these simply are not available. Instead, a topsy-turvy world is rendered stranger still by the unanticipated anger of a parent, the new aloofness of a lover, and the unstated but nonetheless obvious skepticism of a friend. For most rape victims, the experience with familiar support figures is a painful encounter with the awkward silences, inept gestures, and thoughtless remarks of people who might want to be helpful, but somehow are anything but. For other victims, the silences that they encounter amount to abandonment; the gestures are hostile in intent and the remarks are clear and articulate denunciations of the victim.

The phenomenon of failed social support can be quite subtle. Doubt, in the victim's story is evident though not intended in the "I was just wondering . . ." or "Gee, you didn't scream?" remarks of a friend. Avoidance of reality, denial of the trauma, and minimization of the victim's feelings is apparent though not intended in the "Thank God it wasn't worse," or, "Let's just not talk about it" statements of a parent. And rejection is communicated though not intended by a lover's anxious statement, "I'm sorry but I really can't handle seeing you like this." In these examples, the failure of social support lies in the ineptitude of the transaction between rape victim and natural support figure: in the anxious, insensitive, and possibly ill-informed gestures of the latter and the hypervigilant, exquisitely sensitive, and ultimately distorted perceptions of the former. In the breach between her husband's positive intent and Georgia's reaction to him, she is alone in the recovery process and so is he.

When Georgia calls the rape crisis center for information about a survivors' group, she is reaching for a new source of social support. It is not surprising that rape victims turn to these settings in search of outside support. Research indicates that victims frequently experience a failure of support in their home communities. In their study of internal and external mediators of the long- and short-term effects of rape among a multicultural sample of victims, for example, Wyatt, Notgrass, and Newcomb (1990) found the support behaviors of people in the victim's natural environment greatly lacking. No "natural support" variable that they studied was found to mediate positive recovery and few, if any, of the rape victims who comprised their sample (which included victims of multiple rapes and victims of both stranger- and acquaintance-perpetrated rape) reported having experienced positive social support in the aftermath of their assault.

From the vantage point of social support research, then, the rape survivors' group may offer to Georgia reparative opportunities not present in her "natural support network." Research suggests that the process of social support is a complex one, involving much more than the existence and relative goodwill of significant others (Heller, Swindle, & Dusenbury, 1986; Lieberman, 1986). Coyne and Delongis (1986), for example, suggest that the overall quality of a relationship (e.g., of the relationship pretrauma) will influence the nature of specific social support efforts and the intended recipient's perception of that support. The efficacy of any attempt at support, therefore, lies as much with the perception as with the intent. And in their study of social support in the aftermath of traumatic bereavement, Lehman, Ellard, and Wortman (1986) found that close and caring individuals frequently found themselves overwhelmed by face-to-face contact with bereaved survivors. Their attempts at social support may have failed not because of their ignorance or lack of empathy but because of their own anxiety and distress. These findings suggest that significant others who are wanting to help may themselves require assistance. Like Georgia's husband, they may benefit from participating in the public education and support services of grass-roots victim advocacy agencies.

Well-intended but nonetheless failed attempts to provide support emanate not from fundamentally impaired relationships with natural support figures, but from relationships that will continue and no doubt can be repaired. While they are not acts of outright hostility, it is important to recognize that these failures do entail a reluctance to accept the victim's story, to deal with the nature and intensity of her feelings, and/or to affirm her competence in the here and now. Rape victims find in these transactions hurtful challenges to their credibility, negations of their experience, and affirmation of their self-doubt.

When a rape victim meets with outright rejection and active hostility by and from key support figures, her inward self-doubt and self-blame not only are confirmed, but amplified. These reactions are not separate from, but continuations of, the victimization process. A wife who has been sexually assaulted by her husband, for example, is neither free nor physically safe when family member, close friend, or clergy responds to her disclosure with admonitions that "a wife's place is with her husband" or that she has "made her bed and now must lie in it." The college coed who may have had too much to drink before being raped by her date is not in a position to begin her recovery when classmates, friends, and family are berating her for her behavior, counseling her to keep quiet, or telling her that she somehow deserved what happened to her. And the daughter who discloses incest only to be told that she is "lying" or "exaggerating" is not safe; her so-called natural support network is aligned with her abuser and she herself is alone. These reactions are more than failures of social support; they are offenses in themselves, and they signal the need for whole new sources of support.

Social support research underscores the potential importance of new social support figures and resources. Thoits (1986) equates effective social support with support that fosters successful coping by the support recipient. She posits that similarity of experience and background plus a related capacity for empathic understanding are the critical attributes of effective support providers. While these attributes may characterize family, friends, and intimates, they may be more readily available in altogether new support figures: in members of self-help groups, for example, and among others who have shared the recipient's experience. These are the support figures whom Georgia will meet when she enters a rape survivors' group.

Attachment and trust. Van der Kolk (1987b) relates the benefits of group therapy to the social context of psychological trauma. That context may involve the loss of attachment figures, betrayal by them, and/or fundamental disruption of the victim's sense of connectedness to and trust in others. Noting that "the essence of the trauma response is the disruption of secure affiliative bonds" (van der Kolk, 1987b, p. 153), he contrasts the loss of community that can occur to victims in the aftermath of traumatic events with the protective role of group membership and group cohesion among concentration camp survivors subjected to extreme circumstances. In the aftermath of trauma, groups offer a safe and alternative social context in which members can establish a high degree of cohesion and use one another to reflect and examine traumatic memories and feelings. By doing so, they are able to tell their stories, make the past public, bear witness to one another's pain, and engage in a shared reliving of the trauma—a reliving that confirms and validates their experiences and feelings and further solidifies the bond among group members. Over time, van der Kolk (1987b) proposes, participation in group will bring to the surface differences as well as commonalities among group members. Sensitive leadership and clear rules about group boundaries and behavioral norms can contain and direct the group's exploration of differences and enable group members to maintain their attachments across these differences. The experience of developing and maintaining safe attachments with others in the group helps to rebuild the victim's capacity for trust and paves the way for new relationships outside of the group.

GROUP TREATMENT AND RECOVERY

In Chapter 5 we considered seven indices of recovery (Harvey, 1990). These are presented again in the paragraphs that follow, along with a brief discussion of how group treatment is supposed to facilitate the rape victim's recovery on each recovery dimension. Included when applicable is a brief discussion of how specific group treatment approaches might be of particular value.

Memory. A sign of recovery and a goal of treatment is that the rape victim exerts greater personal authority over the remembering process—that she can elect to recall or not recall traumatic events that previously intruded unbidden into awareness and that she is better able to manage distressing associations.

Because group treatment involves for each member the responsibility to hear and bear witness to the stories told by every other member, each member's own recall is likely to be "triggered" by the stories she hears. And, as she relates the details of her own story and responds to questions from other members (questions that will come from their own similar experience), her memory will be clarified further. The process can be a painful one, but as others are present to hear the stories and to provide support and assistance, it can be helpful too. Moreover, the group offers leadership and guidance, boundaries of time, and rules of conduct that help to contain the process. Members must, for example, share the time available in group and frequently lay their own stories aside to hear and respond to the stories of others. The process embodies a "pacing" of traumatic disclosures. Through such pacing, members come to model for one another a more controlled remembering process.

Specific group approaches may focus on particular aspects of traumatic memory. Behavioral groups and groups with a psychoeducational focus, for example, will educate members about the nature of flashbacks and other modes of traumatic recall and may introduce strategies by which members can track, chart, and study their vulnerability to these intrusions. Supportive psychotherapy groups may schedule time for each member to review her story and search for missing data.

Linking memory with feelings. In the wake of trauma, some victims will have clear memories of their assault and yet feel nothing as they recall it. Others will experience waves of terror or rage that they cannot connect to precipitants in the present or events in the past. Memory and affect are separate. A second sign of recovery and a second goal of treatment is that cognitive recollections of traumatic events become linked to and integrated with the affects and bodily states that accompanied those events initially: that events are remembered with affects that are appropriate in valence and intensity to the thing remembered and that the precipitants of feeling states are known, understood, and connected to the past. Sad memories elicit sadness once again; anger, fear, and other emotions are similarly connected to the events recalled.

In group, the process of linking memories and affects is mediated, first, by the feelings being felt for others about events that they report. The victim who can feel no anger or sadness at her own assault can feel both anger and sadness for other group members. The hope of group treatment is that as she allows herself to feel for others, she will develop a new emotional fluency and begin to feel her own feelings as well. Similarly, the victim who can make no connections between her own fits of rage and the sexual assault that she experienced three years prior can feel some of that rage in the context of group on behalf of other group members as they name their experiences and recount their stories. As she witnesses the connections between their experience and feelings, the hope is that she will begin to make these connections for herself as well.

Groups that include an educational component can be particularly helpful in this aspect of recovery. In educating members about the nature of psychological trauma, group leaders can suggest connections that group members may not recognize on their own (noting, for example, that one member's seasonal depression may be a reflection of the time of year and the occasion when an assault occurred, or that another's lack of feeling around specific memories may relate to a dissociative experience that happened during the assault). Both behavioral and supportive psychotherapy groups may teach and allow group members to practice in group guided imagery and other strategies for finding the linkages between memories and affects.

Affect tolerance. A third goal of group treatment and an important sign of recovery is that the affects and feelings associated with traumatic events are bearable: that they have lost their terrible intensity and immediacy; that the rape victim is able to recall her experiences, have her feelings, and tolerate them;

and that she is free of overwhelming arousal, dissociation, and numbing in the face of traumatic recall.

Depending on the nature and focus of the group, group process may pursue this particular goal in any of several ways. The supportive psychotherapy group will offer group members information about trauma and the psychological sequelae of traumatic events. Hopefully, this information will give individual members a cognitive frame for understanding their more intense feelings and techniques for anticipating, preparing for, and managing them. An expressive group might incorporate psychodrama and other expressive techniques for integrating and containing affect. A behavioral group might include guided-imagery techniques and other strategies for containing and modulating feelings.

In virtually all groups, as one rape victim after another recounts her experience and shares her feelings, group members not only feel fear or anger or rage at the details of her assault, they also feel admiration for her courage, warmth at her humor, and closeness to her grief. Together, these many and varied emotions yield a more encompassing sense of empathy and compassion. It is, we think, this empathic response that enables group members to bear one another's pain and which, when extended inward to themselves, enables them to bear even their own. There are other ways of describing this experience. It may be, for example, that repeated but bearable exposures to painful stimuli develop among group members a resiliency that is finally represented even in the neural processing of traumatic recall. Nonetheless, the way in which individual group members experience the process is as one of empathy and compassion overcoming fear and rage and yielding a calmer, fuller sense of self.

Symptom mastery. Another aim of group treatment is that other posttraumatic symptoms subside or become more manageable: more tolerable, more predictable, and more subject to conscious control.

Virtually all trauma groups and certainly all groups for survivors of sexual assault hope to explain and help victims manage lasting symptoms of posttraumatic stress disorder. These symptoms may include sleep and dream disturbances, eating difficulties, a persistent hypervigilance, any number of bodily reactions, anxiety attacks, and episodic depression. Group treatment aims to explain and destigmatize these symptoms and by doing so rob them of some of their mystery and power.

Specific kinds of groups may teach particular symptom management techniques as well. Stress-management groups, for example, will introduce rape survivors to relaxation techniques that may help with sleeping or teach stress-inoculation practices (e.g., diet, hard exercise, problem-solving techniques) that increase resiliency to contemporary life stressors (Flannery, 1987). Self-defense courses may teach physical and psychological defense skills that reduce one's sense of vulnerability and lessen the need for intense hypervigilance. Groups employing cognitive-behavioral strategies will introduce members to techniques for managing anxiety and combating depressive thought processes. Supportive and psychodynamic therapy groups will help victims understand their distress in terms of its relationship to the original trauma.

Self-esteem. Probably no sign of recovery and no treatment goal is as fundamentally important as that of improved or restored self-esteem. With recovery, feelings of guilt, self-blame, and shame are replaced by new feelings of self-worth and personal value. Critical, obsessive review of the past is replaced by a more realistic assessment of it. The burden of responsibility for rape is transferred to the offender.

In the aftermath of rape, many victims will experience self-doubt and self-blame. Janoff-Bulman (1985b) has drawn a distinction between "behavioral self-blame"—typified by a victim's critical review of her own behavior and a search for clues as to what, if anything, she might have done to avoid being raped—and "characterological self-blame" in which the victim finds explanation for rape in a sense of herself as basically flawed. She has proposed that in fact behavioral self-blame can be understood as a search for control, an effort that comes after the belief that one could have done something. In this sense, she posits that behavioral self-blame can be seen as a sign of recovery. More recently, Katz and Burt (1988) have reported findings that challenge Janoff-Bulman's (1985b) somewhat positive view of behavioral self-blame. In their study, 80 rape victims completed a personal interview and two standardized questionnaires: their own "How I see myself now" instrument to assess self-blame (Burt & Katz, 1987) and the Rosenberg self-esteem scale (Rosenberg, 1987). Their findings revealed no indication that behavioral self-blame was positively correlated with any measure of recovery. Instead, self-blame tended to decline over time and, when persistent, to be associated with other indicators of continuing distress and negatively correlated with positive self-esteem. These findings are somewhat consistent with those of Kilpatrick et al. (1984), who report that the post-traumatic impact of rape is predictable from early signs of intense distress and lowered self-esteem. These authors suggest that educating victims about PTSD and rebuilding self-esteem are two important focal points of treatment.

However one understands victim self-blame, it is critical that group leaders address rather than collude with the view that rape victims bear responsibility for rape, and that they remind victims, first, that no behavior on their part constitutes an invitation to rape or a reason for rape, and second, that their choices as victims do not explain the choices that offenders make.

Virtually all survivor groups promote self-esteem in a wide variety of ways: (a) by developing cohesion among members and cultivating self-respect through the mechanism of mutual regard and bonding; (b) by confronting rape myths and misconceptions; (c) by placing sexual assault in a societal context; (d) by fostering resumed control and, most importantly, (e) by hearing, listening to, and taking seriously each victim's story, each woman's efforts after recovery.

Attachment. A final aim of group treatment is that the individual rape victim will use the group to combat isolation, stigma, and shame and that in doing so she will come to know, care about, and trust those who go through the group experience with her. For many victims, these will be the first people with whom she can feel safe and the first in whom she can place her trust.

The modality of group treatment is meant to provide members with a quality of attachment and connectedness that is not available in individual therapy for all of the reasons already discussed. It is also structured to offer safety: the safety of rules and limits and the safety that comes with choice and self-determination. In survivor groups, members are encouraged to share what they can and to disclose to others only what they wish to disclose. They are not pushed to share more than they can handle, nor are they encouraged to push one another. The atmosphere is one of support, safety, and consent. In this way, the attributes of the group are directly opposite the attributes of forced sexual assault. In the same way that rape is the essence of an unsafe human relationship (i.e., it is violent, nonconsensual, and involves the abuse of power), the group provides a context in which closeness and intimacy can safely develop and finally thrive.

Depending upon the nature of the group and the degree of recovery already acquired by group members, specific groups may address attachment issues differently. Some groups, for example, will simply assume that the supportive and educative milieu of a survivors' group is in itself reparative. Other groups will focus on the severe impairments in attachment capabilities that may follow upon brutal assault or chronic abuse. In these groups, sitting quietly in a room with other people or going on walks with one another may be major survival tasks. Still others will emphasize the importance of esprit de corps among group members and will incorporate group wilderness trips and collective participation in social action (e.g., in "Take Back the Night" demonstrations).

Meaning. Ultimately, recovery will require that the victim assign to her experience some kind of meaning: a meaning that enables her to locate her rape in the past and to anticipate her future with greater confidence in herself and greater hopefulness about her relationships with others. Some victims will discard the sense of having been damaged by their experience and will embrace instead the belief that identifiable personal strengths and new capacities for empathy, compassion, and action are victories wrested from the trauma of rape.

Different types of groups will approach the task of meaning-making differently. In psychodynamic groups, the emphasis will be on a deeply personal reassessment of self, others, and relationships. In supportive groups, the goal may be more limited: simply that the victim come to view herself as a survivor and not as a victim. Self-help groups may encourage collective action or provide opportunities for group members to assume the role of group leader or facilitator. Sprei and Goodwin (1983) report that besides the cotherapists, their survivors' group includes as facilitators two women who have previously participated in group and who are now bringing their experience as victims and their experience as group members to bear on the healing of others.

A RANGE OF GROUP TREATMENT APPROACHES

In the weeks, months, and years following a rape, individual rape victims may take advantage of a wide range of group offerings. These include self-help groups and drop-in support groups available through grass-roots feminist rape crisis centers and other women's advocacy organizations and groups for victims with complicating psychiatric complaints or substance-abuse problems, as well as short- and long-term psychotherapy groups and groups for special populations. Groups have been developed for child and adolescent victims, elderly victims, male survivors, victims of particularly brutal rape, victims of homophobic violence, and for partners and family members of rape victims. A complete discussion of these diverse groups is beyond the reach of this chapter. They are, however, listed and at least briefly described and discussed below.

Self-Help and Grass-Roots Support Groups

A wide variety of self-help and support groups are available through community-based rape crisis centers, self-help organizations, and other grass-roots community settings. Included among them are the types of groups described in the sections that follow.

Drop-In Discussion Groups

Most rape crisis centers offer drop-in discussion groups for rape victims at all stages of recovery. Typically, these groups are organized around particular themes, which may include the social context of rape, myths and misconceptions about rape, what recovery looks like, issues of trust, and many others. Often these groups are organized into 4- or 6-week series of topical discussions, and rape victims at particular stages of recovery are invited to attend particular sessions or are referred to particular sessions by rape hot-line services. While these groups have many attributes of self-help groups, and while they may be led by group leaders who are themselves survivors, they are not "self-help" groups per se, for they rely on leadership for organization and guidance.

Crisis-Oriented Support Groups

Rape crisis centers, family court clinics, battered women's shelters, safe houses, and victim-witness advocacy programs may offer support groups for victims still in crisis as a result of their assault. Such groups may be particularly helpful for victims of marital rape and battering and to provide support to women who have sought safety and protection by filing abuse petitions.

Survivor Support Groups

Most rape crisis centers also offer time-limited support groups for survivors of sexual assault. These groups combine a therapeutic with an educative mission and are typically co-led by women therapists who have clinical training and who have completed the rape crisis center's training about rape, rape trauma, and rape crisis work. These leaders may or may not be survivors themselves and, depending upon their own point of view or center policy, those who are survivors may or may not share their history with group members. Most rape crisis centers that utilize leaders who are themselves survivors also encourage careful thinking through of the decision to do this work, and many provide special supervision for leaders who are also survivors.

Self-Help Groups

In addition to the drop-in discussion and support groups that may be available to victims in local rape crisis centers, victims with complicating histories of substance abuse, family alcoholism, or eating disorders may be encouraged to take advantage of the self-help groups available through self-help organizations like Alcoholics Anonymous and Narcotics Anonymous. These groups can be critical aids to recovery among victims who might otherwise be tempted to manage their posttraumatic stress with alcohol or drugs.

Psychotherapy Groups

Psychotherapy groups designed to serve victims of sexual assault typically incorporate themes and methodologies that were developed initially in rape crisis centers and have since been combined with more traditional group psychotherapy approaches. These approaches include both supportive and psychodynamic or insight-oriented group psychotherapy and behavioral or cognitive-behavioral approaches. They include short-term, time-limited models and long-term or ongoing approaches.

Short-Term, Time-Limited Groups

Short-term groups likely to benefit rape survivors include supportive psychotherapy and behavioral stress-management groups.

Supportive psychotherapy groups for rape survivors are, like their grass-roots counterparts, time limited and relatively short term. Between 10 and 12 90-minute to 2-hour sessions are usual, 20 sessions an outside limit. Groups are typically co-led by two female therapists and are comprised of 7 to 10 members chosen into group through a pregroup screening interview. Members may or may not be in individual therapy as well. They are usually required to be at least six months postrape and to have been sober and drug-free for a reasonable period of time. Members with substance-abuse problems may be asked to participate in AA or NA programs or to be involved in some other form of substance-abuse treatment. The primary aims of supportive psychotherapy groups for rape victims are (a) to provide information and emotional support; (b) to facilitate understanding, acceptance, and mastery of depression, anger, and other difficult emotions; and (c) to foster self-esteem and connectedness among group members (Sprei & Goodwin, 1983; Yassen & Glass, 1984). Special support groups for child or adolescent victims, elderly victims, male victims, and victims of particularly brutal assault have been developed along similar lines.

Short-term, *stress-management groups* are designed to help victims of psychologically traumatizing events, including rape, to understand, anticipate, and manage symptoms of posttraumatic stress. These groups are most appropriate for victims exhibiting a high degree of physiological distress, victims who are living in unstable circumstances (e.g., homeless women), and victims who for various reasons may be unable to make use of the more relationally oriented support group. Stress-management groups are educative in nature—they are as much classroom as group—

and are structured around three goals: (a) identifying and explaining posttraumatic symptoms; (b) teaching specific skills for reducing and managing these symptoms; and (c) utilizing the group context to accomplish these other ends. The rationale is that accomplishing something in collaboration with others may be a first step to making fuller use of others (Flannery, 1987).

The rationale for short-term groups. In their description of groups for adult incest survivors, Goodwin and Talwar (1989) examine therapists' rationales for short- and long-term group treatment models. Much of the thinking they report seems apropos to rape survivor groups as well. Therapists who prefer short-term models suggest that the time-limited model (a) sets a framework with clearly defined boundaries; (b) offers limits to the pain and regression that can occur in group; (c) focuses members on the specific issue of incest and its sequelae; (d) underlines the issue of termination, since group members prepare for termination from the first session forward and through this process rework grief over previous losses of support and nurturance; (e) avoids the problem of introducing new members and disrupting the precarious commitment of group members to sharing the incest secret; (f) reflects the limits of the tolerance of group leaders for listening to and processing this stressful material; and (g) decreases the potential for distracting conflicts among group members that tend to emerge if they are exposed to a longer relationship that requires more developed social skills and greater capacity for intimacy than they have yet mobilized. Herman and Schatzow (1984) add that a time-limited group is less likely to solidify a victim identity and that following short-term group treatment, survivors can be encouraged to enter more generic women's therapy groups.

Long-Term and Open-Ended Group Treatment

According to Goodwin and Talwar (1989), those therapists who prefer long-term and open-ended group treatment models argue that the resolution of chronic symptoms requires long-term therapeutic work, that long-term work is sometimes required simply to recover memories, and that some survivors need immediate placement in group as soon as they disclose. These arguments seem less apropos to rape survivors generally and more applicable to those rape victims who may have complicated psychiatric histories and/or who also may have early or chronic abuse histories.

To our knowledge few long-term psychotherapy groups have been developed specifically for rape survivors. An exception is the long-term survivor group currently being developed by therapists at the Rape Crisis Program of Beth Israel Hospital in Boston, Massachusetts. This group consists of five to seven members meeting in 90-minute sessions with two therapist coleaders (both women). The group is being developed in recognition of the fact that among those survivors who are referred to a hospital-based program for follow-up mental health care are a significant number of women with earlier or more chronic abuse histories. In this sense, the group is similar in purpose and format to ongoing and long-term groups for multiply and chronically traumatized women.

Other Group Contexts for Healing

In addition to the foregoing group treatment options, it is important to remember that some of the healing attributes of groups exist in the context of other community endeavors. Women's groups, feminist action groups, neighborhood crime-watch programs, the subcommittees and advisory boards of various political groups, and public policy organizations also offer opportunities for rape victims to join with other women (and men) to address the phenomenon of sexual assault and to experience recovery benefits by doing so.

The Women's Group

When one recalls that sexual assault has a social and a political context and that that context shapes the lives and developmental possibilities of women from all classes, races, ethnic groups, and economic and educational backgrounds, it is clear that women talking to women about their lives, their histories, and their beliefs ultimately will incorporate a discussion of rape and fear of rape. In communities where rape is rampant and largely endorsed by prevailing values, it may be very difficult for a woman to identify herself as a victim of rape and to seek the assistance that a rape survivors' group might offer. It is in recognition of this difficulty that many settings have begun sponsoring "women's discussion groups," "women's rap sessions," and groups that focus on parenting issues and domestic stresses. Typically, these groups are free and very informally organized, with child care options on or near the site. They may provide for the rape victim who is isolated and afraid an alternative and culturally appropriate route to recovery. Authors who have written about the shame associated with rape in certain cultures suggest that these groups may provide the only opportunity that some women will have to share their story and receive understanding in the face of it (Mollica & Son, 1989).

Social Action for Change

Rape is among the many violent crimes that plague our society and threaten its citizens throughout their developmental life span. It is a crime that will go away only as a result of major societal reform. Rape victims can choose to be part of this reform and to seek their recovery in this kind of group process. In writing *Real Rape*, for example, Susan Estrich (1987) made use of her experience as rape victim and her training as an attorney to further not only her own recovery but also the cause of social and legal reform. Other victims have done and are doing similar things: joining antirape task forces, participating in "Take Back the Night" marches, offering volunteer services to local rape crisis centers, and speaking out for women's rights. When clinicians consider how they might aid the recovery of rape victims they encounter as patients, they need to think of referrals to these groups, too.

DESIGNING A SURVIVORS' GROUP

When therapists consider forming a psychotherapy group for rape survivors, they will need to consider and decide upon their response to a number of questions. These are presented below.

What Is Our Understanding of Rape and Rape Trauma?

Therapists wanting to conduct groups for survivors of sexual assault must be clear about their own view of rape, its causes, and its consequences, and they must have an understanding of rape trauma that prepares them to anticipate and address the concerns of group members. A feminist analysis of rape (see Chapter 4) will emphasize the societal roots of sexual violence and will have as a goal the empowerment of group members.

Why Do We Think Group Treatment Might Help?

Therapists also need to be aware of their own expectations of group treatment. Why should it be helpful? How will its benefits differ, if at all, from those of individual therapy? Why might rape victims find a group useful? There are many—and differing—answers to each of these questions, and it is important that therapists know their own particular answers so that they can offer their thoughts about group treatment to prospective groups members who may be quite ambivalent about the prospects of sharing their hurt with others.

What About Group Leadership?

In most settings (but not all) rape survivor groups are co-led by two women therapists. The rationale is that women victims feel safer with women leaders, are more comfortable with them, and are not distracted from their recovery goals by the added task of dealing with a powerful male figure in group. A notable exception to this position is the Austin Rape Crisis Center in Austin, Texas, which for over a decade has made use of male rape crisis workers and male coleaders. Their rationale is that it is sexist to exclude the possibility of male humanity and sensitivity and that the ARCC is, first of all, a setting designed to embody nonsexist, humanistic values (Harvey, 1985).

What Is the Relevance of a Leader's Own Trauma History?

Group leaders differ in their views on this question and in their level of comfort with personal disclosures by therapists generally. One argument is that the leader's own trauma history adds to her credibility with group members and increases their confidence in her competence and compassion. An opposite argument is that the leader's history is not at issue and should not distract group members from working on their own. Whatever position group leaders arrive at, it should be consistent not only with their training, beliefs, and values, but also with their personal preferences. To share one's trauma history when one is fundamentally uncomfortable doing so is contrary to the whole aim of empowerment through assertion of choice. And, whatever decision is made with respect to therapist disclosures in group, it is important that the group leader with her own history of sexual assault be prepared for the impact of group on her own psychological status and continuing recovery process. Outside consultation, supervision, and group support can be helpful in this regard.

What view of group treatment do we prefer? What is implied for group goals, composition, structure, and process? Therapists differ in their theoretical orientation to clinical work with individuals and in their orientation to group treatment. That orientation may be cognitive, behavioral, psychodynamic, psychoeducational, supportive, feminist, or include various combinations of these. Whatever the orientation, it will have implications for the

design, structure, and conduct of group sessions. Will these include topical discussions or a focus on group process? Will it
include education about rape trauma and training in stress-
management skills or will it involve sharing and giving feedback? And, given the orientation of group leaders and the
structure of group, which clients are most likely to benefit from
the group? Need they be relatively high-functioning individuals
with the crisis largely behind them or is the group intended for
much more distressed individuals with psychiatric or other histories that greatly complicate rape trauma? Do we take all who
express interest in the group or should we be more selective?
Who should not be in group? Are there people who might be
harmed by the group or become more distressed as a result of it?
At the present time we have no evidence that one approach and
one set of answers is more or less useful than another—only
fairly consistent evidence that therapists need organizing constructs and a clear theoretical framework if their efforts are to be
effective.

*How will we handle our own reactions to rape? What shall we do
about supervision and/or consultation?* Conducting any kind of
trauma group can be greatly distressing at times for the group
leaders. In rape survivor groups, there is always the story that
one leader was simply not prepared to hear that night or that
caused another leader to experience her own distress symptoms.
Moreover, with or without particularly strong reactions to any
one story, the fact is that group leaders are exposed week in and
week out to a great deal of human tragedy and pain. It is important that group leaders identify ahead of time how they will
handle and process their reactions, both as a way of taking care
of themselves and as a means of understanding group dynamics
and needs. Coleadership is one resource for handling the material: coleaders can on a session-by-session basis discuss and
discharge some of the distress that they are experiencing, and
they can develop ways of leaving the work behind them when
they head home. Outside consultation is another resource for
group leaders to call upon, as is regular outside supervision.
Supervision is recommended, particularly, when the leaders are

relatively new to the work and when group members include severely distressed clients and/or survivors of particularly brutal assaults.

GROUP TREATMENT WITHIN THE VICTIMS OF VIOLENCE PROGRAM

Rape victims seen at Cambridge Hospital's Victims of Violence Program in Cambridge, Massachusetts, may enter any of three groups, depending upon their needs, backgrounds, and circumstances. In addition to the 12-week survivors' group adapted from a model developed by the Boston Area Rape Crisis Center (Yassen & Glass, 1984), the program offers short-term stress-management groups to patients with trauma histories and ongoing psychotherapy groups for women with early and chronic abuse histories. Each of these groups has included adult rape victims as well. The program and each of these groups are described briefly below.

The Victims of Violence Program

The Victims of Violence Program was established in 1984 and located in the adult outpatient clinic of Cambridge Hospital's Harvard-affiliated Department of Psychiatry. The hospital is a city hospital serving a multiethnic and multicultural population that includes large numbers of economically disenfranchised citizens and growing numbers of political refugees from Latin America and Haiti. The program serves as a clinical service for victims and as a clinical training program for advanced and postgraduate students in psychology, psychiatry, and social work. Its primary role within the hospital and within the larger community is that of developing outpatient psychiatric services for adult patients with recent and/or prior histories of physical and sexual abuse and violence. Program patients include women and men of diverse ages, economic circumstance, and ethnic heritage. They include individuals in acute distress as a result of criminal violence at the hands of strangers, acquaintances, and family members, and a sizable number of chronically traumatized patients. These patients include some men, but mostly women, whose life histories since childhood and adolescence literally are punctuated with recurrent incidents of physical and sexual violence. Its patients include a considerable number of rape victims, some entering the hospital in crisis due to a recent assault, some seeking individual or group treatment months or even years later. Toward the goal of serving this broad client population, the program offers a wide range of individual and group services to victims, witnesses, families, and others. Since 1988, the program has sponsored a multiagency community crisis response team as well.

The program is supported primarily by federal Victim of Crime Act funding awarded it by the Massachusetts Board of Victim Assistance. It enjoys city and state funding as well and is the recipient of private foundation awards and grants. In 1988 the program was awarded the American Psychiatric Association's Gold Award for outstanding and innovative hospital and community service (Hospital & Community Psychiatry, 1988). It was the first time in that organization's history that a feminist program and/or a program of services to crime victims had received such recognition. The program's orientation is decidedly feminist and community oriented. It enjoys close ties with a wide variety of grass-roots feminist organizations, and its senior staff includes founding and continuing members of the Boston Area Rape Crisis Center and Women's Mental Health Collective.

Group Services

Since 1984, the size of the Victims of Violence staff, the numbers of patients served by its programs, and its array of group services have steadily increased. During the 1990-1991 fiscal year, the program will offer the following groups: two time-limited rape survivor groups; two time-limited incest survivor groups, adapted from the model developed by Herman and Schatzow (1984) at the Women's Mental Health Collective; two to three short-term stress-management groups for male and female victims of traumatic events (Flannery, 1987); its second time-limited group for male survivors of sexual assault; an ongoing group for mothers of sexually victimized children; two ongoing and one 9-month group for women with early and multiabuse histories. In addition, the program will begin working with shelters for homeless women and families and with them develop shelter-based group services for this population.

Organizing Themes and Values

Unifying these diverse interventions and providing them with common ground and shared direction are (a) a shared set of program values; (b) a common understanding of psychological trauma; (c) mutual treatment goals; and (d) common structural attributes.

Program Values

Guiding the development of services within the Victims of Violence Program is a common and well-articulated set of program values. These values include (a) a feminist view of sexual abuse; (b) a clear affirmation of the validity of nonpsychiatric, community-based services and providers; (c) an equally clear recognition that psychiatric treatment can carry with it the risk of harm and the burden of stigma; (d) an emphasis on the development of service initiatives that make positive use of the psychiatric setting; (e) an emphasis on the relevance of emotional and social support in the recovery process; and (f) a commitment to fostering recovery through the promotion of choice, self-determined problem solving, altruistic commitment to others, and social action.

Psychological Trauma

Program services assume that life-threatening and violent events have traumatic impact: that these are real events in the lives of patients, that they often induce overwhelming feelings of terror and rage, and that trauma emanates from the experience of profound powerlessness in the face of unavoidable harm. Psychological trauma thus entails shattered beliefs in one's self, in others, and in the world at large, as well as persistent symptoms of extreme distress and feelings of shame, helplessness, and guilt. The program assumes that for many victims these feelings have been compounded by posttraumatic encounters with mental health service providers that confirm their powerlessness, threaten to rearouse without allowing for a reworking of traumatic reactions, undermine their coping capabilities, and exacerbate their trauma.

The Role of Treatment

In the face of these realities, the goals of psychotherapeutic treatment, whether group or individual, must be (a) to normalize or at least depathologize individual reactions to traumatic events; (b) to empower or reempower the individual by fostering mastery—mastery of physiological symptoms, mastery through the accomplishment of specific recovery tasks, and mastery through the modulation of affect and assumption of authority over the remembering process; (c) to aid in the restoration of attachments—by reducing isolation and promoting empathic connection; and (d) to help individuals assign a life-affirming, self-affirming meaning to their experience.

Common Structural and Thematic Elements

In the Victims of Violence Program all groups (a) are co-led and supervised by therapists experienced in group work and in the treatment of psychological trauma; (b) formally or informally incorporate psychoeducational intervention to enhance understanding of posttraumatic stress and recovery; and (c) give attention to the social context of victimization as well as to physiological symptoms of distress and issues of safety, mastery, attachment, and meaning-making.

Three Victims of Violence Groups for Rape Victims

Adult women victimized by sexual assault may be referred to any of three Victims of Violence groups. These groups are described below.

The Rape Survivors' Group. Rape survivors' groups at the Victims of Violence Program are modeled after the feminist support groups initially developed by members of the Boston Area Rape Crisis Center. The model has been described in detail by Yassen and Glass (1984). It was brought to the hospital-based program in order to ensure a full continuum of community- and hospital-based services for a wider range of sexual assault victims than can be easily served by a grass-roots setting. Since 1985 when the model first was introduced to the Victims of Violence Program, the populations served by the two agencies have turned out to be quite overlapping—with the program serving a slightly more distressed population and a somewhat greater number of victims with complex psychiatric and substance-abuse histories. Today, the two settings refer victims to one another's services and stagger their scheduling of groups to ensure a year-round calendar of group offerings.

The survivors' group model described by Yassen and Glass (1984) was transferred to the hospital-based program with little change in structure, format, or process. It embodies a feminist view of rape and a feminist approach to treatment. This approach integrates individual and class advocacy and combines therapeutic intervention with education about rape and rape trauma. The groups typically include six to seven members who meet for a total of 12 90-minute sessions. Each session combines open-ended discussions in which individual members claim time for issues of personal concern and more structured, topic-oriented discussions. Group members participate with one another and with group leaders in defining and scheduling discussion topics. The process adds control and predictability to the group experience and ensures that sessions are organized around themes of mutual interest. Regardless of which topics are selected for discussion, several themes emerge and reemerge throughout the 12 weeks. These include self-esteem, trust, power and control, guilt, mourning and loss, and anger.

During the life of the group, group members move through three relatively distinct stages of group development. The first stage involves "bonding" with other group members and includes such tasks as developing trust, setting individual goals, and negotiating group norms and guidelines. During the second stage, group members begin to share more about themselves, their outside lives, and their assaults. They get closer to one another, solidify their commitment to the group, and become active sources of support for one another. The final stage incorporates grief and mourning. In this stage, a first task is to acknowledge, integrate, and then mourn the pain and humiliation of sexual assault with the support and encouragement of group members. The second task is to mourn the group's ending: to say goodbye to other group members, to separate and individuate from the group. Throughout the process, the group leaders act to create safety, model and facilitate supportive interaction, provide information, and affirm each member's contribution to the group process. Prospective group members are generally one year or more postrape. They are jointly interviewed by both coleaders. Screening interviews assess each woman's readiness for group work (women in crisis are dissuaded from entering this group), her ability to participate in, benefit from, and contribute to group process, and her willingness to make a firm commitment to group attendance and participation. Women with substance-abuse histories are required to be involved in a 12-step or other appropriate treatment program, and individual therapy as well as group is generally recommended (sometimes required) for women entering group with prior trauma histories and/or complicated psychiatric concerns.

The Stress-Management Group. The client population of the
Victims of Violence Program includes rape victims who cannot
fully benefit from the 12-week rape survivors' support group.
Some are hindered by persistent symptoms of physiological distress and arousal. Others are deeply depressed or frightened
and have withdrawn from others to live terribly isolated and
painful lives. They include women (and men) who have been
subjected to extremely brutal, life-threatening rapes and individuals who enjoy little or no emotional support from their
so-called "natural support" networks. For many of these individuals, the program's 8-week stress-management groups can
be a helpful first use of group treatment.

The stress-management group model sponsored by the Victims of Violence is adapted from a model described by Flannery
(1987). It is designed to educate members about the nature of
psychological trauma and stress and to teach, model, and facilitate the in- and out-of-group practice of specific stress-
management and stress-reduction skills. The skills focused on in
group have been associated with stress-resiliency and include
regular relaxation; daily hard exercise; dietary modifications to
reduce intake of stress-inducing stimulants (e.g., sugar, nicotine,
and caffeine); purposive, problem-solving behaviors; and utilization of social support. Prospective group members are interviewed individually over the telephone and, when appropriate,
referred to a group screening in which the aims of the group,
group structure, and process are reviewed. Individuals interested in entering the group are asked to see a physician to get
approval for the hard exercise component of the group and to
complete for themselves and group leaders a series of questionnaires concerning contemporary symptoms and stressors. Those
who complete the group complete these same questionnaires
again at the close of group and generally are able to see concrete
evidence of their progress over time. Each member of the group
is encouraged to establish modest but achievable week-to-week
goals for diet modifications (e.g., to reduce coffee intake by one
cup a day) and personal exercise (e.g., to take a daily walk), to
learn and practice specific relaxation techniques, and to utilize
group members for encouragement and support.

Group sessions are largely didactic and include (a) weekly reporting on goals and progress; (b) practice of relaxation techniques in group; (c) participation in stress-inoculation and problem-solving exercises to anticipate and prepare for daily life stressors; and (d) a 15-minute group walk in which group members may chat freely with one another or remain silent as they choose. In the course of conducting several of these groups, the model originally described by Flannery (1987) was modified to include week-to-week evaluation of group sessions by group members—with an emphasis on identifying what aspects of group are and are not proving helpful—and greater discussion of PTSD symptoms, how they are triggered, and how stress-management techniques might modify them. A second modification has to do with the relaxation component, a component which for some highly distressed trauma victims has proven very difficult. It seems that for some survivors, relaxation challenges a hypervigilance that they require for even a minimal sense of safety. Today, group leaders will introduce several relaxation techniques to group members—including sitting quietly with one's eyes open and listening to music—so that individual members can self-select the least distressing, most personally helpful technique available (Flannery, Harvey, & Perry, 1991).

Ongoing groups for women with early and multiabuse histories. Each year, the client population served by the Victims of Violence Program has included increasing numbers of adult women whose histories of physical and sexual assault reach back into their childhoods and whose lives have entailed repeated encounters with violence and abuse. Within this population are adult victims of rape for whom sexual assault is but one of many traumas endured. On behalf of these women, the program has initiated long-term and ongoing groups for women with early and multiabuse histories. In fact, the initial group developed for this client population employed a short-term model similar to the incest survivor group model described by Herman and Schatzow (1984), which also has been transferred intact to the Victims of Violence Program. However, because many of the women referred to these groups were terribly isolated in the community and coping with greater levels of distress and anxiety, the short-term model proved inappropriate. The group was ending by the time the women in group had begun to bond with one another and allow the group to serve a healing function. With this population, the abrupt ending of group appeared to deprive them of the opportunity to utilize this bonding in the interests of a supportive recovery process. The ongoing model has addressed these issues and enabled group members to use the group as a laboratory for exploring the impact of lifelong and early trauma on their relational functioning.

Today, the program offers two ongoing groups and is developing a long-term, time-limited model that we hope will (a) preserve the benefits of the ongoing model; (b) incorporate some of the benefits associated with time-limited models; and (c) better conform to the annual calendar of a clinical training program (a calendar that sees clinical trainees coming and going at the end of each training year). All the groups are co-led by a staff person and an advanced clinical trainee. They are supervised by a feminist therapist experienced in group work with women survivors. The groups are comprised of five or six members who meet in weekly 90-minute sessions. Prospective members are screened by both coleaders in a series of two pregroup interviews. The first interview is conducted to explain the group, its structure and process, and to assess the woman's ability to participate in, benefit from, and contribute to the group process. All members are required to be in a stable, ongoing individual psychotherapy with a therapist who is prepared to work closely with the group leaders, and they should be at least three months away from their last psychiatric hospitalization. Women with substance-abuse issues must have been sober and straight for at least three months and must be enrolled in a 12-step or other appropriate treatment program. In addition, each member must be living a contemporary life-style in which her physical safety is secure. Women who are still living with battering mates, for example, are referred to shelter-based groups in the community and asked to reconsider joining this group when their physical safety has been established.

The second interview focuses on recovery and on the identification of specific goals that each woman might pursue in group and on specific tasks that might reflect progress toward these goals. One woman, for example, might hope to recover more memories and another might simply want to feel better about herself. In the first instance, group leaders might encourage the victim to solidify what she already knows; to share existing memories with others in group; to review intrusive memories and gain control over their sudden, disorganizing influence on her contemporary life; and to "pace" traumatic recall and manage its impacts before reaching for more distressing information. In the second instance, group leaders might think with the member about how she can soothe her distress and reduce her sense of isolation, and how she can use group members to rethink her sense of self and to identify self-caring skills she might develop and practice. Like the survivors' group, the group format combines open-ended discussions and topical discussions. It is more highly structured, however, to ensure that each member gets and claims personal time and that group leaders are able to bring to the group's attention whatever concerns may be arising out of the group process. Each session begins with a brief "check-in" by each group member in which she indicates her general status and whether or not she wishes to claim time in group. The leaders divide up group time among members and, when appropriate, also claim time for topical discussions or other concerns. The group ends with a brief report by each member of her feelings and thoughts about group. The groups begin and end on time, and time-keeping becomes an important element of group process in group. In every way possible, the rules and aims of group are made explicit, the boundaries clear, and the emphasis upon safety maintained.

Group members have included women with a wide range of diagnoses, including chronic PTSD, borderline and multiple personality disorder, major depression, anxiety states, and phobias. Some reenter and leave the hospital during the course of their membership in group. Most remain in group for at least one year; others anticipate much longer enrollments. When an individual member is ready to terminate, the termination process is structured to take place over a four-week period in which she gives and receives feedback about her progress in group and the work she may still have to do, and during which she and other members (and each of the group leaders) prepare and say thoughtful good-byes.

CONCLUSION

Group treatment has become a treatment of choice for survivors of sexual assault. There exists today a wide range of self-help, support, and psychotherapy groups for rape victims and a variety of social action settings in which rape victims also can experience benefits of group interchange. Within the mental health field, psychotherapy groups for rape survivors vary widely according to theoretical orientation, goals, format, and structure. Many trace their beginnings to the feminist support groups initiated by rape crisis centers nationwide. In Cambridge, Massachusetts, the hospital-based Victims of Violence Program exemplifies the community-oriented mental health setting with strong and affiliative ties to the grass-roots feminist community and to its formative view of rape, rape trauma, and treatment.

SEVEN

Preventing Sexual Assault

Amy S. is a 15-year-old, middle-class teenage girl. At 8:00 on this fall evening, she has slammed out of her family home, enraged at parents who, in her view, are overly critical and overly restrictive of her. Angry, and for the moment at least intent on defying them, she decides to leave her own neighborhood and walk to a friend's house several blocks away. While she is walking, a car pulls up driven by a boy from her high school. He is two grades ahead of her and doesn't hang around with her friends, but she does know him—"sort of." After talking with her a few minutes, he offers to give her a ride. Amy is nervous. She doesn't particularly like this boy or the way he smiles at her when offering her a ride. But, recalling how angry she is at her parents and how far it is to her friend's house, she puts on a false smile and hops in.

Three hours later, raped, beaten, and dumped out of the car, Amy sits in a hospital emergency room, waiting for her parents to arrive, waiting for needed medical care, waiting to be interviewed by the police officers who found her stranded on a highway not far from her home.

This scene describes the experience of one individual who, as a result of rape, will deal with a variety of medical, mental health, and law-enforcement personnel. It also portrays events and circumstances that contribute—all too typically—to acquaintance rape statistics in community after community. Amy S. is far from the exception in this society. She is white but could be black; she is middle-class, but could be either rich or poor; she's in high school but could well be in college: a young woman raped not far from her home by someone she "sort of" knows. As such, she is but one member of a much larger population.

In the face of incident after incident like this, of Amy after Amy, of acquaintance rape after acquaintance rape, women, parents, community groups, and professionals debate the issue of preventive intervention. What, if anything, might have prevented this assault? What, if anything, can be done to reduce the trauma that this young woman may face? Most importantly, what can be done to reduce and eliminate the incidence of rape among an entire population and among adolescent girls and young adult women at elevated risk of rape?

Rape prevention is an organizing theme in the sexual assault field. Virtually all community-based rape crisis centers and anti-rape projects at local, regional, or national levels sponsor rape prevention initiatives. The approaches are varied and some are the subject of considerable controversy. Aims of specific rape prevention strategies may include any or all of the following:

- to eliminate rape by challenging societal beliefs and cultural values that promote and condone sexual violence;
- to foil attempted rapes by educating potential victims about risk, risk avoidance, and self-defense;
- to reduce the emotional and physical trauma of rape by early and appropriate attention to the needs of individual rape victims; and/or
- to prevent recurrent instances of rape by offender incarceration and treatment.

This chapter examines preventive initiatives in the sexual assault field and touches at least briefly on activities directed toward each of these goals. Primary attention is given, however, to activities that promote *rape elimination* through public education and social change and *rape avoidance* through competence-building, risk-awareness and self-defense training. These activities are unambiguously preventive in nature. Generally inspired by a feminist analysis of rape (see Chapter 4), they implement the preventive intervention themes of community psychology and illustrate the contrast between medical and public health models of care.

PREVENTIVE MENTAL HEALTH CARE

Within the mental health field, prevention has been a familiar but elusive goal and, until the middle 1960s, an all too secondary one. Then, in 1965, a group of psychologists concerned with the limits of traditional clinical practice, and with the need to address social-environmental variables affecting the mental health status of individuals and groups at risk, met in Swampscott, Massachusetts, to formally "inaugurate" the field of community psychology. They began by charting federal legislation to transform constructs like community care, social support, and preventive intervention into concrete programs. As a result of these efforts, and as the rape crisis center movement was developing in parallel and sympathetic fashion (see Chapter 4), the 1970s witnessed nationwide federal sponsorship of local community mental health centers. These settings experimented with new modes of mental health service and utilized new kinds of mental health workers (Alley et al., 1979; Bloom, 1984; Gonzales et al., 1983). Typically staffed by a mix of noncredentialed, paraprofessional community residents and traditionally credentialed but change-oriented professionals, community mental health centers pursued aims and embraced social ideologies and organizational forms highly compatible with those of the rape crisis center movement.

Authors who have chronicled the history of the community mental health field draw a distinction between clinical and community modes of intervention and trace their differences to those that distinguish "medical" and "public health" models of care (Albee, 1982; Bloom, 1984; Heller & Monahan, 1977). The distinctions are noteworthy in the sexual assault field as well.

The Medical Model

The phrase "medical model" implies primary concern for the health status of *individual patients* and the credentialed practitioner's expert application of medical arts and skills. Foremost among these arts are *diagnosis, prognosis,* and *treatment.* Diagnosis requires thoughtful interpretation of the patient's medical history and presenting symptoms. Rare conditions and exotic symptoms can pose intriguing diagnostic puzzles and consume more time, money, and attention than more mundane but more prevalent disorders. Prognosis requires an integration of diagnostic data with knowledge of various treatment alternatives. Treatment approaches can include the prescription of antibiotic drugs, the performance of difficult surgical techniques, and (some say) short- or long-term psychotherapy. The efficacy of any treatment almost always is measured, in part if not entirely, by the alleviation of symptoms.

Medical constructs such as these have long governed the clinical traditions of mental health practice. Their "fit" has long been far from perfect. Within psychiatry, for example, diagnosis has remained much more "an art" than in some fields of medicine. Psychiatric practitioners often have interpreted the same symptoms quite differently, and research findings continue to suggest that seemingly extraneous demographic factors (e.g., age, race, sex, and social class) exert considerable and unwarranted influence on both diagnosis and treatment. DSM-III, the diagnostic manual of the American Psychiatric Association (1980), and its successors, represent an attempt within psychiatry to systematize its many views of mental illness and "to improve the reliability of diagnostic judgments" (American Psychiatric Association, 1980, p. 1). Practitioners using the DSM-III are, however, deeply divided about the legitimacy of various diagnostic categories. Feminist clinicians have argued, for example, that the diagnosis of masochistic personality disorder typically is assigned only to female patients and is fundamentally woman-blaming. They do not see the latest compromise—"self-defeating personality"—as much of an improvement. Similarly, clinicians interested in psychological trauma are proposing that a second diagnosis of posttraumatic stress disorder (i.e. DESNOS—Disorders of Extreme Stress Not Otherwise Specified) be added to DSM-IV—this one to reflect awareness of the more complicated sequelae of early and chronic trauma. As the Association prepares to publish DSM-IV, fierce debate continues.

The relationship between specific psychiatric diagnoses and psychiatric treatment recommendations also has been less straightforward than one might wish. When virtually all diagnoses seem to call for long-term individual psychotherapy, for example, the value of differential diagnosis is called into question. Finally, the efficacy of psychotherapeutic treatment has been, and indeed remains, a subject of some dispute (Gurman & Razin, 1977; Hogan, 1979; Strupp, 1973). Researchers have examined the efficacy of specific approaches to psychotherapy (e.g., psychoanalytic, psychodynamic, social learning, humanistic, cognitive, behavioral); their collective efficacy; and the attributes of effective, demonstrably competent providers of these services (Durlack, 1979; Gurman & Razin, 1977; Harvey, 1980). While there is general agreement with Jerome Frank's (1961) conclusion that, taken collectively across varied patients, providers, and schools of thought, psychotherapy *is* a treatment of established effectiveness, much more remains to be known about the conditions under which such efficacy is achieved. Research also is required to examine the relative efficacy of various treatment approaches with specific diagnostic presentations.

The Public Health Model

As clinical work emulates a medical model of physician-directed patient care, community mental health initiatives emulate the model provided by public health care activities. This model addresses the incidence and prevalence of disease and disease-inducing conditions within *entire populations*. Attention is given not to the exotic symptoms of individuals suffering from rare disorders, but to afflictions that threaten entire populations or groups at risk.

The aims of a public health care system are not to treat and alleviate the symptoms of disease, but to identify and track the spread of specific symptom complexes, to eliminate the environmental conditions that promote disease, and to inoculate all or all at-risk members of the population against disease. If the medical model sees physicians prescribing quinine to individual malaria patients, public health sees threatened communities draining the swamps that provide safe habitat for malaria-carrying mosquitoes. If the medical model finds physicians battling to save the lives of AIDS patients and providing them access to experimental modes of treatment, the public health model finds researchers tracking the course of the disease and public health educators promoting safe sex practices among the sexually active. And, if medical model care finds in long-term psychotherapy adult women once victimized by incestuous abuse, a public health model finds teachers and social service providers being taught to recognize and respond to early signs of child sexual abuse and children being educated to trust their feelings and seek safety in the face of ongoing abuse. One model seeks to treat, the other to prevent, child sexual abuse.

PREVENTION, PUBLIC HEALTH, AND EPIDEMIOLOGY

Because they focus on disease reduction in entire populations, public health initiatives depend for content and direction upon *epidemiological research*. Epidemiology is the study of disease and disease-inducing conditions in populations of interest. Bloom (1984) distinguishes between three interrelated modes of epidemiological inquiry. *Descriptive epidemiology* studies the incidence, scope, distribution, and severity of particular disease entities. Researchers examine the descriptive information and search the data on afflicted persons and environments for evidence of risk factors that are correlated with and may be causal of disease incidence. These factors may become the targets of preventive intervention. *Experimental epidemiology* makes use of descriptive and analytic findings and employs applied research techniques to study the efficacy of specific public health initiatives. These initiatives may entail *environmental repair* to eliminate conditions conducive to disease and *citizen inoculation* programs designed to create immunity and aid resistance to disease. Inoculation efforts may be directed to the total population or specific at-risk populations. In either case, inoculation strategies will be judged effective only if they are followed by reduced prevalence, lowered incidence, and generally less severe occurrences. Inoculation strategies do not always involve medical intervention (e.g., flu shots or polio vaccines). They include AIDS prevention campaigns that encourage the use of condoms and public education efforts to prevent rape by changing prevailing beliefs and values.

Mental Health Analogues

The mental health field has not had a long history of preventive work. While public health constructs have been appealing to many practitioners, these constructs have not been easily extended into the mental health domain. *What, for example, are the mental health correlates of environmental repair and citizen inoculation?* During the 1960s and throughout the 1970s, community psychologists and community mental health practitioners actively considered these questions. Impetus for their inquiry came from many sources: the civil rights and antiwar movements, the war on poverty, the emergence of a "hippie" counterculture, the spread of drug and alcohol abuse to youngsters from affluent families and middle-class communities, and the "zeitgeist" of political activism and social unrest that characterized the 1960s.

In this context, the fact of social injustice in the delivery of mental health services (Hollingshead & Redlich, 1958) and the obvious limits of traditional psychiatric care caused many in the mental health profession to turn their attention to the societal "swamp." Apparent to them was a glaring need for local programs to amplify the efficacy of existing mental health services and develop new services on behalf of unserved and underserved populations. Also needed were early, preventive modes of intervention on behalf of persons at risk for emotional disorder and community action programs to address the social conditions (e.g., poverty, joblessness, discrimination, bigotry) promoting emotional distress. As they experimented with methods of accomplishing these ends, community mental health practitioners developed their own constructs of preventive care. Community psychologists, for example, distinguished primary from other levels of preventive intervention and emphasized the importance of preventive efforts that fostered psychosocial competence and resiliency. These constructs provide a framework for examining prevention efforts in the sexual assault field.

Three Levels of Preventive Intervention

Some clinicians have posited that all mental health initiatives entail preventive aims. If clinical treatment cannot prevent the occurrence of emotional distress, for example, it may at least prevent further deterioration and/or lessen the probability of recurrent distress. Similarly, early detection and early intervention activities may identify and address the needs of persons at risk of mental illness and thus forestall or prevent later disturbance. In this view, three levels of preventive intervention can be identified:

• *Primary prevention* efforts seek to promote emotional well-being and to eliminate or reduce the incidence of emotional disturbance in the total population and in specific at-risk segments of it. When rape is the issue, primary prevention efforts seek to reduce rape incidence by promoting healthier values in the general population and risk awareness and self-defense competence among those at risk.

• *Secondary prevention* strategies are initiated at the first signs of emotional disturbance. They combine early detection with early intervention initiatives. Within the sexual assault field, early, appropriate, and "empowering" responses to rape victims in crisis qualify as secondary prevention, as does the early detection and treatment of men and boys who have not yet raped but who have begun to commit other, so-called "minor" sex offenses (e.g., exhibitionism, obscene phone calls, peeping Tomism).

• *Tertiary prevention* involves interventions that alleviate the severity and forestall the recurrence of emotional distress. Follow-up of rape victims and ongoing treatment of offenders are practices that include these preventive aims.

For many researchers, the distinction between primary, secondary, and tertiary prevention is an invalid one. In their view, secondary prevention is appropriately regarded as early or timely treatment and tertiary prevention is rehabilitative treatment. Only primary prevention is genuinely preventive in nature (Klein & Goldston, 1977).

The Concept of Primary Prevention

Caplan (1964) generally is credited with bringing the concept of primary prevention to the fore and with early articulation of primary prevention aims and methods in the community mental health field.

Aims. The aims of primary prevention parallel those of a public health care system. They are:

• to eliminate or substantially reduce the incidence of emotional disorder in a given population; and
• to promote optimal mental health, resistance to stress, and psychosocial competence among members of that population.

An assumption underlying these goals is that the incidence of specific emotional disorders in a specific population can be known and its reduction measured. Another is that the environmental conditions conducive to illness and the capabilities that individuals require in order to withstand those conditions can be established. Neither of these assumptions is easily verified. They do, however, give rationale and direction to those primary prevention efforts that today characterize the mental health field.

Methods. Goldston (1977) distinguishes between two general strategies of primary prevention: (a) those that strengthen individual capacities and reduce individual vulnerabilities, and (b) those that entail environmental modification through planned social change. Both approaches are analogous to those of a public health care system. Initiatives designed to cultivate the psychological strengths or lessen the vulnerabilities of individuals within a given population, for example, are akin to public health *inoculation* programs. They seek to develop among the general population or among those at risk the competencies they require to withstand stress, combat emotional disturbance, and enjoy positive mental health. Social change programs entail *environmental action* to address conditions contributing to the incidence, prevalence, and risk of specific forms of mental illness. Both types of intervention reveal the interdependence that exists between the individual and the community and both emphasize the educative, *competence-building* nature of primary prevention activities.

An Ecological Conception of Primary Prevention

Community psychologists have adopted an ecological view of communities (see Chapter 3) and, from that perspective, have encouraged the design of preventive interventions that will have an effect upon and improve the dynamic relationship between community and community member. These interventions entail both citizen and social change. Bloom (1984), for example, stresses the importance of preventive interventions that mobilize the competence-building capacities of communities and that distribute social, economic, and political power more equitably among all segments of the community. Similarly, Iscoe (1974) defines the "competent community" as one that cultivates and makes use of the talents and resources of all its citizens. Kelly (1968, 1977, 1979) cautions that primary prevention initiatives must foster both individual and community development.

In studying the process and outcome attributes of primary prevention and social advocacy activities on behalf of disadvantaged groups, Paster (1977) came to similar conclusions. Effective preventive intervention efforts were distinguished by a number of attributes, including:

- early and ongoing participation of community members in planning and carrying out the intervention;
- a high assumption of responsibility for the intervention among community members served by it;
- the ability of community mental health center (CMHC) staff to see themselves as *resources* to the intervention(s) rather than as persons deserving "credit" for it;
- focus on the strengths of individuals identified as targets of intervention; and
- the creation of ongoing and self-renewing social support groups that helped to build individual competency vis-à-vis the larger social system.

In short, an ecological view of primary prevention assumes that virtually all attempts at primary prevention involve some degree of social activism and community change. It also assumes that mobilizing community commitment to change and fostering citizen involvement in change are activities critical to the ultimate success and effectiveness of preventive initiatives in the sexual assault field.

PREVENTION AND THE PROMOTION OF COMPETENCE

Heller and Monahan (1977) distinguish community mental health from clinical care initiatives in terms of:

- the ecological level (individual and small group, organizational, or community) toward which intervention is aimed;
- the timing of intervention efforts (earlier or later in the etiology of a mental health problem); and
- the competence-building or deficit-correcting orientation of interventions.

The distinction between competence-building and deficit-correcting orientations is particularly relevant to the topics of concern in this chapter. Much of what is called "medical model" mental health care can be characterized as targeted to the individual or family level, timed to occur later in the etiology of emotional illness, and deficit-oriented. Even as the attention of mental health practitioners has been drawn to the possibility of prevention through early intervention, these activities have been largely deficit oriented: addressing the early signs of major mental illness, for example, or correcting the presumed deficits of low-income and minority families. A unique contribution of the community mental health field has been its emphasis on psychosocial competence and its interest in developing community intervention strategies to promote and enhance individual competence and to mobilize competence-building community resources on behalf of community members. Initiatives that create new social support networks for individuals at risk (e.g., widow-to-widow or single parent networks) qualify as competence-oriented preventive mental health initiatives as do public education efforts that foster among community residents new knowledge about mental health resources and new knowledge, skill, and resiliency.

Emphasis on competence is not only a distinguishing attribute of prevention initiatives in the community mental health field but also one that differentiates competing approaches to rape prevention and avoidance education. There is, for example, a vast difference between rape avoidance programs that encourage women's reliance on male protectors and those that encourage women to lead lives that are fully independent but informed by accurate knowledge of risk and the choice of self-defense alternatives.

Rape and the Construct of Prevention

The need for preventive intervention is highlighted by any incident of sexual assault or abuse. Too often, however, preventive recommendations place responsibility for rape on people already victimized by rape. For example, in Amy's case (described previously), how easy is it to conclude:

- that had the family not fought, had Amy not run, had she not taken a ride with someone she only "sort of knew," this rape might have been prevented; or that
- if Amy had not taken foolish risks, had she kept her cool, had she fought or not fought back, this rapist would not have been successful and this rape could have been avoided.

Until relatively recently, these kinds of answers formed the core of publicly sponsored rape prevention initiatives. Characterized as public safety efforts, such initiatives encourage potential victims to avoid any circumstances that might place them at risk. Women are cautioned not to be out alone at night; to go certain places only in the company of male escorts or with several women; not to hitchhike; not to invite male acquaintances into their homes; not to unlock doors; and, indeed, to do very little in the way of solitary and independent activity. A problem with this advice is that it builds fear and encourages women to consider themselves helpless in the face of attempted rape.

Storaska—A Deficit-Oriented Approach to Prevention

One such approach to rape prevention is that of Frederic Storaska (1975). Reasoning that murder and mutilation are always possible outcomes of rape, Storaska advises the woman faced with the possibility of rape to avoid angering or upsetting her assailant unless (a) she is certain that he means to kill her no matter what, or (b) she knows that she can incapacitate him and escape (a possibility that Storaska regards as rare). The implication is that to avoid rape, women must give up notions of resistance and escape and must, instead, remain passive in the face of attack. Such recommendations clearly comprise a *deficit-oriented approach to rape prevention:* one that rejects self-defense as a viable option and one that encourages women to act from an assumption of personal powerlessness.

Storaska's approach to rape prevention (once popular among law-enforcement agencies and officers) has been widely criticized by researchers in the sexual assault field and by activists in the rape crisis center movement. Bart (1981) and Bart and O'Brien (1985), for example, compared the interviews of 51 women who had been attacked but avoided being raped with those of 43 women who had been raped. Their findings, and those of others in the field (e.g., Sanders, 1980; McIntyre, 1979) support conclusions directly contrary to the Storaska recommendations. In general, those women who have successfully escaped situations of attempted rape have not been immobilized by fear of death or mutilation and have not tried to plead with or placate their assailants. They are more likely to have actively resisted their assailants from the moment threatened, that is, they were more likely to have fled or attempted to flee (apparently the single most effective rape-avoidance strategy); to have yelled or physically fought back; and to have employed more than one rape-avoidance strategy. It is important to emphasize that all of these studies include interviews with women who were raped despite asserted and continued attempts to fight or flee. It is likely that situational factors beyond the victim's control (e.g., locale, lighting, nearness of others) have much to do with the success or failure of any rape-avoidance strategy she might employ. The main points to be drawn from research findings to date is that cooperation is no guarantee of safety and resistance no guarantee of added danger. There is, in short, little in the data to support Storaska's recommendations.

The Need for Competence-Oriented Primary Prevention

In 1983, the National Coalition Against Sexual Assault (NCASA) strongly condemned Storaska's approach to rape prevention, charging that it

- emphasized unlikely risks over likely ones;
- perpetuated unnecessary fear and encouraged unnecessary passivity;
- invoked women to restrict their personal freedom in deference to and in reliance upon male power and protection; and
- dissuaded women's acquisition of the knowledge, attitudes, and self-defense skills that might increase their comfort with active resistance.

The NCASA critique emphasizes the need for prevention interventions that combat rape by activating rather than paralyzing those at risk and that develop in local communities resources for women's acquisition of needed competence and choice. In this same vein, Brodyaga et al. (1975) stress the importance of assuring women of the validity of virtually *all* victim responses to attempted rape. These include (a) *active resistance* through physical self-defense, screaming, and fleeing; (b) *passive resistance* aimed at persuading a rapist to forgo his attempt at sexual assault (e.g., by talking to him, appealing to his "moral" values, engaging in offensive behavior oneself, promising voluntary sex later on); and (c) *submission* out of fear for one's own or others' personal safety. These authors stress that submission, too, is a response to attempted rape that merits respect, understanding, and compassion. Even the woman who wants to resist and feels prepared by self-defense training and feminist values to do so may find herself in a situation where resistance is neither possible nor wise. She needs to know and hear from others that her survival is the priority and that she need not feel ashamed or guilty for surviving by submission.

Virtually all antirape advocates and researchers in the sexual assault field would agree. While Storaska's approach can be justifiably criticized for discouraging women's resistance, the data do not warrant a recommendation that all women in all circumstances attempt active resistance. What, then, are reasonable alternatives to deficit-oriented approaches to rape prevention?

THE PRIMARY PREVENTION OF SEXUAL ASSAULT

Since the early 1970s, the rape crisis center movement has pioneered unique approaches to the prevention of sexual assault. Many of these are analogous to public health modes of intervention and virtually all share the community mental health field's emphasis upon competence-oriented primary prevention.

Public Health Analogues

Approaches to rape prevention developed by feminist rape crisis centers (see Chapter 4) bear a clear resemblance to the *environmental action* and *citizen inoculation* strategies of a public health care system. Those that embody *environmental action* seek economic and political power for women and the development of community resources to assure women's safety and well-being. These interventions stress the relevance of extensive social change and, in community after community, have led to the creation of new community resources—new settings, new events, and new personal alliances—for combating rape. Community education campaigns, "Take Back the Night" marches, school-based rape education programs, and feminist social support networks are examples of feminist efforts to create competence-building community resources for the primary prevention of sexual assault.

Rape prevention efforts that resemble the *citizen inoculation* activities of a public health care system seek to inculcate knowledge, skills, attitudes, and values incompatible with rape and to cultivate self-defense competence among those at risk. Men and boys and women and girls are encouraged to revise rape-supportive belief systems in light of information that challenges sex role stereotypes and calls into question the legitimacy of social standards that assign to the two sexes differential degrees of latitude and responsibility in sexual encounters. Such activities seek to prevent rape by fostering attitudes and values that, in effect, "inoculate" citizens against committing, condoning, or being victimized by rape.

The theme of citizen inoculation also is recognized in rape prevention programs that disseminate accurate risk information and offer self-defense or other modes of assertion training to those at risk. Such initiatives aim to engender in potential victims personal competencies that can help them avoid, resist, and survive rape attempts.

Both approaches to the primary prevention of sexual assault are evident in a series of four documentary talk shows broadcast in 1984 by the American Public Broadcasting System (PBS). Aimed at parents and other adult caretakers, the program presented in clear and unambiguous language and in vivid but unsensational interviews with victims, the scope and trauma of child sexual assault. The initial broadcast examined what parents and communities could do to protect their children. Remaining programs addressed child audiences directly. Each was designed to "arm" children of a specific age group with age-appropriate information about child sexual abuse: how to recognize, avoid, and respond to it. In one sequence, for example, kindergarten through third-grade pupils talked about the difference between touches that feel good, touches that feel bad, and touches that confuse. With an adult facilitator guiding their discussion, young children associated feelings of fear, anger, sadness, and embarrassment with touches that feel bad and touches that confuse. They encouraged one another to trust their feelings (the "uh-oh" feelings) and to turn for help to adults who can and will provide protection. Parents viewing the series learned about the early warning signs of child sexual abuse and that parental awareness is a primary defense against it. Listening, believing, and acting on behalf of children—helping them to trust their feelings and assuring them of parental availability and support—are the main protections children have against rape, incest, and molestation.

The aims of the PBS series were many: to alert, to inform, to empower and, primarily, to prevent the sexual victimization of children. During each broadcast, viewers were invited to telephone their local stations and direct unanswered questions to program panelists. A national hot line was made available so that child and adult victims could seek referrals to helping resources in their home communities. Following each national broadcast, local public television stations aired discussions among local experts and informed their viewers of nearby protective and preventive resources. The series constituted a nationwide effort toward the primary prevention of child sexual abuse. Its methods were competence-building in nature and included attention to the empowerment of individuals and to the cultivation of new community resources.

Limits of the Public Health Analogy

The aims of these rape prevention activities thus strongly resemble those of a public health care system. To date, however, their proponents have found it difficult to establish the effectiveness of such initiatives by proof of reduced incidence or to offer more than global definitions of at-risk populations.

Reduced incidence. A primary goal of any public health activity is to reduce the incidence of a given disease or other health-threatening event in populations at risk. When rape is the event of concern, however, incident determination is extremely difficult (see Chapter 1). Bowker (1979), for example, reports that FBI records of 56,730 instances of forcible rape in 1976 (1 rape every 9 minutes) in fact represented only one quarter of the rapes detected that same year by a nationwide self-report survey! Studies to date have yielded estimates of actual incidence among adult women (Koss & Oros, 1982); adolescent girls (Ageton, 1983); and children (Herman, 1981). All agree that reported rape statistics fall far short of actual incidence. According to these investigations, it is likely that 20% to 40% of all adult

Preventing Sexual Assault 263

women have experienced at least one incident of sexual abuse as children; 40% to 45% will experience in their adolescent or adult lives at least one assault meeting the legal definition of rape or attempted rape; and approximately 25% will experience at least one incident of complete rape. Rape is a drastically under-reported crime.

If determination of incidence is difficult, the documentation of reduced incidence is even more so. This is due not only to the great disparity between actual and reported rape figures, but also to the multiple aims and achievements of the antirape movement. While some antirape activities promote rape aware-ness and prevention, others offer new services and ongoing ad-vocacy to victims. The availability of such services may help a woman recognize her experience as rape and to report it as such to medical and law-enforcement agencies. Thus the same move-ment that fosters rape prevention also encourages increased re-porting. And, with the growing number and availability of local rape crisis centers, rape victims have additional reporting op-tions. A woman may be reluctant to report her assault to the police or to seek help from a local hospital and yet feel able to consult with a rape crisis center. Thus, in this paradoxical fash-ion, an *increase* in reported rape incidents can be regarded as a positive outcome of an overall effort to address and prevent rape.

Given the enormous and assuredly underestimated scope of rape and the seemingly huge disparity between estimates of actual rape and records of reported incidence, the assessment of a given initiative's preventive impact by evidence of reduced incidence is an elusive goal. Carefully planned and no doubt costly longitudinal research might establish changes in inci-dence over several years of comparison of pre- and post-intervention activity, given appropriate controls for cultural and other changes taking place over time. Such research has not taken place to date. Shorter term research activities would re-quire a highly proscribed intervention, careful delineation of a target population, and the collection of pre- and postinterven-tion data within and across identified experimental and control groups. The following steps would be involved:

(1) Identification of an at-risk population not previously exposed to a particular mode of prevention intervention.

(2) Determination of reported rape incidence within this population.

(3) Data-based estimation of actual incidence by surveying a representative sample of the target population.

(4) Determination of the ratio between reported and actual incidence, and, if possible, determination of how that ratio is changing over time with greater public awareness and more antirape resources.

(5) Initiation of a preventive intervention (e.g., risk awareness and self-defense) with an experimental group within the target population; a nonpreventive but rape-related intervention with another group; a preventive but non-rape-related intervention (e.g., public safety education) with yet another group; and no intervention with a fourth control group.

(6) Redetermination of incidence statistics and ratios at least once if not at several postintervention points.

(7) Replication.

Methodological and design constraints such as these highlight the importance of researchers familiar with primary prevention intervention becoming involved as consultants to the design of preventive initiatives (Kelly, 1984). Even with the implementation of this kind of design, however, any number of factors may operate during the life of a given intervention to confound measures of actual and reported incidence within target groups. For example, because of funding shortages, a rape crisis center may close its doors, thus altering the reporting options for women victimized by rape in that community. Or, a particularly brutal rape may be highly publicized in local media and, for a time, prompt women in the community to seek rape-awareness and self-defense education. While researchers must be encouraged to team up with sponsors of preventive initiatives and while those sponsors should, in turn, be encouraged to work closely with researchers, it remains true that most rape prevention initiatives in the sexual assault field will continue to establish their effectiveness by criteria other than the reduced incidence of rape. Individuals and settings reached by a preventive effort; measured changes in the knowledge, attitudes, and values of persons reached; new organizational support for rape prevention activities; and the emergence of self-sustaining community supports (e.g., self-help groups, town forums, self-defense collectives) constitute some of the measures by which rape prevention initiatives currently assess their impact.

Population(s) at risk. The public health model of care generally asks not only that the incidence and prevalence of given diseases be known, but also that the attributes of at-risk populations and the environmental correlates of risk be determined. Such is true when rape is the "disease" as well. Generally, however, the antirape movement has appropriately defined the at-risk population in very global terms. The data suggest that virtually all women and girls, and indeed a good number of boys, are at risk of being raped. Moreover, researchers have not yet been able to identify attributes that clearly distinguish men likely to commit rape from those who are not. All men and all boys are viewed by some as potential offenders. Given this kind of data base, antirape projects have concentrated on alerting general audiences to the possibility of rape, the reality of acquaintance rape, and the need for new information and skill.

Primarily at the instigation of highly experienced rape crisis centers, more specialized prevention activities are now being developed for particular (though still quite broadly defined) groups at risk: children under 12; adolescent and young adult women ages 12 to 25; women on college campuses; elderly women; minority women; handicapped citizens; and gay men. The incidence of rape and rape attempts among these groups is particularly high, and the attributes of persons and circumstances associated with successful rape attempts within each group are beginning to be known (McDermott, 1979). It is known, for example, that children are more vulnerable to assault by family members, adult caretakers, neighbors, and friends than by persons unknown to child or family. The feared event of stranger rape and kidnap is relatively rare. Rape prevention efforts with children today thus concentrate on providing children and parents with accurate information and stress the importance of even very young children being encouraged to exert control over their own bodies. Parents who insist that their children "kiss Uncle Joe" or "hug Mrs. Smith" may be inadvertently enhancing vulnerability to rape.

Among adolescent and young adult women, acquaintance and date rape are far more typical than stranger rape. Amy S. (whose experience is described at the beginning of this chapter) is the norm, not the young woman mugged and raped by a masked stranger. Both events certainly occur, but the likelihood of one event is considerably greater than the other. In the face of such information, rape prevention activities with young audiences (male and female) emphasize that any and all forced sexuality is rape and warn potential victims and potential perpetrators of the criminal and traumatic nature of forced sex. Adolescent girls are encouraged to heed inner warnings and to assert early and continuous rejection of unwanted sexual overtures. Amy S. knew that she felt uncomfortable with this young man, yet she dismissed her feelings and, by doing so, heightened her own vulnerability. More dangerous than being out alone at night may be a young woman's reluctance to trust and to quickly and decisively act on feelings of discomfort with men she knows.

Koss's (1988) nationwide study of sexual assault on college campuses has established that college women constitute a population at great risk of rape. College campuses have been identified as environments in which rape prevention activities are sorely needed. Roark (1987) has distinguished primary, secondary, and tertiary prevention activities appropriate to the campus milieu. Primary prevention strategies recommended by Roark include the promotion of safety through alterations in the physical environment, attention to the training needs of campus staff, development of skill workshops to address the values and beliefs of potential victims and potential perpetrators, and self-defense training programs.

Risk and Vulnerability Research

Rape prevention activities depend for their effectiveness on continuing research into the risk factors associated with rape and vulnerability to rape. Research to date has focused on offender, victim, and situational correlates of rape and has not yet yielded findings that provide clear guidelines to the development of rape prevention programs.

Offender research, for example, has generally failed to draw stark distinctions between rapists and nonrapists or to yield a predictive profile of persons likely to rape. Rapists, it appears, are more sexually aggressive than nonassaultive men and men incarcerated for other crimes (including violent ones), and their sexual arousal is less inhibited by violence and perhaps enhanced by victim resistance and humiliation. How rapists develop such proclivities, however, is widely debated (see Chapter 1). And, although there appears to be some evidence of differences between rapists who are prone or not prone to sadistic violence, how a woman could determine "which type" of rapist is attacking her and how she could use that knowledge to effectively resist rape is unclear (Brodyaga et al., 1975).

A particularly controversial line of research has attempted to identify personality and behavioral attributes that may distinguish rape victims from nonvictims and women raped from women who have successfully resisted rape attempts. In a very early inquiry of this kind, Amir (1971) drew from police reports of victim character the view that some victims invited sexual assault by provocative, risk-taking behavior. Subsequently, Selkin (1978) found rape victims to score lower than women who had successfully resisted rape on several California Personality Inventory (CPI) scales, including Dominance, Social Presence, Sociability, and Communality. Myers et al. (1984) have reported similar findings. In a study that corrected for the methodological and sampling limitations of these studies, however, Koss (1985) found no evidence of attitudinal or personality differences between victims and nonvictims. It is very unlikely that knowledge of the psychological attributes of rape victims can account for the behavior of their assailants.

Many feminists view these findings as indicative of the need for women to master self-defense competence and to develop comfort with physical and other modes of resistance. In this view, the socialization of women for passive and dependent roles increases their vulnerability to rape. This interpretation has given direction to exciting, competence-building preventive initiatives in the sexual assault field. It is important to remember, however, that available research findings do not warrant the conclusion that physical resistance is appropriate or effective for all women, with all assailants, or across all circumstances. Many victims of completed rape self-report the unsuccessful use of one or more resistance strategies. While it may be important to empower women with the self-defense competence that makes resistance an option, it also is true that women who lack these skills are not responsible for rape or for the success or failure of attempted rape.

Another direction of research on risks associated with vulnerability to rape has examined the relevance of situational factors. There is general agreement that certain circumstances *outside* the home (e.g., safety and familiarity of setting, time of day or night, degree of isolation from others) affect risk. It is also true, however, that most rapes take place *inside* the home or other familiar and once safe setting and that many perpetrators are known to the victim. Police precincts routinely inform citizens of precautions to take inside the home. How effective these are against acquaintance-initiated rape attempts is unclear. A danger is that the existence of these suggested precautions may unwittingly support the view that women who are raped have been careless, have not adequately protected themselves, and are somehow coresponsible for rape (Brodyaga et al., 1975). Medical, mental health, and law-enforcement personnel are well reminded that an unlocked window is not an invitation to rape and that the woman who invites her date in for a cup of coffee (or a glass of wine) has not enticed him into sexual assault.

In recent years, findings yielded by diverse research activities have directed rape prevention activities to the particular importance of widespread attitudinal change. Studies of offender characteristics generally agree that rapists are strong subscribers to rape-supportive beliefs, for example. A disturbing feature of this line of research is the accumulating evidence that these beliefs do not distinguish between men who do and do not rape. In one study, for example, Malamuth (1983) found that roughly 35% of the male university students he studied could be adjudged by multiple criteria as capable of committing rape. These subjects exhibited relatively strong sexual arousal to scenes of sexual violence against women, self-reported a willingness to commit rape under certain circumstances, and adhered strongly to rape-supportive beliefs and attitudes. In all, they exhibited physiological, behavioral, and attitudinal tendencies "strikingly similar" to those of convicted rapists. The alarming epidemic of date-rape on college campuses is further evidence of this.

The findings suggest, in fact, that risk of and vulnerability to rape lies neither in the idiosyncratic and "deviant" characteristics of offenders, nor in the risk-taking behavior or heightened passivity of victims, but in widespread cultural acceptance of given beliefs and values. Goodchilds and Zellman (1984) studied the rape attitudes of high school students in Los Angeles, California, asking male and female subjects if they thought forced sexuality was "okay" in any of nine situations (e.g., when she "gets him sexually excited," "says she's going to have sex with him and then changes her mind," "has had sexual intercourse with other guys," "is stoned or drunk," and so forth). Only 24% of the male adolescents questioned found forced sexuality unacceptable in all nine circumstances. As disturbing, only 44% of female subjects objected to rape regardless of circumstances.

It is apparent, then, that rape-supportive beliefs are shared by large numbers of offenders and nonoffenders, victims and nonvictims. Effective rape prevention activities must focus as much, if not more, on *attitudinal* and *behavioral change* in the general

population as on the detection and reeducation of potential rapists and their prospective victims. Borden, Karr, and Caldwell-
Colbert (1988) evaluated the effects of a university-based rape
prevention program on the attitudes and degree of empathy
male and female students expressed before and after their enrollment in a class designed to cultivate rape awareness and
knowledge of risk. They found, first, that college men were
less empathic and sensitive in their attitudes toward rape than
college women and that this approach to prevention was unsuccessful in reducing the differences. Earlier, however, Malamuth
(1985) and colleagues found that subjects given an educational
debriefing following exposure to sexually violent films became
less accepting of violence against women and less accepting of
rape myths. These researchers conclude that available data support a feminist emphasis upon broad-based social change and
rape prevention through the eradication of cultural supports for
rape within so-called "normal" populations.

COMPETENCE-BASED PRIMARY RAPE
PREVENTION STRATEGIES

What use has been made of these data? What programs today
express competence-building rather than deficit-correcting
themes? Each of the programs described in the paragraphs
below is recognized as having pioneered innovative and highly
effective rape prevention activities.[1] Alternatives to Fear has
made physical self-defense training a central part of its activities. Illusion Theater has mined the preventive possibilities of
theater and fostered new approaches to public education. Community Action Strategies to Stop Rape has demonstrated the
role of feminist social support networks in creating community
support for local rape prevention. Differing in program form
and content but aligned by the common aim of rape prevention,
these programs illustrate the range and diversity of competence-
oriented preventive initiatives that today characterize the sexual
assault field. All combine an emphasis on citizen inoculation

against rape with environmental action at organizational, community, and societal levels.

Alternatives to Fear: Rape Prevention Competence for Individuals at Risk

Alternatives to Fear (ATF) in Seattle, Washington, started in the early 1970s as a self-defense, feminist karate course for women affiliated with the University of Washington. Today it offers self-defense and risk-awareness training for adult, adolescent, elderly, disabled, and parent-child audiences throughout the metropolitan area.

Organizing themes. ATF's approach to preventive intervention emphasizes (a) knowledge of the martial arts, (b) concern with the paralyzing effect of criminal violence upon people's lives, and (c) an affirmation of women's right to live without fear and to develop the self-defense skills that can assure that right. Its goals are

- to train potentially vulnerable individuals in active self-defense methods that may help them to protect themselves from violence;
- to teach individuals preventive strategies that may help them avoid violent confrontations; and
- to provide education services that may effect social and cultural change and thus reduce or eliminate violent victimization.

Self-defense training. ATF offers six training programs: (a) a 4-week workshop for adult women; (b) self-defense training for seniors; (c) self-defense training for disabled citizens; (d) a teens' program; (e) a parent-child workshop; and (f) a three-hour, communitywide, rape prevention workshop. Each program combines physical self-defense and assertion training with accurate rape information, risk-awareness education, and an analysis of personal resources for avoiding and resisting rape. Each gives concrete expression to the assumptions that make up ATF's concept of primary rape prevention. These assumptions are as follows:

(1) That exhaustive, reliable information is crucial in addressing any issue: *knowledge reduces fear and dependence, and increases power and control.*

(2) That *no person is defenseless:* everyone has an arsenal of skills, strengths, and abilities at her or his disposal.

(3) That a person's arsenal of self-defense skills include *psychological as well as physical abilities.* Self-defense competence includes psychological assertiveness and self-confidence as well as physical mastery of self-defense martial arts.

(4) That just as no victim is completely powerless, *neither is any offender all-powerful:* all offenders have physical and psychological vulnerabilities that make self-defense possible.

(5) That *while not all efforts at self-defense will be successful, many can be.* Moreover, all options of psychological and physical self-defense should be known to and explored by potential victims.

(6) Finally, *that an analysis of individual fears, behavior patterns, and life-styles can be a useful means of exploring methods of avoidance,* provided that such analysis does not conflict with individual values regarding personal space and individual freedom.

Each of ATF's courses implements these assumptions. The Women's Self-Defense course, for example, trains women in physical and psychological strategies for self-protection (e.g., breaking out of hold, offense techniques, safe falls, and techniques for special situations). ATF's Teens' Project focuses on acquaintance rape and on situations like that experienced by Amy S. The project provides training in how to recognize potentially dangerous situations and offers instruction in a wide range of self-defense skills, from immediate and clear-cut boundary setting and psychological assertiveness to various self-defense tactics. Self-defense programs for senior and disabled citizens also introduce varied approaches to self-protection and defense, and concentrate on preparing individuals to manage the risks that they are most likely to experience.

Impact. Since 1981, more than 3,000 women have participated in ATF's free-of-charge, communitywide Rape Prevention Workshops. Each workshop provides accurate risk information, and each includes self-defense demonstrations. The training serves as a starting point for citizen inoculation through knowledge development and attitude change.

In the course of its 17-year history, ATF has influenced the service programs and philosophies of rape-related and other service agencies throughout the country, articulated formative prevention constructs, produced needed self-defense training materials for the field, and provided thousands of individuals with self-defense skills and training. In doing so, it has established physical self-defense training as an integral part of competence-oriented primary rape prevention.

Illusion Theater:
Theater as a Vehicle for Preventive Education

On September 17, 1984, when PBS began its series on childhood sexual assault, an articulate member of its panel was Ms. Cordelia Anderson-Kent, Director of the Applied Theater component of Illusion Theater based in Minneapolis, Minnesota. Her presence on the panel—and indeed the broadcast itself—are indices of the pivotal role that Illusion Theater has played in the nationwide effort to prevent rape.

Illusion Theater was founded in 1974 on the premise that theater could serve social and aesthetic aims and that the collective talents of concerned actors, writers, directors, and producers could yield works of unique social impact. Since 1977, when Ms. Anderson-Kent began working with Illusion Theater to create age-appropriate plays that alert children (and parents) to the reality of childhood sexual assault, Illusion Theater has

- produced and widely disseminated imaginative and informative theatrical works for child, adolescent, and adult audiences;
- fostered the development of like programs in diverse communities nationwide;
- provided technical assistance to rape crisis centers and antirape programs in every state of the United States; and

- created a national clearinghouse of information about child sexual abuse and its prevention.

Organizing themes. Several assumptions give content and direction to the Illusion Theater's preventive actions. Among these are the following:

- that educating children about sexual abuse is a means of assuring their *personal body safety;*
- *that keeping children ignorant is the same as keeping children vulnerable.* Children need to be empowered with the knowledge that they can say "no" to unwanted touch; that they can tell secrets when someone is being hurt by a secret; and that they can trust feelings, ask questions, and seek adult protection when they need to;
- *that children can handle clear and balanced information about sexual assault if adults can handle giving it to them;* and
- that while it may be ideal for children to acquire sexual abuse awareness and prevention information from their parents, *many parents need assistance in truthfully communicating these facts to their children.*

In expression of these themes, Illusion Theater offers a wide array of preventive initiatives, including travelling theatrical works, curriculum development, services for special populations, a referral system, professional training, and a sexual assault prevention clearinghouse.

Plays. Play creation at the Theater begins with research. Children from local schools are asked about their knowledge, fears, and understanding of child sexual assault. Data analysis identifies those areas of ignorance and misunderstanding that can be addressed by theater. Play development then begins with collaborative improvisation and continues through tentative scripting, experimental presentations, and constant reworking until a final script and format are realized. The final product must meet social, educational, and artistic criteria. Each play uses a Play Moderator who can stop the action at any time and respond to audience concerns or invite audience discussion.

The most well-known of Illusion's plays is *Touch*, which introduces the "touch continuum." The play uses simple words and entertaining scenes to name and define important terms. It depicts examples of victimization incidents, emphasizes non-stranger abuse, and attempts to dispel myths about offenders, victims, and sexual assault itself. "Good" and "bad" touches are portrayed by three actors and three actresses. At scheduled points in the presentation, the Moderator stops the play to engage the audience in a discussion of the play's content.

Since producing *Touch*, Illusion Theater has developed a second play, *No Easy Answers*, for junior and senior high school students and educational productions for adult audiences. Film and video renditions of its plays as well as formatted scripts have made Illusion Theater's approach to rape prevention widely available. Moreover, the theater has now formed a touring company that, by invitation of local community groups, will present Illusion Theater productions to audiences around the country.

Curriculum development. Illusion Theater staff have developed sexual assault education curricula, touch continuum study cards, posters, and teaching guides to help schools introduce childhood assault prevention activities. Its "Child Sexual Abuse Prevention Project: An Educational Program for Children," contains several sections for teachers and an elementary school curriculum. Anderson-Kent has developed a 24-lesson curriculum and teaching guide for adolescent training called "No Easy Answers: A Sexual Abuse Prevention Curriculum for Junior and Senior High School Students."

Service to special populations. Illusion Theater also has developed sexual abuse prevention programs for mentally retarded citizens. The State of Minnesota is working with the theater to develop prevention curricula for hearing impaired, blind, and physically and mentally handicapped persons.

The prevention clearinghouse. In 1982, Illusion Theater received federal funds for establishing a nationwide clearinghouse for childhood sexual assault prevention materials. Lack of continued funding today prevents the theater from itself disseminating the materials that it continues to compile, but clearinghouse materials remain available to those who write and request access to them.

Impact. A second federal grant enabled Illusion Theater to expand its technical assistance activities and to evaluate its impact on childhood sexual assault prevention efforts nationwide and in each of 13 consultation sites. To date, all of these sites have successfully introduced prevention education into local community settings and have themselves produced unique educational materials, including coloring books, original plays, puppet theater productions, films, and study cards based on Illusion Theater concepts for elementary school children.

The theater's lay and professional audiences expand each year. In 1983-1984, for example, Illusion Theater took 130 performances and workshops to a total of 37,198 children and adults in communities throughout Minnesota and the United States. All of Minnesota's rape crisis centers have received training from Illusion Theater, and each incorporates the "touch concepts" into its prevention activities with school-aged youngsters. Nationally, the theater has provided training to practitioners in at least one community of every state and to more than one community in several states. Finally, Illusion Theater's own play presentations have directly reached more than 300,000 people. With groups trained by the theater now developing their own productions and with national initiatives like the PBS broadcast described earlier in this chapter, it appears that the audiences directly and indirectly reached by Illusion Theater soon will represent a significant portion of the general population.

Community Action Strategies to Stop Rape:
Feminist Networking to Prevent Rape

Community Action Strategies to Stop Rape (CASSR) began as a federally funded research-demonstration project of Women Against Rape, a grass-roots feminist organization in Columbus, Ohio. Among the most self-consciously research-oriented programs in the field, CASSR sought from its inception to integrate the preventive themes of community psychology with feminist theory about rape. The primary aim of CASSR was to build women's competence, thus decreasing vulnerability to rape. A second goal was to increase community support for feminist approaches to rape prevention (Sparks, 1982).

CASSR related rape to three contributing social conditions: (a) lack of rape information and understanding; (b) women's subordinate role and the sense of vulnerability that women develop as a result of sex-role specialization in a patriarchal society; and (c) women's isolation in the community and from one another (Sparks, 1982). Specifying the long-term aim of reducing the incidence of rape in the community, CASSR sought first to create within the community an environment more conducive to rape prevention and more supportive of feminist strategies to oppose rape.

The program applied four criteria to the design of competence-building feminist prevention strategies, requiring that each strategy (a) build women's strength; (b) extend women's mobility; (c) promote women's independence; and (d) guarantee women's freedom. Four programs met these criteria:

• *Rape Prevention Workshops* that combined lecture and discussion with confrontation and self-defense training. The aim of the workshops was to foster an awareness of rape as a political issue and to engage women in their own and one another's defense. A lecture and discussion component of the workshops provided accurate rape information, presented a challenge to rape myths, and presented a feminist interpretation of rape. Confrontation training drew on assertion training techniques and engaged women in role playing methods to anticipate, diffuse, and challenge dangerous situations. Self-defense training explored psychological as well as physical strategies for rape resistance.

• *The Whistle Alert Program.* CASSR's Whistle Alert Program encouraged women to carry and use whistles as a first-line defense against attack. Easy to use, whistles can startle and frighten assailants long enough to permit escape. When used by many in the community, their familiar sound can alert neighbors to solicit aid.

• *Shelter Houses.* CASSR sought to develop emergency shelter houses for women throughout the community to provide needed services and to provide visible evidence of women's capacity to aid one another. Like the Whistle Alert program, the shelter house concept challenges the notion that women must accept violence against themselves as a necessary part of life. Moreover, it gives the community new settings through which to express opposition to violence against women.

• *The Rape Prevention Network.* The first years of CASSR funding concentrated on recruiting women into rape workshops and on developing the Whistle Alert and Shelter House programs. Remaining project years focused on building a communitywide feminist network against rape. Relying initially upon participants in the rape prevention workshops and other programs, CASSR attempted to initiate women's rape-awareness groups in settings throughout the community—in apartment buildings, housing projects, neighborhoods, and university settings. Network organizers recruited women from these settings and gained their assistance in establishing initial groups. CASSR supported network development with monthly bulletins, help on special programs, planning sessions among network organizers, and training in community organization skills. The aim was that the rape prevention network ultimately expand of its own momentum, reaching and providing social support to increasing numbers of women. A community of mutually supportive women, no longer isolated from one another, well informed about rape and prepared to help themselves and one another was the ultimate aim of CASSR's rape prevention network.

Impact. When its four-year demonstration period came to a close, CASSR examined the impact of its four-fold approach to rape prevention, looking for evidence of lasting change in the knowledge, attitudes, ideologies, and self-defense capacities of workshop participants and for widespread community support for CASSR's rape prevention efforts. The data were mixed but clearly encouraging. Workshop participants generally exhibited more accurate knowledge about rape as well as attitudes and beliefs more consistent with a feminist analysis of rape. They also reported increased confrontation and self-defense behavior, decreased fear, and increased confidence in their ability to defend themselves if attacked. These findings held over a two-month follow-up. From the workshops, CASSR's rape prevention network successfully recruited more than 600 women into an information sharing system. It was less successful, however, in motivating these women, themselves, to organize antirape projects that would expand the network.

Based on pre- and postsampling of community attitudes, CASSR concluded that the general public continued to maintain a number of rape myths and to generally support more restrictive rape-prevention strategies; however, the public did exhibit increased awareness of rape and antirape activities. In two target neighborhoods, awareness of the Whistle Stop and Shelter House programs more than doubled over a two-year period. These data suggest that feminist action to prevent rape can realize widespread community impact even in the relatively short span of two experimental program years.

CONCLUSION

Rape prevention is a primary concern of all antirape activities. For the most part, prevention strategies focus on rape avoidance through risk awareness and self-defense capability and on social change to eliminate attitudes and beliefs conducive to rape and victimization. Such activities are an integral part of primary prevention activities in the community mental health field and of the public health model of citizen health care generally. As such, they seek to "inoculate" citizens against rape with accurate information about rape and to rid the larger social environment of attitudes and beliefs that contribute to an enormously high rape incidence. Historically, rape awareness efforts have encouraged women to live somewhat fearful and restricted lives in deference to their assumed inability to avoid and resist rape. Feminist and community mental health approaches to rape prevention emphasize competence building and social activism. Programs like Alternatives to Fear, Illusion Theater, and Community Action Strategies to Stop Rape combine educational activities to build individual competence with action strategies to create new social supports for those at risk.

NOTE

1. Alternatives to Fear and Illusion Theater are two of nine programs included in an NCPCR-sponsored study of exemplary antirape activities (Harvey, 1985). Community Action Strategies to Stop Rape began as an NCPCR-funded research demonstration program of Women Against Rape in Columbus, Ohio (Sparks, 1982).

Epilogue

The conservative milieu of the 1980s dealt serious blows to the antirape movement and to the search for greater understanding of the causes and consequences of rape. After experiencing repeated staff and funding cuts, The National Center for the Prevention and Control of Rape—established by federal law in 1975 and located by Congress in the National Institute of Mental Health—was dismantled just one decade later. In the 1980s, NIMH-sponsored research on rape moved to the Center for the Study of Anti-Social Violent Behavior. Many in the field feared that this administrative shift would also entail a shift in programmatic focus: from concern for victim to concern for offender, and from an interest in social responsibility for rape to greater interest in individual psychopathology. Today that center is being reorganized into the Center for Violence and Traumatic Stress Studies, and there is renewed hope for federally sponsored research on victimization and revived interest in feminist approaches to rape prevention and victim care.

As the 1990s begin, antirape programs at the state and local level and community-based rape crisis centers throughout the country are once again struggling for survival. Some have become discouraged by the frustration of having to compete, year after year, for dwindling funds and volunteer resources. Others are considering again issues of program affiliation and program independence, strategizing their economic and political survival in an "ecosystem" governed by a deficit economy and mandated by the Gramm-Rudman Act. Other social programs also are facing setbacks and frustration. But programs meant to serve the repeatedly underserved—women, children, elderly citizens, ethnic minorities, homeless families—are particularly beleaguered.

WHAT HAVE BEEN THE GAINS?

As they look back on two decades of social activism, service, and scholarship, feminist activists, practitioners, and researchers in the sexual assault field can be justly proud of their accomplishments. Despite the tenacity of patriarchal institutions, sexist values, and rape-supportive beliefs, rape and rape trauma are understood and treated differently now than was the case in 1970. Today, many women victimized by rape have access in their home communities to advocacy, social support and mental health and legal services that were not available then and that were rare even one decade ago. Feminist scholars and researchers in the field have cultivated among medical and mental health practitioners a greater understanding of the trauma invoked by rape and a respect for empowering modes of treatment and intervention. The innovations pioneered by rape crisis centers have found their way into the standard procedures of traditional health and mental health facilities.

Today, the crime of rape is recognized as a terribly familiar event in women's lives. Legal reforms initiated by antirape activists have drastically altered the law-enforcement practices of police and prosecuting attorneys and have accomplished significant change in courtroom procedures pertaining to the prosecution of sexual assault. While the attitudes and values of the larger society are still hostile to women who have been raped, the process of legal reform has begun to erode the degree of formal institutional support for that hostility. These victories will no doubt prove increasingly precious as the sexual assault field and society as a whole adapts to a Supreme Court of unprecedented conservatism and to the ramifications of that conservatism throughout the justice system.

Rape prevention remains an elusive goal in this society. For all the efforts of antirape advocates, each year seems to uncover more sexual assault and more evidence of its traumatic impact. Research into the societal causes, social costs, and psychological consequences of rape is more and more needed if preventive intervention on a nationwide scale is to be accomplished. Cultural values and societal beliefs change slowly, usually in a climate that promotes the consideration of new ideas and the testing of new behaviors. We have yet to learn whether or not the 1990s will offer such a climate.

While the 1980s did not yield a completely positive social response to feminist activism or sweeping and progressive social change, the sheer proportion of criminal violence in this country and the magnitude of sexual violence against women and children is likely to sustain citizen interest in rape, rape prevention and institutional support for anti-rape activities. One expression of citizen concern is women's increasing involvement in rape-awareness, risk-avoidance, and self-defense training. Women are refusing to consider themselves helpless in the face of attack. One expression of institutional support for antirape and victim service activities is found in the federally funded Victims of Crime Act (VOCA) initiative of 1984. Signed into law in 1984, this act provides funds (collected from fines imposed on offenders) to be distributed by the Department of Justice to each state in the United States and, within each state, to local advocacy, treatment, and prevention efforts. Cambridge Hospital's decidedly feminist Victims of Violence Program is but one of several hundred victim care and advocacy programs nationwide that rely on VOCA support.

The 1990s will pose continuing challenges to the sexual assault field and to activists, researchers, and clinical practitioners within the field. Scant resources will once again provide limited opportunity to build knowledge, change values, and successfully instigate lasting change. The prevention of rape

and the successful clinical treatment of its aftermath will require, once again, that advocates for legal reform and activists for community change mobilize a creative response to this
challenge.

References

Abbey, A. (1987). Perceptions of personal avoidability versus responsibility: How do they differ? *Basic and Applied Social Psychology, 8,* 3-19.

Abbey, A. (1990). Misperception as an antecedent of acquaintance rape: A consequence of ambiguity in communication between women and men. In A. Parrot & L. Bechhofer (Eds.), *Acquaintance rape: The hidden crime.* New York: John Wiley.

Ageton, S. S. (1983). *Sexual assault among adolescents.* Lexington, MA: D.C. Heath.

Albee, G. (1982). Primary prevention. *Treatment for Sexual Aggressives, 5*(3), 1-3.

Alley, S., Blanton, J., Feldman, R., Hunter, G., & Rolfson, M. (1979). *Cases studies of mental health paraprofessionals: Twelve effective programs.* New York: Human Sciences Press.

American Psychiatric Association. (1980). *Diagnostic and statistical manual of mental disorders* (3rd ed.). Washington, DC: Author.

American Psychiatric Association. (1987). *Diagnostic and statistical manual of mental disorders* (4th ed.). Washington, DC: Author.

American Psychological Association. (1984, May). *The Monitor,* 22-24.

Amir, M. (1971). *Patterns of forcible rape.* Chicago: University of Chicago Press.

Amir, D., & Amir, M. (1975). Rape crisis centers: An arena of ideological conflicts. *Victimology: An International Journal 4*(2), 247-257.

Anderson, R. E., & Carter, I. (1978). *Human behavior in the social environment: A social systems approach.* New York: Aldine.

Annon, J. S. (1974). *The behavioral treatment of sexual problems* (Vol. 1). Hawaii: Kapiolami Health Services.

Annon, J. S. (1976). *Behavioral treatment of sexual problems: Brief therapy.* New York: Harper & Row.

Atkeson, B., Calhoun, K. S., Resick, P. A., & Ellis, E. (1982). Victims of rape: Repeated assessment of depressive symptoms. *Journal of Consulting and Clinical Psychology, 50,* 96-102.

Bailey, L., Moore, T. F., & Bailar, B. A. (1978). An interviewer variance study for the eight impact cities of the National Crime Survey cities sample. *Journal of the American Statistical Association, 73,* 23-30.

Baron, L., & Strauss, M. A. (1989). *Four theories of rape in American society.* New Haven, CT: Yale University Press.

Bart, P. (1979). Rape as a paradigm of sexism in society: Victimization and its discontents. *Women's Studies International Quarterly, 2,* 347-357.

Bart, P. B. (1981). A study of women who both were raped and avoided rape. *Journal of Social Issues, 37,* 123-136.

Bart, P., & O'Brien, P. (1985). *Stopping rape: Successful survival strategies.* Elmsford, NY: Pergamon.

Beck, A. T. (1972). *Depression: Causes and treatment.* Philadelphia: University of Pennsylvania Press.

Beck, A. T., Ruch, A. J., Shaw, B. F., & Emery, G. (1979). *Cognitive therapy of depression.* New York: Guilford.

Beck, A. T., Ward, C. H., Mendelson, M., Mock, J., & Erbaugh, J. (1961). An inventory for measuring depression. *Archives of General Psychiatry, 4,* 561-571.

Becker, J. V., & Abel, G. G. (1981). Behavioral treatment of victims of sexual assault. In S. M. Turner, K. S. Calhoun, & H. E. Adams (Eds.), *Handbook of clinical behavior therapy.* New York: John Wiley.

Becker, J. V., Abel, G. G., & Skinner, L. J. (1979). The impact of a sexual assault on the victim's sexual life. *Victimology: An International Journal, 4,* 229-235.

Becker, J. V., & Skinner, L. J. (1983). Assessment and treatment of rape-related sexual dysfunctions. *The Clinical Psychologist, 36,* 102-105.

Becker, J. V., Skinner, L. J., Abel, G. G., & Cichon, J. (1986). Level of postassault sexual functioning in rape and incest victims. *Archives of Sexual Behavior, 15,* 37-49.

Becker, J. V., Skinner, L. J., Abel, G. G., & Treacy, E. C. (1982). Incidence and types of sexual dysfunction in rape and incest victims. *Journal of Sex and Marital Therapy, 8,* 65-74.

Belnap, J. (1989). The sexual victimization of unmarried women by nonrelative acquaintances. In M. A. Pirog-Good & J. E. Stets (Eds.), *Violence in dating relationships: Emerging issues.* New York: Praeger.

Beneke, T. (1982). *Men who rape.* New York: St. Martin's.

Bienen, L. B. (1981). Rape III—National developments in rape reform legislation. *Women's Rights Law Reporter,* 171-213.

Binder, R. (1980). Setting up a rape treatment center. *Journal of the American Medical Association, 35*(6), 145-148.

Bloom, B. L. (1984). *Community mental health: A general introduction.* Belmont, CA: Brooks/Cole.

Bohmer, C. (1990). Acquaintance rape and the law. In A. Parrot (Ed.), *Acquaintance Rape.* New York: John Wiley.

Borden, L. A., Karr, S. K., & Caldwell-Colbert, A. (1988). Effects of a university rape prevention program on attitudes and empathy toward rape. *Journal of College Student Development, 29*(3), 132-136.

Borkman, T. (1990). Self-help groups at the turning point: Emerging egalitarian alliances with the formal health care system? *American Journal of Community Psychology, 18*(2), 321-332.

Bowker, L. (1979). The criminal victimization of women. *Victimology: An International Journal, 4*(4), 371-384.

Briere, J. (1988). *Therapy for adults molested as children: Beyond survival.* New York: Springer.

Brodyaga, L., Gates, M., Singer, S., Tucker, M., & White, R. (1975). *Rape and its victims: A report for citizens, health facilities and criminal justice agencies.* Washington, DC: National Institute of Law Enforcement and Criminal Justice.

Brownmiller, S. (1975). *Against our will: Men, women and rape.* New York: Simon & Schuster.

Bulman, R. J., & Wortman, C. B. (1977). Attributions of blame and coping in the "real world": Severe accident victims react to their lot. *Journal of Personality and Social Psychology, 35,* 351-363.

Bureau of Justice Statistics. (1984). *Criminal victimization in the United States, 1982.* Washington, DC: U.S. Department of Justice.

Bureau of Justice Statistics. (1985, March). *The crime of rape* (Report No. NCJ-96777). Washington, DC: U.S. Department of Justice.

Bureau of Justice Statistics. (1987). *Criminal victimization in the United States, 1986.* Washington, DC: U.S. Department of Justice.

Bureau of Justice Statistics. (1988). *Criminal victimization in the United States, 1986.* Washington, DC: U.S. Department of Justice.

Bureau of Justice Statistics. (1989). *Criminal victimization in the United States, 1987.* Washington, DC: U.S. Department of Justice.

Burge, S. K. (1988). Post-traumatic stress disorder in victims of rape. *Journal of Traumatic Stress, 1*(2), 193-209.

Burgess, A. W., & Holmstrom, L. L. (1974a). Rape trauma syndrome. *American Journal of Psychiatry, 131,* 981-986.

Burgess, A. W., & Holmstrom, L. L. (1974b). Crisis and counseling requests of rape victims. *Journal of Nursing Research, 23,* 196-202.

Burgess, A. W., & Holmstrom, L. L. (1976). Coping behavior of the rape victim. *American Journal of Psychiatry, 133,* 413-418.

Burgess, A. W., & Holmstrom, L. L. (1979). Rape: Sexual disruption and recovery. *American Journal of Orthopsychiatry, 49,* 648-657.

Burgess, A. W., & Holmstrom, L. L. (1988, January). Treating the adult rape victim. *Medical Aspects of Human Sexuality,* 36-43.

Burnam, M. A., Stein, J. A., Golding, J. M., Siegel, J. M., Sorenson, S. B., Forsythe, A. B., & Telles, C. A. (1988). Sexual assault and mental disorders in a community population. *Journal of Consulting and Clinical Psychology, 56,* 843-850.

Burt, M. R. (1980). Cultural myths and supports for rape. *Journal of Personality and Social Psychology, 38,* 217-230.

Burt, M. R., Gornick, J., & Pittman, K. (1984). *Feminism and rape crisis centers.* Washington, DC: The Urban Institute.

Burt, M. R., & Katz, B. L. (1985). Rape, robbery, and burglary: Responses to actual and feared criminal victimization, with special focus on women and the elderly. *Victimology: An International Journal, 10,* 325-358.

Burt, M. R., & Katz, B. (1987). Dimensions of recovery from rape: Focus on growth outcomes. *Journal of Interpersonal Violence, 2*(1), 57-81.

Calderwood, D. (1987). The male rape victim. *Medical Aspects of Human Sexuality, 21*(5), 53-55.

Calhoun, K. S. (1990). Lies, sex, and videotapes: Studies in sexual aggression [Presidential address]. Presented at the meeting of the Southeastern Psychological Association, Atlanta, GA.

Calhoun, K. S., Atkeson, B. M., & Ellis, E. M. (1981). Social adjustment in victims of sexual assault. *Journal of Consulting and Clinical Psychology, 49,* 705-712.

Calhoun, K. S., Kelley, S., Amick, R., & Gardner, R. (1986). *Factors differentiating sexually coercive and noncoercive college males.* Paper presented at the meeting of the Southeastern Psychological Association, Orlando, FL.

Caplan, G. (1961). *An approach to community mental health.* New York: Grune & Stratton.

Caplan, G. (1964). *Principles of preventive psychiatry.* New York: Basic Books.

Check, J.V.P., & Malamuth, N. M. (1983). Sex role stereotyping and reactions to depictions of stranger versus acquaintance rape. *Journal of Personality and Social Psychology, 45,* 344-356.

Clark, L., & Lewis, D. (1977). *Rape: The price of coercive sexuality.* Toronto: Women's Press.

Cohen, L. J., & Roth, S. (1987). The psychological aftermath of rape: Long-term effects and individual differences in recovery. *Journal of Social and Clinical Psychology, 5*(4), 525-534.

Cohen, L. J., & Roth, S. (1989). The psychological aftermath of rape: Long-term effects and individual differences in recovery. *Journal of Social and Clinical Psychology, 5*(4), 525-534.

Commonwealth v. Crowe. (1984, March 20). *Trial transcript.* Judge Barton presiding.

Commonwealth v. Vierra. (1984, March 25). *Trial transcript.* Judge Young presiding.

Conte, J. (1988). The effects of sexual abuse on children: Results of a research project. *Annals of the New York Academy of Sciences, 528,* 311-326.

Coons, P. M., Bowman, E. S., Pellow, T. A., & Schneider, P. (1989). Post-traumatic aspects of the treatment of victims of sexual abuse and incest. In R. P. Kluft (Ed.), *Treatment of victims of sexual abuse* (pp. 325-336). Philadelphia: W. B. Saunders.

Courtois, C. A. (1988). *Healing the incest wound.* New York: Norton.

Coyne, J. C., & Delongis, A. (1986). Going beyond social support. *Journal of Consulting and Clinical Psychology, 54*(4), 454-460.

Craig, M. E. (1990). Coercive sexuality in dating relationships: A situational model. *Clinical Psychology Review, 10,* 395-423.

Craig, M. E., & Kalichman, S. C. (1988). *Study on coercive sexuality.* Unpublished data.

Cryer, L., & Beutler, L. (1980). Group therapy: An alternative treatment approach for rape victims. *Journal of Sex and Marital Therapy, 6,* 40-46.

Curtis, L. A. (1976). Present and future measures of victimization in forcible rape. In M. J. Walker & S. L. Brodsky (Eds.), *Sexual assault* (pp. 61-68). Lexington, MA: D.C. Heath.

Deming, M. D., & Eppy, A. (1981). The sociology of rape. *Sociology and Social Research, 65,* 357-380.

Derogatis, L. R. (1977). *SCL-90R Manual-L.* Baltimore, MD: Johns Hopkins University of Medicine.

Deutsch, R. M. (1968). *The key to feminine response in marriage.* New York: Random House.

Dietz, S. R., Blackwell, K. T., Daley, P. C., & Bentley, B. J. (1982). Measurement of empathy toward rape victims and rapists. *Journal of Personality and Social Psychology, 43,* 372-384.

Dodge, R. W., & Lentzer, H. R. (1978, August). *Patterns of personal series incidents in the National Crime Survey.* Paper presented at the annual meeting of the American Statistical Association, San Diego, CA.

Draucker, C. B., (1989). Cognitive adaptation of female incest survivors. *Journal of Consulting and Clinical Psychology, 57,* 668-670.

Durlack, J. A. (1979). Comparative effectiveness of paraprofessional and professional helpers. *Psychological Bulletin, 86*(1), 80-92.

Ellis, E. M. (1983). A review of empirical rape research: Victim reactions and response to treatment. *Clinical Psychology Review, 3,* 473-490.

Ellis, E. M., Atkeson, B. M., & Calhoun, K. S. (1981). An assessment of long-term reactions. *Journal of Abnormal Psychology, 90,* 263-266.

Ellis, E. M., Calhoun, K. S., & Atkeson, B. M. (1980). Sexual dysfunctions in victims of rape: Victims may experience a loss of sexual arousal and frightening flashbacks even one year after the assault. *Women and Health, 5,* 39-47.

Ellis, L. (1989). *Theories of rape: Inquiries into the causes of sexual aggression.* New York: Hemisphere.

Ellis, R., & Harper, R. A. (1961). *A guide to rational living.* Englewood Cliffs, NJ: Prentice-Hall.

Essock-Vitale, S. M., & McGuire, M. T. (1985). Women's lives viewed from an evolutionary perspective. I. Sexual histories, reproductive success, and demographic characteristics of a random sample of American women. *Ethology and Sociobiology, 6,* 137-154.

Estrich, S. (1987). *Real rape.* Cambridge, MA: Harvard University Press.

Federal Bureau of Investigation. (1982). *Uniform Crime Reports.* Washington, DC: U.S. Department of Justice.

Feild, H. S. (1978). Attitudes toward rape: A comparative analysis of police, rapists, crisis counselors, and citizens. *Journal of Personality and Social Psychology, 36,* 156-179.

Feldman-Summers, S., Gordon, P. E., & Meagher, J. F. (1979). The impact of rape on sexual satisfaction. *Journal of Abnormal Psychology, 88,* 101-105.

Feldman-Summers, S., & Lindner, K. (1976). Perceptions of victims and defendants in criminal assault cases. *Criminal Justice and Behavior, 3*(2), 135-150.

Federal Bureau of Investigation. (1989). *Uniform Crime Reports.* Washington, DC: U.S. Department of Justice.

Flannery, R. B. (1987). From victim to survivor: A stress-management approach in the treatment of learned helplessness. In B. A. van der Kolk (Ed.), *Psychological trauma* (pp. 217-232). Washington, DC: American Psychiatric Association.

Flannery, R., Harvey, M., Perry, J. (1991). Stress management groups for patients with histories of victimization and trauma. Manuscript submitted for publication.

Foa, E. B. (1989). Manual for stress inoculation training and prolonged exposure treatment [mimeo]. Philadelphia: Eastern Psychiatric Institute.

Foa, E. B., & Kozak, M. J. (1986). Emotional processing of fear: Exposure to corrective information. *Psychological Bulletin, 99,* 20-35.

Foa, E. B., Olasov, B., & Steketee, G. (1987). *Treatment of rape victims.* Paper presented at the conference, State-of-the-Art in Sexual Assault, Charleston, SC.

Foa, E. B., Rothbaum, B. O., Riggs, D. S., & Murdock, T. B. (1990). *Treatment of posttraumatic stress disorder in rape victims: A comparison between cognitive-behavioral procedures and counseling.* Unpublished manuscript.

Foa, E. B., Steketee, G., & Olasov, B. (1989). Behavioral/cognitive conceptualization of post-traumatic stress order. *Behavior Therapy, 20,* 155-176.

Forman, B. (1980). Psychotherapy with rape victims. *Psychotherapy: Theory, Research, and Practice, 17,* 304-311.

Forman, B. D. (1982). Reported male rape. *Victimology: An International Journal, 7*(1-4), 235-236.

Forman, B. (1983). *Assessing the impact of rape and its significance in psychotherapy. Psychotherapy: Theory, Research, and Practice, 20,* 315-519.

Frank, E. (1979, December). *Cognitive therapy in the treatment of rape victims.* Paper presented at the Association for the Advancement of Behavioral Therapy, San Francisco, CA.

Frank, E., & Anderson, B. P. (1987). Psychiatric disorders in rape victims: Past history and current symptomatology. *Comprehensive Psychiatry, 28,* 77-82.

Frank, E., & Stewart, B. D. (1983). Treating depression in victims of rape. *The Clinical Psychologist, 36,* 95-98.

Frank, E., & Stewart, B. D. (1984). Depressive symptoms in rape victims: A revisit. *Journal of Affective Disorders, 7,* 77-85.

Frank, E., Turner, S. M., & Duffy, B. (1979). Depressive symptoms in rape victims. *Journal of Affective Disorders, 1,* 269-277.

Frank, E., Turner, S. M., & Stewart, B. D. (1980). Initial response to rape: The impact of factors within the rape situation. *Journal of Behavioral Assessment, 2,* 39-53.

Frank, E., Turner, S. M., Stewart, B. D., Jacob, J., & West, D. (1981). Past psychiatric symptoms and the response to sexual assault. *Comprehensive Psychiatry, 22,* 479-487.

Frank, J. (1961). *Persuasion and healing.* Baltimore, MD: Johns Hopkins University Press.

Friedrich, W. N., Beilke, R. L., & Urquiza, A. J. (1988). Behavior problems in young sexually abused boys. *Journal of Interpersonal Violence, 3,* 1-12.

Galvin, J., & Polk, K. (1983, January). Attrition in case processing: Is rape unique? *Journal of Research in Crime and Delinquency,* 126-153.

Gartner, A., & Riessman, F. (1977). *Self-help in the human services.* San Francisco: Jossey-Bass.

Geisinger, D. L. (1969). Controlling sexual interpersonal anxieties. In J. D. Krumboltz & C. E. Thoreson (Eds.), *Behavioral counseling: Cases and techniques.* New York: Holt, Rinehart & Winston.

George, W. H., & Marlatt, G. A. (1986). The effects of alcohol and anger on interest in violence, erotica, and deviance. *Journal of Abnormal Psychology, 95,* 150-158.

Gidycz, C. A., & Koss, M. A. (1990). A comparison of group and individual sexual assault victims. *Psychology of Women Quarterly, 14,* 325-342.

Girelli, S. A., Resick, P. A., Marhoefer-Dvorak, S., & Hutter, C. K. (1986). Subjective distress and violence during rape: Their effects on long-term fear. *Violence and Victims, 1*, 35-45.

Glidewell, J. (1976). A theory of induced social change. *American Journal of Community Psychology, 4*, 227-242.

Gold, E. R. (1986). Long-term effects of sexual victimization in childhood: An attributional approach. *Journal of Consulting and Clinical Psychology, 54*, 471-475.

Goldfried, M. R. (1980). Toward the delineation of therapeutic change principle. *American Psychologist, 35*, 991-999.

Golding, J. M., Stein, J. A., Siegel, J. M., Burnam, M. A., & Sorenson, S. B. (1988). Sexual assault history and use of health and mental health services. *American Journal of Community Psychology, 16*(5), 625-644.

Goldston, S. (1977). An overview of primary prevention programming. In D. Klein and S. Goldston (Eds.), *Primary prevention: An idea whose time has come.* Washington, DC: Government Printing Office.

Gonzales, L. R., Hays, R. B., Bond, M. A., & Kelly, J. G. (1983). Community mental health. In M. Herson, A. E. Kazdin, & A. S. Bellack (Eds.), *The clinical psychology handbook.* Elmsford, NY: Pergamon.

Goodchilds, J., & Zellman, G. (1984). Sexual signaling and sexual aggression in adolescent relationships. In N. Malamuth & E. Donnerstein (Eds.), *Pornography and sexual aggression.* New York: Academic Press.

Goodchilds, J., Zellman, G., Johnson, P. B., & Giarrusso, R. (1988). Adolescents and their perceptions of sexual interactions. In A. W. Burgess (Ed.), *Rape and sexual assault* (Vol. 2, pp. 245-270). New York: Garland.

Goodwin, J. M., & Talwar, N. (1989). Group psychotherapy for victims of incest. In R. P. Kluft (Ed.), *Treatment of victims of sexual abuse* (pp. 279-294). *The Psychiatric Clinics of North America, 12*(2). Philadelphia: W. B. Saunders.

Gornick, J., Burt, M., & Pittman, K. (1983). *Structure and activities of rape crisis centers in the early 1980s.* Washington, DC: The Urban Institute.

Gottlieb, B. H., & Todd, D. (1979). Characterizing and promoting social support in natural settings. In R. Munoz, L. Snowden, & J. G. Kelly (Eds.), *Social and psychological research in community settings.* San Francisco: Jossey-Bass.

Goyer, P. F., & Eddleman, H. C. (1984). Same-sex rape of nonincarcerated men. *American Journal of Psychiatry, 141*(4), 576-579.

Green, B. L., Wilson, J. P., & Lindy, J. D. (1985). Conceptualizing post-traumatic stress disorder: A psychosocial framework. In C. R. Figley (Ed.), *Trauma and its wake: The study and treatment of post-traumatic stress disorder* (pp. 53-69). New York: Brunner/Mazel.

Greendlinger, V., & Byrne, D. (1987). Coercive sexual fantasies of college men as predictors of self-reported likelihood to rape and overt sexual aggression. *Journal of Sex Research, 23*, 1-11.

Griffin, S. (1971, September). Rape: The all-American crime. *Ramparts, 10*, 26-36.

Gurman, A. S., & Razin, A. M. (1977). *Effective psychotherapy: A handbook of research.* Elmsford, NY: Pergamon.

Hall, E. R., & Flannery, P. J. (1984). Prevalence and correlates of sexual assault experiences in adolescents. *Victimology, 9*, 398-406.

Hall, G.C.N. (1990). Prediction of sexual aggression. *Clinical Psychology Review, 10*, 229-245.

Harvey, M. (1980). *Competence-based mental health service: A synthesis for social planning.* Washington, DC: National Center for the Study of Professions.

Harvey, M. (1982a). Helping victims and preventing rape: A look at three effective programs. *Response, 5*(4), 4-6.

Harvey, M. (1982b). Helping victims and preventing rape: Underpinnings of program effectiveness and success. *Response, 5*(5), 7-9.

Harvey, M. (1985). *Exemplary rape crisis program: Cross-site analysis and case studies.* Washington, DC.

Harvey, M. (1990). *An ecological view of psychological trauma and recovery from trauma.* Manuscript submitted for publication.

Harvey, M., & Passy, L. (1978). The creative use of marginality. *Journal of Alternative Human Services, 4*(4), 29-32.

Hassell, R. A. (1981, March). *The impact of stranger vs. nonstranger rape: A longitudinal study.* Paper presented at the eighth annual conference of the Association for Women in Psychology, Boston, MA.

Haynes, S. N., & Mooney, D. K. (1975). Nightmares: Etiological, theoretical and behavioral treatment considerations. *Psychological Record, 25,* 225-236.

Heller, K., & Monahan, J. (1977). *Psychology and community change.* Homewood, IL: Dorsey.

Heller, K., Swindle, R., & Dusenbury, L. (1986). Component social support processes: Comments and integration. *Journal of Consulting and Clinical Psychology, 54*(4), 466-470.

Herman, J. (1981). *Father-daughter incest.* Cambridge, MA: Harvard University Press.

Herman, J., & Schatzow, E. (1984). Time-limited group therapy for women with a history of incest. *International Journal of Group Psychotherapy, 34*(4), 605-616.

Hicks, D. J. (1988, November). The patient who's been raped. *Emergency Medicine,* 106-122.

Hindelang, M. J., & Davis, B. J. (1977). Forcible rape in the United States: A statistical profile. In D. Chappel, R. Geis, & G. Geis (Eds.), *Forcible rape: The crime, the victim, and the offender* (pp. 87-114). New York: Columbia University Press.

Hogan, D. B. (1979). *The regulation of psychotherapists.* Cambridge, MA: Ballinger.

Hollingshead, A. B., & Redlich, F. C. (1958). *Social class and mental illness.* New York: John Wiley.

Holmes, M. R., & St. Lawrence, J. S. (1983). Treatment of rape induced trauma: Proposed behavioral conceptualization and review of the literature. *Clinical Psychology Review, 3,* 417-433.

Holmstrom, L., & Burgess, A. (1975). Rape: The victim and the criminal justice system. *International Journal of Criminology and Penology, 3*(2), 101-110.

Horowitz, M., Wilner, N., & Alvarez, W. (1979). Impact of event scale: Measure of subjective stress. *Psychosomatic Medicine, 41*(3), 209-218.

Horowitz, M., Wilner, N., Marmar, C., & Krupnick, J. (1980). Pathological grief and the activation of latent self-images. *American Journal of Psychiatry, 137,* 1137-1162.

Hospital & Community Psychiatry. (1988). Gold award: A regional resource for psychiatric treatment of victims of violence: The Victims of Violence Program, Department of Psychiatry, Cambridge [MA] Hospital. *Hospital and Community Psychiatry, 39*(1).

Iscoe, I. (1974). Community psychology and the competent community. *American Psychologist, 29,* 607-613.

Jackson, S. (1978). The social context of rape: Sexual scripts and motivation. *Women's Studies International Quarterly, 1,* 27-38.

Jacobson, A., & Richardson, B. (1987). Assault experiences of 100 psychiatric inpatients: Evidence of the need for routine inquiry. *American Journal of Psychiatry, 144,*(7), 909-913.

Jacobson, E. (1938). *Progressive relaxation.* Chicago: University of Chicago Press.

Jamison, K. M., & Flanagan, T. J. (1989). *Sourcebook of criminal justice statistics—1988.* (BJS Report No. NCJ-100899). Washington, DC: U.S. Department of Justice, Bureau of Justice Statistics.

Janoff-Bulman, R. (1979). Characterological versus behavioral self-blame: Inquiries into depression and rape. *Journal of Personality and Social Psychology, 37,* 1798-1809.

Janoff-Bulman, R. (1985a). Criminal vs. non-criminal victimization: Victim's reactions. *Victimology: An International Journal, 10,* 498-511.

Janoff-Bulman, R. (1985b). The aftermath of victimization: Rebuilding shattered assumptions. In C. R. Figley (Ed.), *Trauma and its wake: The study and treatment of post-traumatic stress disorder* (pp. 15-35). New York: Brunner/Mazel.

Janoff-Bulman, R., & Frieze, I. H. (1983). A theoretical perspective for understanding reactions to victimization. *Journal of Social Issues, 39,* 1-17.

Javorek, F. J. (1979). *When rape is not inevitable: Discriminating between completed and attempted rape cases for nonsleeping targets* (Research Bulletin 75-2). Denver, CO: Violence Research Unit.

Jenkins, M. J., & Dambrot, F. H. (1985). The attribution of date rape: Observers' attitudes and sexual experiences and the dating situation. *Journal of Applied Social Psychology, 17,* 875-895.

Jenny, C., Hooton, T. M., Bowers, A., Copass, M. K., Krieger, J. N., Hiller, S. L., Kiviat, N., & Corey, L. (1990). Sexually transmitted diseases in victims of rape. *The New England Journal of Medicine, 322,* 713-716.

Johnson, J. D., & Jackson, L. A. (1988). Assessing the effects of factors that might underlie the differential perception of acquaintance and stranger rape. *Sex Roles, 19,* 37-44.

Kanin, E. J. (1957). Male aggression in dating-courtship relations. *American Journal of Sociology, 63,* 197-204.

Kanin, E. J. (1967). Reference groups and sex conduct norm violations. *Sociological Quarterly, 8,* 495-504.

Kanin, E. J. (1970). Sexual aggression by college men. *Medical Aspects of Human Sexuality, 4,* 25-40.

Kanin, E. J. (1985). Date rapists: Differential sexual socialization and relative deprivation. *Archives of Sexual Behavior, 14,* 219-231.

Kanin, E. J., & Parcell, S. (1977). Sexual aggression: A second look at the offended female. *Archives of Sexual Behavior, 14,* 219-231.

Kaplan, H. S. (1974). *The new sex therapy: Active treatment of sexual dysfunctions.* New York: Brunner/Mazel.

Katon, W., Ries, R., & Kleinman, A. (1984). The prevalence of somatization in primary care. *Comprehensive Psychiatry, 25,* 208-215.

Katz, B., & Burt, M. (1988). Self-blame in recovery from rape: Help or hindrance? In A. Burgess (Ed.), *Rape and Sexual Assault II* (pp. 151-169). New York: Garland.

Katz, S., & Mazur, M. A. (1979). *Understanding the rape victim: A synthesis of research findings.* New York: John Wiley.

Kaufman, A., DiVasto, P., Jackson, R., Voorhees, D., & Christy, J. (1980). Male rape victims: Noninstitutionalized assault. *American Journal of Public Health, 67,* 221-223.

Kegel, A. H. (1952). Sexual functions of the pubococcygeus muscle. *Western Journal of Surgery, 60,* 521-524.

Kelly, J. G. (1968). Towards an ecological conception of preventive interventions. In J. W. Carter, Jr. (Ed.), *Research contributions from psychology to community mental health.* New York: Behavioral Publications.

Kelly, J. G. (1970). Antidotes for arrogance. *American Psychologist, 25,* 524-531.

Kelly, J. G. (1971). Qualities for the community psychologist. *American Psychologist, 26,* 897-903.

Kelly, J. G. (1977). The ecology of social support systems: Footnotes to a theory. In J. Rappaport (Chair), *Toward an understanding of natural helping systems.* Symposium conducted at the meeting of the American Psychological Association, San Francisco, CA.

Kelly, J. G. (1979). T'aint what you do, it's the way that you do it. *American Journal of Psychology, 7*(3), 244-261.

Kilpatrick, D. G. (1983, Summer). Rape victims: Detection, assessment and treatment. *The Clinical Psychologist,* 92-95.

Kilpatrick, D. G., & Amick, A. E. (1985). Rape trauma. In M. Hersen & C. G. Last (Eds.), *Behavior therapy casebook* (pp. 86-103). New York: Springer.

Kilpatrick, D. G., & Best, C. L. (1990, April). Sexual assault victims: Data from a random national probability sample. Presented at the 36th Annual Meeting of the Southeastern Psychological Association, Atlanta, GA.

Kilpatrick, D. G., Best, C. L., Veronen, L. J., Amick, A. E., Villeponteaux, L. A., & Ruff, G. A. (1985). Mental health correlates of criminal victimization: A random community survey. *Journal of Consulting and Clinical Psychology, 53,* 866-873.

Kilpatrick, D. G., Best, C. L., Veronen, L. J., Ruff, M. H., Ruff, G. A., & Allison, J. C. (1985, August). *The aftermath of rape: A three-year longitudinal study.* Paper presented at the annual convention of the American Psychological Association, Los Angeles, CA.

Kilpatrick, D. G., Resick, P. A., & Veronen, L. J. (1981). Effects of a rape experience: A longitudinal study. *Journal of Social Issues, 37,* 105-121.

Kilpatrick, D. G., Saunders, B. E., Amick-Mullen, A., Best, C. L., Veronen, L. J., & Resnick, H. S. (1989). Victim and crime factors associated with the development of crime-related post-traumatic stress disorders. *Behavior Therapy, 20,* 199-214.

Kilpatrick, D. G., Saunders, B. E., Veronen, L. J., Best, C. L., & Von, J. M. (1987). Criminal victimization: Lifetime prevalence, reporting to police, and psychological impact. *Crime and Delinquency, 33,* 479-489.

Kilpatrick, D. G., & Veronen, L. J. (1982). Treatment for rape-related problems: Crisis intervention is not enough. In L. H. Cohen, W. Claiborn, & G. Specter (Eds.), *Crisis intervention.* New York: Human Sciences Press.

Kilpatrick, D. G., & Veronen, L. J. (1984). *Treatment of fear and anxiety in victims of rape.* (Final Report, Grant No. R01 NG29602). Rockville, MD: National Institute of Mental Health.

Kilpatrick, D. G., Veronen, L. J., & Best, C. L. (1984). Factors predicting psychological distress among rape victims. In C. R. Figley (Ed.), *Trauma and its wake: The study and treatment of post-traumatic stress disorder* (pp. 113-141). New York: Brunner/Mazel.

Kilpatrick, D. G., Veronen, L. J., & Resick, P. A. (1979a). The aftermath of rape: Recent empirical findings. *American Journal of Orthopsychiatry, 49,* 658-669.

Kilpatrick, D. G., Veronen, L. J., & Resick, P. A. (1979b). *The rape victim: Issues in treatment failure.* Paper presented at the meeting of the American Psychological Association, New York.

Kirkpatrick, C., & Kanin, E. J. (1957). Male sexual aggression on a university campus. *American Sociological Review, 22,* 52-58.

Klein, D., & Goldston, S. (1977). *Primary prevention: An idea whose time has come.* Washington, DC: Government Printing Office.

Kleinbaum, D. G., Kupper, L. L., & Morgenstern, H. (1982). *Epidemiologic research: Principles and quantitative methods.* Belmont, CA: Lifetime Learning.

Klerman, G., Weissman, M., Rounsaville, B., & Chevron, E. (1984). *Interpersonal psychotherapy of depression.* New York: Basic Books.

Koss, M. P. (1985). The hidden rape victim: Personality, attitudinal, and situational characteristics. *Psychology of Women Quarterly, 9,* 193-212.

Koss, M. P. (1988). Hidden rape: Sexual aggression and victimization in a national sample of students in higher education. In A. W. Burgess (Ed.), *Rape and sexual assault* (Vol. 2, pp. 3-25). New York: Garland.

Koss, M. P. (1990a, August). Testimony before the United States Senate, Committee of the Judiciary.

Koss, M. P. (1990b). Violence against women. *American Psychologist, 45*(3), 374-380.

Koss, M. P., & Burkhart, B. R. (1989). The long-term impact of rape: A conceptual model and implications for treatment. *Psychology of Women Quarterly, 13* (528), 133-147.

Koss, M. P., & Dinero, T. E. (1989a). Predictors of sexual aggression among a national sample of male college students. In R. A. Pretkney & V. L. Quinsey (Eds.), *Human sexual aggression: Current perspectives, Annals of the New York Academy of Science, Vol. 528,* 113-146.

Koss, M. P., & Dinero, T. E. (1989b). Discriminant analysis of risk factors for sexual victimization among a national sample of college women. *Journal of Consulting and Clinical Psychology, 57,* 242-250.

Koss, M. P., Dinero, T. E., Seibel, C., & Cox, S. (1988). Stranger, acquaintance, and date rape: Is there a difference in the victim's experience? *Psychology of Women Quarterly, 12,* 1-24.

Koss, M. P., Gidycz, C. A., & Wisniewski, N. (1987). The scope of rape: Incidence and prevalence of sexual aggression and victimization in a national sample of higher education students. *Journal of Consulting and Clinical Psychology, 55,* 162-170.

Koss, M. P., Koss, P., & Woodruff, W. J. (1990). Relation of criminal victimization to health perceptions among women medical patients. *Journal of Consulting and Clinical Psychology, 58,* 147-152.

Koss, M. P., Koss, P., & Woodruff, W. J. (in press-a). Deleterious effects of criminal victimization on women's health and medical utilization. *Archives of Internal Medicine*.

Koss, M. P., & Oros, C. (1982). The sexual experiences survey: A research instrument investigating sexual aggression and victimization. *Journal of Consulting and Clinical Psychology, 50*, 455-457.

Koss, M. P., Woodruff, W. J., & Koss, P. G. (in press-b). Criminal victimization among primary care medical patients: Prevalence, incidence, and physician usage. *Behavioral Sciences and the Law*.

Koziey, P. W., & McLeod, G. L. (1987). Visual-kinesthetic dissociation in the treatment of victims of rape. *Professional Psychology: Research and Practice, 18*, 276-282.

LaFree, G. (1989). *Rape and criminal justice: The social construction of sexual assault*. Belmont, CA: Wadsworth.

Lang, P. J. (1977). Imagery in therapy: An information processing analysis of fear. *Behavior Therapy, 8*, 862-886.

Lang, P. J. (1979). A bio-informational theory of emotional imagery. *Psychophysiology, 16*, 495-512.

Largen, M. (1988). *Rape-law reform: An analysis*. In A. Burgess (Ed.), *Rape and Sexual Assault* (Vol. 2, pp. 105-132). New York: Garland.

Lazarus, A. A. (1966). Behavioral rehearsal vs. non-directive therapy vs. advice in effecting behavioral change. *Behavioural Research and Therapy, 4*, 209-212.

Lazarus, A. A. (1981). *The practice of multimodal therapy*. New York: McGraw-Hill.

Lazarus, A. A., & Rachman, C. (1960). The use of systematic desensitization in psychotherapy (pp. 181-187). In H. J. Eysenck (Ed.), *Behavior therapy and the neuroses*. Elmsford, NY: Pergamon.

Ledray, L. (1986). *Recovering from rape*. New York: Henry Holt.

Legrand, C. E. (1977). Rape and rape law: Sexism in society and law. In D. Chappell & R. Geis (Eds.), *Forcible rape*. New York: Columbia University Press.

Lehman, D. R., Ellard, J. H., & Wortman, C. B. (1986). Social support for the bereaved: Recipients' and providers' perspectives on what is helpful. *Journal of Consulting and Clinical Psychology, 54*(4), 438-446.

Lerner, M. J. (1980). *The belief in a just world*. New York: Plenum.

Levine-MacCombie, J., & Koss, M. P. (1986). Acquaintance rape: Effective avoidance strategies. *Psychology of Women Quarterly, 10*, 311-320.

Lieberman, M. A. (1986). Social supports—The consequences of psychologizing: A commentary. *Journal of Consulting and Clinical Psychology, 54*(4), 461-465.

Liese, B. S., Larson, M. W., Johnson, C. A., & Hourgan, R. J. (1989). An experimental study of two methods for teaching sexual history taking skills. *Family Medicine, 21*, 21-24.

Linsky, A. S., Straus, M., & Backman-Prehn, R. (1990). *Social stress and the cultural context of rape in the United States*. Paper presented at the International Conference on Social Stress Research, London, England.

Lisak, D., & Roth, S. (1988). Motivational factors in nonincarcerated sexually aggressive men. *Journal of Personality and Social Psychology, 55*, 795-802.

Lott, B., Reilly, M. E., & Howard, D. R. (1982). Sexual assault and harassment: A campus community case study. *Signs: Journal of Women in Culture and Society, 8*, 296-319.

Lundberg-Love, P., & Geffner, R. (1989). Date rape: Prevalence, risk factors, and a proposed model. In M. A. Priog-Good & J. E. Stets (Eds.), *Violence in dating relationships: Emerging issues.* New York: Praeger.

Mahoney, E. R., Shively, M. D., & Traw, M. (1986). Sexual coercion and assault: Male socialization and female risk. Sexual Coercion and Assault, 1, 2-8.

Malamuth, N. M. (1983). Factors associated with rape as predictors of laboratory aggression against women. *Journal of Personality and Social Psychology, 45,* 432-442.

Malamuth, N. M. (1986). Predictors of naturalistic sexual aggression. *Journal of Personality and Social Psychology, 5,* 953-962.

Malamuth, N. M. (1988). A multidimensional approach to sexual aggression: Combining measures of past behavior and present likelihood. In R. A. Pretkney & V. L. Quinsey (Eds.), *Human Sexual Aggression: Current Perspectives, Annals of the New York Academy of Science, Vol. 528,* 113-146.

Malamuth, N. M. (1989a). The attraction to sexual aggression scale: Part one. *The Journal of Sex Research, 26,* 26-49.

Malamuth, N. M. (1989b). The attraction to sexual aggression scale: Part two. *The Journal of Sex Research, 26,* 324-354.

Malamuth, N. M., & Ceniti, J. (1986). Repeated exposure to violent and nonviolent pornography: Likelihood of raping ratings and laboratory aggression against women. *Aggressive Behavior, 12,* 129-137.

Malamuth, N. M., & Dean, K. (in press). Attraction to sexual aggression. In A. Parrot (Ed.), *Acquaintance rape: The hidden crime.* New York: John Wiley.

Marquis, J. N. (1970). Orgasmic reconditioning: Changing sexual object choice through controlling masturbation fantasies. *Journal of Behavior Therapy and Experimental Psychiatry, 1,* 263-271.

Marsh, J. C. (1982, April). Testimony before the U.S. Senate, Committee of the Judiciary, Subcommittee on Criminal Justice.

Marsh, J., Caplan, N., Geist, A., Gregg, G., Harrington, J., & Sharphorn, D. (1980). *Criminal sexual conduct in Michigan: The law reform solution.* University of Michigan: Institute for Social Research.

Masters, W. (1986). Sexual dysfunction as an aftermath of sexual assault of men by women. *Journal of Sex and Marital Therapy, 12,* 35-45.

Masters, W., & Johnson, V. E. (1970). *Human sexual inadequacy.* Boston: Little, Brown.

McCahill, T. W., Meyer, L. C., & Fischman, A. M. (1979). *The aftermath of rape.* Lexington, MA: D.C. Heath.

McCann, I. L., Sakheim, D. K., & Abrahamson, D. J. (1988). Trauma and victimization: A model of psychological adaptation. *The Counseling Psychologist, 6,* 531-594.

McEvoy, A. W., & Brookings, J. B. (1984). *If she is raped: A book for husbands, fathers and male friends.* Holmes Beach, FL: Learning Publications.

McIntyre, J. (1979). *Victim response to rape: Alternative outcomes.* Final report on grant MH-29045. National Center for the Prevention and Control of Rape, National Institute of Mental Health, Rockville, MD.

Meyer, C. B., & Taylor, S. E. (1986). Adjustment of rape. *Journal of Personality and Social Psychology, 50,* 1226-1234.

Michenbaum, D. (1977). *Cognitive behavioral modification.* New York: Plenum.

Miller, B., & Marshall, J. C. (1987). Coercive sex on the university campus. *Journal of College Student Personnel, 28,* 38-47.

Miller, W. R., Williams, A. M., & Bernstein, M. H. (1982). The effects of rape on marital and sexual adjustment. *The American Journal of Family Therapy, 10,* 51-58.

Mollica, R. F., & Son, L. (1989). Cultural dimensions in the evaluation and treatment of sexual trauma: An overview. In R. P. Kluft (Ed.), *Treatment of victims of sexual abuse* (pp. 363-381). *The Psychiatric Clinics of North America, 12*(2). Philadelphia: W. B. Saunders.

Moore, K. A., Nord, C. W., & Peterson, J. L. (1989). Nonvoluntary sexual activity among adolescents. *Family Planning Perspectives, 21*(3), 110-114.

Mosher, D. L., & Anderson, R. D. (1986). Macho personality, sexual aggression, and reactions to guided imagery of realistic rape. *Journal of Research in Personality, 20,* 77-94.

Mosher, D. L., & Sirkin, M. (1984). Measuring a macho personality constellation. *Journal of Research in Personality, 18,* 150-163.

Muehlenhard, C. L., Friedman, D. E., & Thomas, C. M. (1985). Is date rape justifiable? The effects of dating activity, who initiated, who paid, and men's attitudes toward women. *Psychology of Women Quarterly, 9,* 297-310.

Muehlenhard, C. L., & Hollabaugh, L. (1988). Do women sometimes say no when they mean yes? The prevalence and correlates of women's token resistance to sex. *Journal of Personality and Social Psychology, 54,* 872-879.

Muehlenhard, C. L., & Linton, M. A. (1987). Date rape and sexual aggression in dating situations: Incidence and risk factors. *Journal of Counseling and Psychology, 34,* 186-196.

Muehlenhard, C. L., & Shrag, J. (1990). Nonviolent sexual coercion. In A. Parrot & L. Bechhofer (Eds.) *Hidden rape: Sexual assault among acquaintances, friends and intimates.* New York: John Wiley.

Murphy, S. M., Amick-McMullan, S., Kilpatrick, D. G., Haskett, M. E., Vernonen, L. J., Best, C. L., & Saunders, B. E. (1988). Rape victims' self-esteem: A longitudinal analysis. *Journal of Interpersonal Violence, 3*(3), 355-370.

Myers, M. P., Templer, D. L., & Brown, R. (1984). Coping ability of women who become rape victims. *Journal of Consulting and Clinical Psychology, 52,* 73-78.

Nadelson, C., Notman, M., Zackson, H., & Gornich, J. (1982). A follow-up study of rape victims. *American Journal of Psychiatry, 139,* 1266-1270.

National Center for the Prevention and Control of Rape (1981). *National directory: Rape prevention and treatment resources.* Washington, DC: Government Printing Office.

National Center for the Prevention and Control of Rape. (1982). *Research program notice.* Rockville, MD: National Institute of Mental Health.

National Coalition Against Sexual Assault. (1982). *Historical summary of NCASA,* (pamphlet).

National Legal Data Center. (1975). *Rape legislation: A digest of its history and current status.* Seattle, WA: Battelle Law and Justice Study Center.

National Organization for Victim Assistance. (1987). *Debriefing outline for crisis response team members.* Washington, DC: Author.

Neiderland, W. G. (1982). The survivor syndrome: Further observations and dimensions. *Journal of the American Psychoanalytic Association, 30,* 413-425.

Neisser, U. (1976). *Cognition and reality: Principles and implications of cognitive psychology.* San Francisco: Freeman.

Niles, P. L., & White, J. W. (1989). *Correlates of sexual aggression and their accessibility.* Paper presented at the Southeastern Psychological Association meeting, Washington, D.C.

Ohio Revised Code. (Supp. 1980). 2907.01A, 2907.02.

Ohio Revised Code for Rape. (Ann. of 1988). 2907.01A (Definitions), 2907.02 (Provisions).

Orlando, J. A., & Koss, M. P. (1983). The effect of sexual victimization on sexual satisfaction: A study of the negative association hypothesis. *Journal of Abnormal Psychology, 92,* 104-106.

O'Sullivan, E. (1976). What has happened to rape crisis centers? A look at their structures, members and funding. *Victimology: An International Journal, 3* (1-2), 45-62.

Palmer, C. T. (1988). Twelve reasons why rape is not sexually motivated: A skeptical examination. *The Journal of Sex Research, 25,* 512-530.

Parrot, A. (1989). Acquaintance rape among adolescents: Identifying risk groups and intervention strategies. *Social Work and Human Sexuality, 8,* 47-61.

Parson, E. R. (1985). Ethnicity and traumatic stress: The intersecting point in psychotherapy. In C. R. Figley (Ed.), *Trauma and its wake: The study and treatment of post-traumatic stress disorder* (pp. 314-337). New York: Brunner/Mazel.

Paster, V. B. (1977). Organizing primary prevention programs with disadvantaged community groups. In D. C. Klein & S. E. Goldston (Eds.), *Primary prevention: An idea whose time has come.* Washington, DC: Government Printing Office.

Pearson, M. A., Poquette, B. M., & Wasden, R. E. (1983). Stress-inoculation and the treatment of post-rape trauma: A case report. *The Behavior Therapist, 6,* 58-59.

Peterson, D. L., Olasov, B., & Foa, E. B. (1987). *Response patterns in sexual assault survivors.* Paper presented at the Third World Congress on Victimology.

Pittman, K., Burt, M., & Gornick, J. (1984). *The internal dynamics of rape crisis centers.* Washington, DC: The Urban Institute.

Quackenbush, R. L. (1989). A comparison of androgynous, masculine sex-typed, and undifferentiated males in dimensions of attitudes toward rape. *Journal of Research in Personality, 23,* 318-342.

Rapaport, K. R., & Burkhart, B. R. (1984). Personality and attitudinal characteristics of sexually coercive college males. *Journal of Abnormal Psychology, 93,* 216-221.

Rapaport, K. R., & Burkhart, B. R. (1987). *Male aggression symposium: Responsiveness to rape depictions.* Paper presented at the Society for the Scientific Study of Sex, Atlanta, GA.

Rapaport, K. R., & Posey, C. D. (1990). Sexually coercive college males. In A. Parrot & L. Bechhofer (Eds.), *Hidden rape: Sexual assault among acquaintances, friends, and intimates.* New York: John Wiley.

Resick, P. A. (1986, May). *Reactions of female and male victims of rape or robbery.* Final report of NIMH Grant No. MH 37296.

Resick, P. A. (1987, September). *The impact of rape on psychological functioning.* Paper presented at the conference, State of the art in sexual assault, Charleston, SC.

Resick, P. A., Jordan, C. G., Girelli, S. A., Hutter, C. K., & Marhoefer-Dvorak, S. (1989). A comparative outcome study of behavioral group therapy for sexual assault victims. *Behavior Therapy, 19*, 385-401.

Richardson, D., & Hammock, G. (1990). The role of alcohol in acquaintance rape. In A. Parrot & L. Bechhofer (Eds.). *Acquaintance rape: The hidden crime.* New York: John Wiley.

Riger, S., & Gordon, M. T. (1981). The fear of rape: A study of social control. *Journal of Social Issues, 37*, 71-92.

Robin, G. (1977). Forcible rape: Institutionalized sexism in the criminal justice system. *Crime and Delinquency, 23*(2), 136-153.

Rodkin, L., Hunt, E., & Cowan, S. (1982). A men's support group for significant others of rape victims. *Journal of Marital and Family Therapy, 8*, 91-97.

Rosenberg, M. (1987). Society and the adolescent self-image. Princeton, NJ: Princeton University Press.

Ross, V. M. (1977). Rape as a social problem: A byproduct of the feminist movement. *Social Problems, 25*, 75-89.

Ross, R. J., Ball, W. A., Sullivan, K. A., & Caroff, S. N. (1989). Sleep disturbance as the hallmark of post-traumatic stress disorder. *American Journal of Psychiatry, 146*(6), 697-707.

Roth, S., & Lebowitz, L. (1988). The experience of sexual trauma. *Journal of Traumatic Stress, 1*(1), 79-107.

Rothbaum, B. O., Foa, E. B., & Hoge, L. A. (1988, November). *Responses following sexual and non-sexual assault.* Paper presented at the 22nd Annual Association for the Advancement of Behavior Therapy Convention, New York, NY.

Rouse, L. P. (1988). Abuse in dating relationships: A comparison of blacks, whites, and Hispanics. *Journal of College Student Development, 29*, 312-319.

Ruch, L. O., Gartrell, J. W., Amedeo, S., & Coyne, B. J. (in press). Dimensions of initial sexual assault trauma: The victim's perspective. *Psychological Assessment: A Journal of Consulting and Clinical Psychology.*

Ruch, L. O., Gartrell, J. W., Ramelli, A., & Coyne, B. J. (1990, May). The sexual assault symptom scale: Measuring self-reported sexual assault trauma in the emergency room.

Ruch, L. O., & Leon, J. J. (1983). Sexual assault trauma and trauma change. *Women and Health, 8*, 5-21.

Russell, D.E.H. (1982). *Rape in marriage.* New York: Macmillan.

Russell, D.E.H. (1984). *Sexual exploitation.* Beverly Hills, CA: Sage.

Russell, D.E.H. (1990). *Rape in marriage* (rev. ed.). Bloomington: Indiana University Press.

Sales, E., Baum, M., & Shore, B. (1984). Victim readjustment following assault. *Journal of Social Issues, 37*, 5-27.

Sanders, W. (1980). *Rape and women's identity.* Beverly Hills: Sage.

Saunders, B. B., Mandoki, C. A., & Kilpatrick, D. G. (1990). Development of a crime related post-traumatic stress disorder scale for women within the symptom checklist—90 revised. *Journal of Traumatic Stress, 3*(3), 439-448.

Schatzow, E., & Herman, J. (1989). Breaking secrecy: Adult survivors disclose to their families. In R. P. Kluft (Ed.), *Treatment of victims of sexual abuse* (pp. 337-350). *The Psychiatric Clinics of North America, 12*(2). Philadelphia: W. B. Saunders.

Schepple, K. L., & Bart, P. B. (1983). Through women's eyes: Defining danger in the wake of sexual assault. *Journal of Social Issues, 39*, 63-81.

Scully, D., & Marolla, J. (1984). Convicted rapists' vocabulary of motive: Excuses and justifications. *Social Problems, 31*, 530-544.

Scurfield, R. M. (1985). Post-trauma stress assessment and treatment: Overview and formulations. In C. R. Figley (Ed.), *Trauma and its wake: The study and treatment of post-traumatic stress disorder* (pp. 219-256). New York: Brunner/Mazel.

Searles, P., & Berger, R. J. (1987). The current status of rape reform legislation: An examination of state statutes. *Women's Rights Law Reporter*, 25-43.

Seligman, J. (1984, April 16). The date who rapes. *Newsweek*, pp. 91-92.

Selkin, J. (1978). Protecting personal space: Victim and resister reactions to assaultive rape. *Journal of Community Psychology, 6*, 263-268.

Shields, W. M., & Shields, L. M. (1983). Forcible rape: An evolutionary perspective. *Ethnology and Sociobiology, 4*, 115-136.

Siegel, J. M., Sorenson, S. B., Golding, J. M., Burnam, M. A., & Stein, J. A. (1989). Resistance of sexual assault: Who resists and what happens? *American Journal of Public Health, 79*(1), 27-31.

Silver, R. L., Boon, C., & Stones, M. L. (1983). Searching for meaning in misfortune: Making sense of incest. *Journal of Social Issues, 39*, 83-103.

Silverman, D. (1977). First do no more harm: Female rape victims and the male counselor. *American Journal of Orthopsychiatry, 47*, 91-96.

Skogan, W. G. (1981). Issues in the measurement of victimization (NCJ-74682). Washington, DC: Government Printing Office.

Sorenson, S. B., & Golding, J. M. (1990). Depressive sequelae of recent criminal victimization. *Journal of Traumatic Stress, 3*(2), 337-350.

Sorenson, S. B., Stein, J. A., Siegel, J. M., Golding, J. M., & Burnam, M. A. (1987). Prevalence of adult sexual assault: The Los Angeles Epidemiologic Catchment Area Study. *American Journal of Epidemiology, 126*, 1154-1164.

Sparks, C. (1982). *Community action strategies to stop rape.* Final Report of NIMH Grant No. R18 MH29049. National Center for the Prevention and Control of Rape, National Institute of Mental Health.

Spergel, I. (1969). *Community problem solving: The delinquency example.* Chicago: University of Chicago Press.

Spiegel, D. (1987). Dissociation and hypnosis in post-traumatic stress disorders. *Journal of Traumatic Stress, 1*, 17-33.

Sprei, J., & Goodwin, R. A. (1983). The group treatment of sexual assault survivors. *Journal for Specialists in Group Work, 8*, 34-46.

Stark, E., Flitcraft, A., Zuckerman, D., Grey, A., Robison, J., & Frazier, W. (1981). *Wife abuse in the medical setting: An introduction for health personnel.* Rockville, MD: National Clearinghouse on Domestic Violence (Domestic violence monograph series No. 7).

Stewart, B. D., Hughes, C., Frank, E., Anderson, B., Kendall, K., & West, D. (1987). The aftermath of rape: Profiles of immediate and delayed treatment seekers. *Journal of Nervous and Mental Disease, 175*, 90-94.

Storaska, F. (1975). *How to say no to a rapist and survive.* New York: Random House.

Strupp, H. H. (1973). On the basic ingredients of psychotherapy. *Journal of Consulting and Clinical Psychology, 43*, 1-8.

Sudman, S., & Bradburn, N. M. (1974). *Response effects in surveys: A review and synthesis.* Chicago, IL: Aldine.

Sutherland, S., & Scherl, D. J. (1970). Patterns of response among victims of rape. *American Journal of Orthopsychiatry, 28,* 527-529.

Symonds, M. (1975). Victims of violence: Psychological effects and aftereffects. *American Journal of Psychoanalysis, 35,* 19-26.

Symonds, M. (1976). The rape victim: Psychological patterns of response. *American Journal of Psychoanalysis, 36,* 27-34.

Taylor, S. E. (1983). Adjustment to threatening events: A theory of cognitive adaptation. *American Psychologist, 38,* 1161-1173.

Taylor, S. E., & Brown, J. D. (1988). Illusion and well-being: A social-psychological perspective on mental health. *Psychological Bulletin, 103,* 193-210.

Taylor, S. E., Wood, J. V., & Lichtman, R. R. (1983). It could be worse: Selective evaluation as a response to victimization. *Journal of Social Issues, 39,* 19-40.

Teens express themselves (1988, May 3). *South Carolina State Newspaper,* p. 2A.

Thoits, P. (1986). Social support as coping assistance. *Journal of Consulting and Clinical Psychology, 54*(4), 416-423.

Tieger, T. (1981). Self-rated likelihood of raping and the social perception of rape. *Journal of Research in Personality, 15,* 147-158.

Trickett, E., Kelly, J. G., & Todd, D. (1972). The social environment of the high school: Guidelines for individual change and organizational redevelopment. In S. E. Golann and C. Eisdorfer (Eds.), *Handbook of community mental health.* New York: Appleton-Century-Crofts.

Turner, S. M. (1979). *Systematic desensitization of fears and anxiety in rape victims.* Paper presented at the Association for the Advancement of Behavioral Therapy.

van der Kolk, B. A. (1987a). The psychological consequences of overwhelming life experiences. In B. A. van der Kolk (Ed.), *Psychological trauma* (pp. 1-30). Washington, DC: American Psychiatric Press.

van der Kolk, B. A. (1987b). The role of the group in the origin and resolution of the trauma response. In B. A. van der Kolk (Ed.), *Psychological trauma* (pp. 153-171). Washington, DC: American Psychiatric Press.

van der Kolk, B. A. (1989). Compulsion to repeat the trauma: Reenactment, revictimization and masochism. In R. P. Kluft (Ed.), *Treatment of victims of sexual abuse* (pp. 389-412). *The Psychiatric Clinics of North America, 12*(2). Philadelphia: W.B. Saunders.

Veronen, L., & Kilpatrick, D. G. (1983). Stress management for rape victims. 341-374. In D. Meichenbaum & M. Jaremko (Eds.) *Stress prevention and management: A cognitive behavioral approach* (pp. 341-374). New York: Plenum.

Warner, C. G. (1978). The psychological reactions of victims and the response of attending personnel. In C. G. Warner, J. Koerper, D. Spaulding, and S. McDevitt (Eds.), *San Diego County protocol for the treatment of rape and sexual assault victims.* [Mimeo].

Webster's Ninth New Collegiate Dictionary. (1985). Springfiled, MA: Merriam-Webster.

Weis, K., & Borges, S. (1973). Victimology and rape: The case of the legitimate victim. *Issues in Criminology, 8,* 71-115.

White, C., & Shuntich, R. (1990). *Some relationships between the father's approach to sexuality and the son's propensity to date rape*. Paper presented at Southeastern Psychological Association, Atlanta, GA.

White, J. W., & Humphrey, J. A. (1990). *A theoretical model of sexual assault: An empirical test*. Paper presented at symposium on Sexual Assault: Research, Treatment and Education. Southeastern Psychological Association meeting, Atlanta, GA.

White, J. W., & Koss, M. P. (in press). Adolescent sexual aggression within heterosexual relationships: Prevalence, characteristics, and causes. In H. E. Barbee, W. L. Marshall, & D. R. Laws (Eds.), *The juvenile sex offender*. New York: Guilford.

Williams, J. E., & Holmes, K. A. (1981). *The second assault: Rape and public attitudes*. Westport, CT: Greenwood.

Wilson, W., & Durrenberger, R. (1982). Comparison of rape and attempted rape victims. *Psychological Reports, 50,* 198.

Winfield, I., George, L. K., Swartz, M., & Blazer, D. G. (1990). Sexual assault and psychiatric disorders among a community sample of women. *American Journal of Psychiatry, 147*(3), 335-341.

Wirtz, P. W., & Harrell, A. V. (1987). Assaultive versus nonassaultive victimization: A profile analysis of psychological response. *Journal of Interpersonal Violence, 2*(3), 264-277.

Wolberg, L. R. (1967). *The technique of psychotherapy* (Volumes I and II). New York: Grune & Stratton.

Wolberg, L. R. (1980). *Handbook of short-term psychotherapy*. New York: Thieme & Stratton.

Wolfe, J., & Baker, V. (1984). Characteristics of imprisoned rapists and circumstances of the rape. In C. Warner (Ed.), *Rape and assault*. London: Aspen.

Wolff, D. A. (1977). Systematic desensitization and negative practice to alter the aftereffects of a rape attempt. *Journal of Behavior Therapy and Experimental Psychiatry, 8,* 423-425.

Wolpe, J., & Lazarus, A. A. (1966). *Behavior therapy techniques: A guide to treatment of neuroses*. Elmsford, NY: Pergamon.

Wortman, C. B., & Silver, R. C. (1989). The myths of coping with loss. *Journal of Consulting and Clinical Psychology, 57,* 349-357.

Wyatt, G. E. (1984). *Wyatt sexual history questionnaire*. Los Angeles, CA: Neuropsychiatric Institute, University of California.

Wyatt, G. E. (June, 1990). Testimony before the United States House of Representatives Select Committee on Children, Youth and Families.

Wyatt, G. E., Notgrass, C. M., & Newcomb, M. (1990). Internal and external mediators of women's rape experiences. *Psychology of Women Quarterly, 14* (2), 153-157.

Yassen, J., & Glass, L. (1984). Sexual assault survivors groups: A feminist practice perspective. *Social Work, 29*(3), 252-257.

Yescavage, K. M., & White, J. W. (1989). *Relating self-monitoring and sexual aggression*. Paper presented at the Southeastern Psychological Association, Washington, DC.

Index

Acquaintance rape, 5, 17, 21, 29, 74, 245-246, 265, 266
  case example, 245
Adolescents:
  at-risk population, 246, 265-266
  incidence of rape, 12-13
Aggravated rape, 118
Albuquerque Rape Crisis Center, 119, 141
Alcohol
  rape and, 57
Alternatives to Fear (Seattle, WA), 146, 149, 217-273
  an exemplary program, 146
  impact, 272-273
  organizational themes, 271
  self-defense training in, 271-272
  Teens Project, 272
American Psychiatric Association, 48
Anderson-Kent, Cordelia. *See also* Illusion Theater, 273
Anti-rape citizen action groups, 120, 122, 246, 259, 265
Anti-rape movement, 146, 259, 279, 281
Anxiety, 59-61
  treatment for, 194-195
Attachment, 210, 223-224
  as a criteria for recovery, 223-224

as a focal point of group treatment, 210, 216-217, 223-224
Attempted rape, 12, 25, 26, 27

Beck Depression Inventory, 61, 200
Boston, Massachusetts:
  Beth Israel Hospital, 228-229
  Boston Area Rape Crisis Center, xi, 119, 130, 206, 234, 235-236, 238

California Psychological Inventory (CPI), 34-35
Cambridge, Massachusetts:
  Cambridge Hospital. *See also* Victims of Violence Program, xi, 119, 130, 206, 234-244
Center for Anti-Social Violence and Traumatic Stress Studies, 121
Center for the Study of Anti-Social Violent Behavior, 121, 181
Center for the Study of Mental Health Emergencies, 181, 212
Center for Women's Policy Studies, 130
Children:
  at risk, 250, 265-266
  rate of victimization, 10, 12-13
Child sexual abuse:
  prevention of, 250, 261-262, 265, 273-276

Clinical treatment of rape,
  challenges, 156-159
    burnout, 157
    feelings of vulnerability, 156-157
    special problems for male clini-
      cians, 157-159
  cognitive approaches to treatment
    for depression, 199-201
    in group, 218, 219, 220, 221, 227,
      240-241
  coping skills, 196-199
  criteria for recovery, 176-177
  group treatment, 205-244
  integrative treatment of nonrecent
    rape
    assessing rape resolution, 180-183
    effectiveness, 179
    processing memories, 185-189
    reformulating beliefs, 189-191
    restoring mastery, 191-193
    selection criteria, 178
    treating target symptoms, 194
  relationship difficulties, 202-204
  screening, 82-88
    assault history, 82-85
    psychometric assessment, 85-88
      Clinical Trauma Assessment, 86
      Impact of Event Scale, 86
      Rape Aftermath Symptom Test,
        87
      Rape Trauma Syndrome Rating
        Scale, 87
      Sexual Assault Symptoms Scale,
        87
  single session debriefing, 159-176
  treatment for recent victims
    attending to immediate needs,
      164-168
    establishing supportive relation-
      ship, 160-164
Community:
  -based rape crisis centers. *See* rape
    crisis centers
  change, x, 99-101, 102-103
    adaptive nature of community
      change, 102-103
    initiating change in a
      community's response to rape,

    community needs assessment
      tool, 115, 116
  community-wide response to rape,
    components of, 107-115
    crisis services, 107-108, 225
    hospital care, 108-109
    police services, 109
    Sexual Assault Unit, 109
    specialized victim services, 110
    24-hour hotline, 107
  defining community, 92-93, 113-115
  as "ecosystem," 96-100, 139
    case example, 100-101
    a resource perspective, 97-99
  education programs, 113-115
    preventive themes in, 252, 261,
      270-271, 279
  prevention programs, 114-115
  specialized victim services
    groups. *See* Groups, Group treat-
      ment, 205-244
  -wide response to rape, x, 103-104,
    107-115
    components of, 107-115
Community Action Strategies to Stop
  Rape (CASSR) 270, 277-280
  Rape Prevention Network, 278
  Rape Prevention Workshops, 277
  Shelter Houses, 278
  Whistle Alert Program, 278
Community mental health field, 129,
  149, 205, 234, 247
  group services, 205, 234
Community psychology, vii, 247, 251-
  252
  competence-based prevention, 246,
    252, 254-257, 259-260, 268, 270-
    280
  ecological view of primary preven-
    tion, 254-259
  preventions interventions, 251-257,
    260-270, 280
  preventive constructs, 247, 251-257,
    279
  the concept of primary prevention,
    247, 252, 253-257

Date rape, 6, 7, 118

Depo-Provera, 113
Depression, cognitive-behavioral
    treatment for, 199-201
Diagnostic and Statistical Manual,
    American Psychiatric Associa-
    tion, 78, 248, 249
District attroney's offices, 109
Drug abuse, 57

Ecology, Ecological analogy, ecologi-
    cal perspective, vii, 43-47, 254-
    259
  view of primary prevention, 254-259
  view of rape trauma, ix, 43-47
Empowerment, 133-135
  addressing rape-supportive belief
      systems, 246, 260-261, 266, 270-
      280
  and rape prevention 246, 252, 256-
      257, 260-261, 266, 270-280
  empowering service (case exam-
      ples), 194
  through risk awareness education,
      246, 252, 256-257, 266, 270-280
  through self-defense training, 246,
      252, 257, 266, 270-273
Epidemiology, 250-251
  and prevention, 251
  epidemiological research, 250-251

Federal Bureau of Investigation
    definition of rape, 2-3
    Uniform Crime Reports (UCR), 2, 9,
        11, 13
Feminist:
  approaches to rape prevention, 246-
      247, 256, 260-262, 268, 270-280
  services
    models of group treatment, 206,
        224-230, 234-244
Feminist activists. *See also* Rape crisis
    centers:
  accomplishments, 123-124
  efforts for reform, 127-133

Gang rape, 89-91
  trials, 90-91, 132-133
Gramm-Rudman Act, 282

Groups, group treatment, vii, xi, 110,
    205-244
  and empowerment, 205, 212-213,
      236, 237
  and rape trauma, 205, 231
  and recovery (toward recovery cri-
      teria), xi, 206, 217-224
    affect tolerance, 219-220
    attachment, 210, 223-234
    linking memory and feeling, 218-
        219
    meaning, 210, 224
    memory, 2210, 218
    self-esteem, 221-222
    symptom mastery, 220-221
  and self-blame, 209, 221-222
  and social support, 209, 213-216, 236
  and survivorship, 205, 238
  as a treatment of choice, xi, 205, 244
  at Beth Israel Hospital (Boston), 228-
      229
  at Cambridge Hospital. *See also* Vic-
      tims of Violence Program, 206,
      234-244
  at the Austin Rape Crisis Center, 232
  at the Boston Area Rape Crisis Cen-
      ter, 206, 234, 235-236, 238
  at the Victims of Violence Program,
      xi, 206, 234-244
    ongoing groups for women with
        early and multi-abuse histories,
        241-244
    stress management groups, 240-
        241
    the male survivor's group, 234
    the rape survivor's group, 223-
        224, 238-239
  at the Women's Mental Health Col-
      lective, 206, 235-236
  behavioral and cognitive-behav-
      ioral approaches, 218, 219, 220,
      221, 227, 240-241
  case example, 211-215
  designing a survivors group, 231-
      234
  expressive approaches in group, 220
  feminist models of, 206, 224-230,
      234-244

group goals and structure, 217, 232-233, 237-238
in community mental health settings, 205, 236
in rape crisis centers. *See also* Rape Crisis Centers, 205, 225-226, 232
leadership and co-leadership, 208, 231-232, 237-238
leader's own trauma history, 232
male co-leadership, 207-208, 231-232
rationale for co-leadership, 233
of psychological trauma, 205-206, 214-217, 221, 237
of PTSD. *See* of psychological trauma
rational for, 208-217, 228, 231, 237
in the Victims of Violence Program, 237
research on groups, 207-208
stages of group development, 237
supervision and consultation, 233-234
the women's group, 229-230
to foster attachment and trust, 210, 216-217, 223-224
varied models of, xi, 110, 205-206, 224-239, 234-244
crisis oriented groups, xi, 225
drop in discussion groups, xi, 205, 244
psychotherapy groups, 226-229, 241-244
at the Victims of Violence Program, xi, 206, 234-244
long-term and open-ended, xi, 228-229, 241-244
short-term, time-limited, xi, 227-228
supportive psychotherapy groups, xi, 207, 218, 219, 220, 224, 226-228
self-help (and grass roots support) groups, 205, 224, 225-226
social action as a context for group work, 224, 230-231, 236
stress management, stress inoculation groups, 207, 221, 227, 240-241

Illusion Theater, 146, 151, 273-276, 280
Anderson, Cordelia Kent, 273
an exemplary program, 146
curricula, 148, 275
impact, 149
organizing themes, 274
plays, 148, 274-275

Las Vegas:
Community Action Against Rape, 141, 152
Law enforcement agencies
crime against property (rape), 125
LEAA recommendations for change, 130
rape response team, 106
Law Enforcement Assistance Administration (LEAA), 130, 138
Legal reform, 131-133, 282
feminist legal reform activities, 131-133
Legislation about rape
reform in, 130-133
Lexington Rape Crisis Center, 146, 147

Medical field
change in, 128-129
patriarchal values in, 129
Medical model, 247, 248-249
Medical treatment for rape victim, 128-129
Mental health profession:
change in, 129
Miami Rape Treatment Center, 128-129, 144, 146, 149
Michigan Sexual Conduct Law, 131-132

National Center for the Prevention and Control of Rape (NCPCR), 121-122, 142
National Coalition Against Sexual Assault (NCASA), 122, 143
Storaska's approach opposed, 138
National Crime Survey, 2, 11-22
National Institute of Mental Health, 121
monograph on anti-rape, 145

National Organization for Women
    (NOW), 120, 124, 144
National Youth Study, 12
New Bedford, Massachusetts, 89-90,
    93
  ethnic community, 93, 97
  gang rape in, 89-90
  media coverage, 89-90
  rape crisis center, 89
  reactions to rape, 89-90, 93
  sentences of assailants, 132-133
New Bedford Coalition Against Sex-
    ist Violence, 89

Offender treatment, 110-113
  arrest and prosecution, 111
  courts, 111-112
  treatment alternatives, 112

Parents:
  services for, 147
Philadelphia:
  services to rape victims, 119
  Women Organized Against Rape,
    119, 128, 141
Pittsburgh Action Against Rape, 146,
    147, 149
Police practices, 130-132
Populations at risk, 246, 249, 250-251,
    260, 265-270, 279
Post-traumatic stress disorder. See
    also Trauma of rape, 43-47, 77-80
  diagnostic criteria, 78
  prevalence, 79
Psychological trauma. See also Post-
    traumatic stress disorder, x, 43-
    47
  determinants of posttraumatic re-
    sponse and recovery, 45-46
  ecological view of, 43-47
  group treatment of, 205-206, 214-
    217, 221, 237
Psychotherapy. See also Clinical Treat-
    ment and Groups, x
  research on effectiveness of, 249

Rape
  acknowledged and unacknowl-
    edged, 6

a community issue, 89-117. See also
    Community
aftereffects, 80-82
aggravated rape, 118
assault history, 82-85
attitudes of social institutions, 257,
    269, 289
blame for
  victim blame, 69-70, 257, 269
causes of rape
  attitudes, 39
  cognitive restructuring, 41
  cultural values, 30
  demographic characteristics, 38
  early family experiences, 31
  institutional influences, 31
  masculinity and gender schema,
    40
  miscommunication, 36
  peer-group influences, 32
  personality, 39
  relationships, 33
  sex and power motives, 40
  sexual scripts, 30
  situational characteristics, 37
  victim characteristics, 34
cognitive impact, 68-74
  altered schemas, 70-74
    esteem, 72
    intimacy, 73
    power, 72
    safety, 71
    trust, 71-72
  causal explanations, 68-70
  traumatic memories, 68
disinhibitors, 37
early detection and intervention,
    160, 246, 250, 252, 261
early laws, 125
effect on mental health, 66-67. See
    also Trauma of rape
incidence figures, 8-16
  adolescents, 12-13
  adult women, 13
  legal definition, 2
  post-traumatic stress, 77-80. See also
    Trauma of rape
prevalence studies, 22-29
  adult women, 25-27

adolescent girls, 23-24
college students, 24-25
"real" versus spurious, 162
reported, 6
response to, 74-77
simple rape, 118, 126
state laws on, 125-126
stigma of, 17
symptoms, 57-67
trauma. *See* Trauma of rape
types, 5-6, 7
  acknowledged and unacknowledged, 6, 8
  acquaintance, 5, 7, 8, 17, 21, 29, 74,
  date, 6, 7
  hidden, 6, 8
  individual, 5, 8
  marital, 6, 7, 8, 145
  multiple, 5, 7, 8
  pair, 5
  partially planned, 6
  planned, 6
  stranger, 5
  unplanned, 6
victim to survivor process, ix
why victims do not report, 17, 83
Rape avoidance, 114, 246, 256-257, 279
  situtational factors in, 259, 266, 268
  studies of, 258, 267-268
  successful resistors, 258, 267-268
Rape crisis centers, 118-154
  diversity and change, 135-139
  early programs, 120-121, 140
  feminist organizations, 135-138, 144
  feminist origins, 120, 123-138
    analysis of rape, 124-127
    approaches to prevention, 127
    empowering services, 133-135
    funding opportunities, 136, 137-138
    ideological debate among, 136-137
    proliferation, 120-123
    research, 139-153
      exemplary project, 141-142
      study of nine exemplary centers,
        142-153
      survey, 139-141
    services, 128-130, 139, 140-149
    social action, 143-144

social change initiatives, 113, 127-
  133
  legal advocacy, 130-133
  rape prevention, 114-115, 127-128
  service reforms, 125, 128
Rape hot lines, 107-108
Rape myths, 30, 91
  examples, 30
Rape prevention, 114-115
  Alternatives to Fear, 146, 271-273
  Community Action Strategies to
    Stop Rape, 270, 277-280
  competence-based prevention, xi,
    246, 252, 254-257, 259-260, 268,
    270-280
  Illusion Theater, 146, 273-276, 280
  public health model, public health
    approaches, 247, 249-250, 279
  and rape prevention, 256, 260-262
  citizen inoculation, 251, 260-261,
    279
  enviromental repair, 251, 279
  indices of effective intervention,
    262
  reduced incidence of rape, 252,
    262-264
  mental health analogs, 251-252,
    279
Rape prevention education, 115
Rape response, 57-67
  anxiety/fears, 59-61
  depression, 61-62
  effects on health, 66-67
  sexual functioning, 63-66
  social adjustment, 62-63
Rape supportive beliefs, 91
Recovery from rape. *See also* Clinical
  treatment of rape; Trauma of
  rape, 45-47, 206, 217-224
  ecological view of outcomes, x, 45-
    47
  group treatment and, 206, 217-224
Resistance to rape. *See also* Rape
  avoidance
  and self-defense. *See* defense
    training
  resistance strategies, 246, 258, 266,
    267-268

studies of, 258, 267-268
submission to rape, 258, 259
successful resistors, 258, 267-268

San Joaquin, California, Sexual
    Assault Center, 146, 147, 150-
    157
Seattle, Washington, Alternatives to
    Fear, 146, 271-273
Self-defense skills and training, 246,
    252, 264, 270, 271-273
    Alternative to Fear program, 270,
        271-273
Sex offenses, 55
Sex stereotyping, 4
Sexual arousal:
    studies. 41
Sexual assault, 3, 14, 24, 25, 27, 28, 37,
    64, 65, 75, 83-85, 176, 181
Sexual coercion, 6, 36
Sexual contact, 3, 7, 24, 26, 38
Sexual dysfunction, 43, 57, 58, 64, 65
Sexually aggressive men
    prevention implications of, 267-268
    research on, 39-41
    studies of, 267
Sexual trauma. See Trauma of Rape
Significant others, 16
Sleep disturbances, 53
Social support
    and group treatment, 209, 213-216,
        236
Storaska, Fredric, 257-258, 259
    NCASA reaction, 259
    the Storaska approach to preven-
        tion, 257-258
Stress management, 207, 221, 227,
    240-241
Sweetwater County Task Force on
    Sexual Assault, 146, 147-148
Syracuse Rape Crisis Center, 146, 149

Trauma of rape
    beliefs affected, 70-73, 81-82
    determinants of posttraumatic
        response and recovery, 45-57
    ecological model, 42-47
        assumptions, 43-44
        recovery outcomes, 45-47

formal diagnosis of aftereffects, 57-
    58, 80-82
group treatment of, 205-244, 282
phases of response, 47-55
    anticipatory, 48
    expressive styles, 50
    impact, 48
    reconstitution phase, 54
    resolution, 55
    somatic reactions, 53
recovery process, 45-47, 206, 217-224
    criteria, 45-47
    ecological view of, 45-47
    group treatment and, 206, 217-224
symptomatic responses
    anxiety/fears, 59-61
    depression, 61-62
    effects on health, 66-67
    sexual functioning, 63-66
    social adjustment, 62-63
    talking about the rape, 181
    term of disequilibrium, 182
    traumatic memories, 68
    unresolved sexual trauma, 181
Trial of rape
    Grand Slamm rock group, 132
    in New Bedford, Massachusetts, 89-
        90, 132-133
    in New York City, 90-91
    legal reform, 132

Victim blame, 2, 57, 257, 266
Victimization
    coping with, 196
    effects on health, 66
    mental health relevance, 67
    rates, 8, 11
Victims of Crime Act (VOCA), 235,
    283
Victims of rape:
    male, 55
    recovery, 45-47. See also Clinical
        treatment of rape; Trauma of
        rape
Victims of Violence Program. See also
    Cambridge Hospital
American Psychiatric Association
    Gold Award, xi, 130, 235

and the Boston Area Rape Crisis
Center, 119, 130, 206, 234, 235,
238
and the Women's Mental Health
Collective, 206, 234, 235, 236
at the Cambridge Hospital, xi, 119,
130, 206, 234
clinical training in, 130, 234
community ties, 130, 235
feminist origins, 130, 206, 235
funding, 235
mental health services at, 206, 234-
235
group treatment at, 206, 234-244
population served, 234-235
program values, 236
understanding of psychological
trauma, 237

Violence, 14
studies of arousal and, 41
victim's health problem, 66, 67
Vulnerability
offender, 272
research on vulnerable populations,
262-263, 265-266

Women:
rape incidence among, 11-12, 15
rape prevalence among, 22-23, 25-29
sex stereotyping, 4
victimization rate, 8, 10
Women's Mental Health Collective,
206, 235-236

Young, Judge William, 132-134

About the Authors

Mary R. Harvey, Ph.D., is a clinical and community psychologist. She is a cofounder (with Judith Herman, M.D.) and the director of the Victims of Violence Program at Cambridge Hospital in Cambridge, Massachusetts, and a Lecturer in Psychiatry at Harvard Medical School. The Victims of Violence Program was founded in 1985 and in 1988 was awarded the American Psychiatry Association's Gold Award for innovative hospital and community service. Dr. Harvey served as Visiting Psychologist to the National Center for the Prevention and Control of Rape (NCPCR) at the National Institute of Mental Health. While there, she conducted a nationwide study of exemplary rape crisis programs, authored *Exemplary Rape Crisis Programs: A Cross-Site Analysis and Case Studies,* and worked with Mary Koss on the development of the *Ms.* magazine study of hidden rape on college campuses. Dr. Harvey has initiated, studied, and provided consultation to community-based service initiatives throughout the United States. She lectures widely concerning the social and political context of sexual violence against women and the nature and treatment of psychological trauma. In addition to her work at Cambridge Hospital, Dr. Harvey is a licensed clinician and founding partner of Cambridge Associates in Psychotherapy and Mediation.

Mary P. Koss, Ph.D., is a Professor of Psychiatry (with a joint appointment in the Department of Psychology) at the University of Arizona College of Medicine. For more than 10 years she has conducted research on *hidden rape,* that is, sexual aggression and victimization among the general population. For this work she was awarded a Distinguished Publication Award in 1986 from the Association of Women in Psychology. Dr. Koss directed a national study of more than 6,000 college students that was the subject of the book, *I Never Called it Rape: The Ms. Report on Recognizing, Fighting, and Surviving Date and Acquaintance Rape.* Under contract from the National Institute of Mental Health she prepared a mental health research agenda in the area of violence against women. She is associate editor of *Psychology of Women Quarterly* and *Violence and Victims* and is a member of the editorial boards of the *Journal of Consulting and Clinical Psychology* and the *Journal of Interpersonal Violence.* In 1989, she was the recipient of the Stephen Schafer Award for outstanding research contributions to the victim assistance field from the National Organization for Victim Assistance. In August, 1990, Dr. Koss testified on behalf of the American Psychological Association before the United States Senate Judiciary Committee hearings on the Violence Against Women Act.

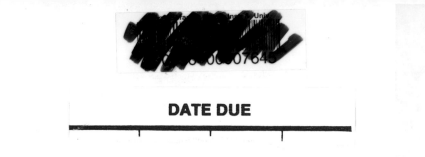